Security in Cyberspace

Security in Cyberspace

Targeting Nations, Infrastructures, Individuals

Edited by
Giampiero Giacomello

B L O O M S B U R Y
NEW YORK • LONDON • NEW DELHI • SYDNEY

Bloomsbury Academic

An imprint of Bloomsbury Publishing Inc

1385 Broadway	50 Bedford Square
New York	London
NY 10018	WC1B 3DP
USA	UK

www.bloomsbury.com

Bloomsbury is a registered trade mark of Bloomsbury Publishing Plc

First published 2014

© Giampiero Giacomello and contributors, 2014

Library of Congress Cataloging-in-Publication Data

A catalog record for this book is available from the Library of Congress.

ISBN: HB: 978-1-6235-6803-0
ePub: 978-1-6235-6699-9
ePDF: 978-1-6235-6570-1

Typeset by Fakenham Prepress Solutions, Fakenham, Norfolk NR21 8NN
Printed and bound in the United States of America

To Angela, Jacopo and Emma Michela

Contents

List of Abbreviations   viii

List of Figures and Tables   xiv

Acknowledgements   xv

Foreword *Carlo Schaerf*   xvi

List of Contributors   xx

Introduction: Security in Cyberspace *Giampiero Giacomello*   1

Part 1   The Nation

1   The 'State(s)' of Cybersecurity *Rossella Mattioli*   23
2   Reducing Uncertainties in Cyberspace through Confidence and
    Capacity-Building Measures *Patryk Pawlak*   39
3   WikiLeaks and State Control of Information in the Cyber Age
    Judith Reppy   59
4   Leaks: Secure Communications and Achieving Nuclear Zero
    Bruce D. Larkin   83
5   Establishing Norms of Behaviour in Cyberspace: The Chinese
    Viewpoint *Chunmei Kang*   113

Part 2   The Infrastructure and The Individual

6   Einstein on the Breach: Surveillance Technology, Cybersecurity and
    Organizational Change *Andreas Kuehn and Milton Mueller*   127
7   Artificial or 'Legitimate' Barriers to Internet Governance?
    Francesco Giacomini and Laura Cordani   161
8   Public-Private Partnerships: A 'Soft' Approach to Cybersecurity?
    Views from the European Union *Maria Grazia Porcedda*   183
9   Being Publicly Private: Extreme Nationalist User Practices on Social
    Networks *Andra Siibak*   213

Index   229

List of Abbreviations

ACLU   American Civil Liberties Union

ACTA   Anti-Counterfeiting Trade Agreement

APT   Advanced Persistent Threats

ARF   ASEAN Regional Forum

AS   Autonomous Systems

ASEAN   Association of Southeast Asian Nations

BBC   British Broadcasting Corporation

BGP   Border Gateway Protocol

BT   British Telecom

C&C   Command-and-Control

CBS   Columbia Broadcasting System

CBMS   Confidence Building Measures

CCBMS   Civil Confidence Building Measures

CD-RW   Readable and [re]Writable Compact Disk

CEO   Consumer Electronics Association

CERT   Computer Emergency Response Team

CESG   Communications-Electronics Security Group

CIA   Central Intelligence Agency

CI   Critical Infrastructure

CII   Critical Information Infrastructure

CIIP   Critical Information Infrastructure Protection

CISPA	Cyber Intelligence Sharing and Protection Act
CNCI	Comprehensive National Cybersecurity Initiative
CNCERT	National Computer Network Emergency Technical Team Coordination Center
CNO	Computer Network Operations
CS/IA	Cybersecurity/Information Assurance
CSBMS	Confidence and Security Building Measures
CSDP	Common Security and Defence Policy
CSIS	Canadian Security Intelligence Service
CSO	Chief Security Officer
CSP	Commercial Service Providers
DCM	Deputy Chief of Mission
DDOS	Distributed Denial of Service
DECS	DIB Enhanced Cybersecurity Services
DHS	Department of Homeland Security
DIB	Defence Industrial Base
DMCA	Digital Millennium Copyright Act
DNS	Domain Name System
DNSEC	Domain Name System Security Extensions
DOD	Department of Defence
DPD	Data Protection Directive
DPI	Deep Packet Inspection
DRM	Digital Rights Management
EC3	European Cybercrime Center
EC	European Community

ECS	Enhanced Cybersecurity Services
EEAS	European External Action Service
EEC	European Economic Community
ENISA	European Network and Information Security Agency
EP3R	European Public-Private Partnership for Resilience
EU	European Union
EUMC	EU Military Committee
EUMS	EU Military Staff
FBI	Federal Bureau of Investigation
FEDCIRC	Federal Computer Incident Response Center
FISA	Foreign Intelligence Surveillance Act of 1978
FISMA	Security Management Act of 2002
FOIA	Freedom of Information Act of 1966
FTP	File Transfer Protocol
GAO	Government Accountability Office
GDP	Gross Domestic Product
GGE	Group of Governmental Experts
GSA	General Service Administration
H.R.	House of Representatives bill
HSPD	Homeland Security Presidential Directive
JCSP	Joint Cybersecurity Services Pilot
KGB	Committee for State Security
ICANN	Internet Corporation for Assigned Names and Numbers
ICS	Industrial Control Systems
ICT	Information and Communication Technologies

IDS	Intrusion Detection System
IETF	Internet Engineering Task Force
IGF	Internet Governance Forum
IMPACT	International Multilateral Partnership Against Cyber Threats (ITU)
IP	Internet Protocol
IPS	Intrusion Prevention System
IRC	Internet Relay Chat
ISO	International Organization for Standardization
ISOC	Internet Society
ISP(S)	Internet Services Providers
ITU	International Telecommunication Union
LE(A)	Law Enforcement (Agency)
MC	Management Costs
MERCOSUR	Mercado Común del Sur
MTIPS	Managed Trusted IP Service
NATO	North Atlantic Alliance Organization
NCSD	National Cybersecurity Division
NIS	Network Information Systems
NIST	National Institute for Standard and Technology
NM	Nautical Miles
NOAA	National Oceanic and Atmospheric Administration
NOFORN/NF	No Foreign Dissemination
NOGS	Internet Network Operators' Groups
NPT	Non-proliferation Treaty

NSA	National Security Agency or Non-State Actors
NSLS	National Security Letters
NSPD	National Security Presidential Directive
NWFZ	Nuclear Weapon Free Zone
NYRB	*New York Review of Books*
OECD	Organization for Economic Co-operation and Development
OIG	Office of the Inspector General
OMB	Office of Management and Budget
OSCE	Organization for Security Co-operation in Europe
PAA	Protect America Act
PAT	Principal-Agent Theory
PII	Personally Identifiable Information
PIPA	Protect IP Act
PKE	Public Key Encryption
PKI	Public Key Infrastructure
PPP	Public-Private Partnership
QRC	Quick Reaction Capability
RCMP	Royal Canadian Mounted Police
REVCO	Review Conference of the NPT
RFC	Request for Comment
RIRS	Regional Internet Registries
SCADA	Supervisory Control and Data Acquisition
SCI	Sensitive Compartmented Information
SIEM	Security Incident and Event Management
SNS	Social Network Sites

SOPA	Stop Online Piracy Act
SOPS	Standard Operating Procedures
TC	Transaction Costs
TCBMS	Transparency and Confidence Building Measures
TCP	Transmission Control Protocol
TIC	Trusted Internet Connections Initiative
TICAP	TIC Access Provider
UN	United Nations
UNIDIR	United Nations Institute for Disarmament Research
UNODC	United Nations Office on Drugs and Crime
USB	Universal Serial Bus
US-CERT	United States Computer Emergency Readiness Team
USG	United States Government
VGT	Virtual Global Taskforce
W3C	World Wide Web Consortium
WCIT	World Conference on International Telecommunications
WTO	World Trade Organization
WWW	World Wide Web

List of Figures and Tables

Figure 5.1 Comparative Internet users and development levels in China and the United States

Figure 5.2 Amount of tampered Chinese government websites compared with total number of tampered websites (mainland China)

Figure 5.3 Example of the main page of a tampered government website

Figure 6.1 TIC access service options – interaction of TIC and Einstein

Figure 6.2 Timeline

Figure 8.1 Taxonomy based on eight criteria

Figure 8.2 Integration between NIS, LEAs and defence

Table 2.1 Cyber alphabet soup: Who does what?

Table 2.2 Performances of EU Member States on cybersecurity

Table 2.3 Types of cyber-exercises

Table 6.1 Possible methods of organizing IDS/IPS signature production

Table 6.2 Overview Einstein and ECS program

Table 6.3 Changes in pattern of secure Internet access production for government agencies

Acknowledgements

The project originated with the 25th ISODARCO (International School on Disarmament and Research on Conflict) Winter Course in 2012 that, for the third time, specifically focused on information technologies and their relation to war and international relations (previous courses were held in summer 1999 and summer 2002). The discussion, among students and instructors was extremely broad, touching topics such as cyberwarfare, cyberterrorism, privacy and freedom of speech, WikiLeaks and many others. So valuable was the experience for all the participants that we decided to put it down in writing. But the process, from the idea to the actual volume, was truly a 'long and winding road'. The first big thanks go to Judith Reppy, who not only contributed a chapter but was also a real 'co-editor' for the volume, and to Carlo Schaerf, director of ISODARCO, for supporting the idea from the very beginning. I would like to express my gratitude to all the present contributors who decided to 'stick' with the project and, in the end, made it possible. Many thanks to Matthew Kopel and Kaitlin Fontana of Bloomsbury Publishing, for their support and patience. Gianluca Pescaroli's help and assistance were truly indispensable. This book is dedicated to my family, Angela, Jacopo and Emma Michela, who unwaveringly helped me go through a particularly difficult time, when finishing this work was not really at the top of my list of worries.

Foreword

Carlo Schaerf

Most of the chapters in this book are the result of the lectures delivered at the 25th ISODARCO Winter Course held in Andalo (Trento, Italy) on 8–15 January 2012 with the title 'Security in Cyberspace: Targeting Nations, Infrastructures, Individuals'. The course gathered a total of 55 scholars who spent one week together in a small hotel in the mountain resort of Andalo to discuss the problems of information technologies and their relation to war and international relations.

This course had a broad scope, addressing topics such as cyberwarfare, cyberterrorism, privacy and freedom of speech, organized crime, WikiLeaks and others. The entire realm of cyberspace is now at risk of being 'securitized'. It would then be removed from public debate and left into the sole hands of law enforcement agencies and defence and military professionals. Therefore our goal, as in all ISODARCO courses, is to shed some light, tackle controversial issues and provide a forum for high-level general discussion among participants and speakers alike. This course is the third ISODARCO course on information technologies and security in Cyberspace; previous courses were held in summer 1999 and summer 2002 and have resulted in a volume: Cyberwar, Netwar and the Revolution in Military Affairs published by Palgrave (Macmillan).

ISODARCO is an NGO (non-government organization) founded in 1966 by two Italian professors of physics, Edoardo Amaldi and myself, that offers a unique international forum on security problems throughout the world. ISODARCO's purpose is to bring together people with a great variety of experiences and approaches relating to security problems. Their discussions focus on commissioned expert papers.

ISODARCO's main activity has always been the organization of residential courses with senior lecturers and junior participants sharing the same living environment for 7–10 days. This encourages informal exchanges among lecturers and participants during the sessions and free time. Since 1966, ISODARCO has organized about 65 meetings that have resulted in the publication of 28 books by such British and American publishers such as Macmillan, John Wiley,

St Martin's Press, Dartmouth-Ashgate and Stanford University Press. Overall, the organization's characteristics are the following:

Participants in meetings held in the last decade have come from 68 countries. In ISODARCO's informal atmosphere, with Pugwash and Chatham House rules applying, traditional adversaries have been encouraged to debate with each other with a minimum of acrimony. For example, recent meetings have seen an Israeli coming into contact with a Syrian; Taiwanese sitting together with Chinese; Pakistanis and Indians equally encouraged to present their opinions. Twenty-five different nationalities are present at an average course.

Those attending come from a great variety of professions and backgrounds: military personnel and peace campaigners; diplomats and professors; nuclear scientists and historians. The common requirement ISODARCO sets for them all, however, is that they should be willing to engage in intellectually rigorous debate.

ISODARCO always places great emphasis on the importance of young people participating in the meetings. Typically half of them are in their twenties and early thirties: senior or graduate students or junior faculty members in a relevant discipline. In each session, half of the time is devoted to the discussion and during this period people chairing the sessions are required to give priority to younger participants to offer their views and ask questions.

The original purpose of ISODARCO was to provide reliable scientific and technical information on the political problems of disarmament, arms control, the nuclear arms race, and so on. However, already during the Cold War, ISODARCO has sensed the changing international environment and the new, emerging threats to world security. For example, it held sessions and published books relating to terrorism during the 1970s long before this subject became fashionable with mainstream security analysts. And it has similarly taken a long-standing interest in world security issues connected with energy, refugees, the environment, natural resources, and ethnic tensions.

The various ISODARCO meetings traditionally have been held in Italy. But there has been some internationalization in this respect, with meetings held in Germany, Jordan, twice in Taipei, and, on 13 occasions, in China. As a result, many more than 200 from Mainland China, and nearly as many from Taiwan, are ISODARCO alumni. The fact that it has been possible for ISODARCO to co-host meetings both in Beijing and Taipei demonstrates the extent of its credibility in East Asia. Probably no other security-related NGO has, or could have, achieved this. A meeting on Middle East security, with a broad range of participants (including Israelis) took place in Amman in 1997.

All opinions expressed in this book are of a purely personal nature and do not necessarily represent the official view of either ISODARCO or the organizers of the course or of the organizations with which the writers may be affiliates. The organization of this specific course has been made possible by the generous support and financial contributions of several institutions and foundations. In particular, it is pleasure to thank the Physics Department of the University of Rome 'Tor Vergata' and several local institutions such as, the Fondazione Opera Campana dei Caduti, the Giunta della Provincia Autonoma di Trento, the Regione Trentino Alto Adige, the Presidenza del Consiglio Regionale and the Presidenza del Consiglio della Provincia Autonoma di Trento. For the organization and operation of the course it is a pleasure for me to thank Dr Mirco Elena for the overall organization in Trentino, the management and staff of the Hotel Gruppo Brenta for their practical support during the course and Ms Svetlana Ignatyuk for administrative help during the course and its preparation.

Hic liber est scriptus, qui scripsit sit benedictus.
Propter Christum librum bene condidit istum.
Qui scripsit scribat, semper cum Domino vivat.
Qui scripsit scribat, et bona vina bibat.
Finito libro pinguis detur auca magistro.
Detur pro penna scriptori pulchra puella[*]

'Explicit of the XII Century'
Charles H. Haskins,
The Renaissance of the Twelfth Century (1955)

---

[*] This ode is a praise for the author(s) for completing the book, thank the Lord! Now they can toast and celebrate (with good wine) and collect all the benefits for their hard work. It is written in a 'collegiate' tone (probably by a friar in a convent); any literal translation would fail to render the significance and bonhomie of the piece.

List of Contributors

Laura Cordani, *Research Assistant, Department of Political and Social Sciences, University of Bologna*
Laura Cordani is a research assistant with the Department of Political and Social Sciences, University of Bologna and an intern in a London-based art gallery. She received her BA in International Studies and European Institutions from the University of Milan, Italy, in 2010 and completed a Master's Degree in International Relations at the University of Bologna, in 2013. Ms. Cordani's areas of interests are international conflicts, arms control, security and defence questions, cyber strategy, NATO, Russia and Iran.

Giampiero Giacomello, *Assistant Professor of International Relations in the Department of Political and Social Sciences, University of Bologna*
Giampiero Giacomello is Assistant Professor of International Relations with the Department of Political and Social Sciences, University of Bologna. Previously he held research and teaching positions (visiting) at several American universities. His research interests include strategic theory, cybersecurity, and foreign policy analysis. He has authored and co-edited seven volumes and published several articles in *European Political Science*, *International Studies Review*, *European Security*, *Contemporary Politics* and *International Political Science Review*. Dr Giacomello reports on Italy for the yearly publication *Freedom of the Net* (Freedom House) and is a contributor on defence and security issues for Italian dailies. Before becoming a scholar and an academic, he briefly considered a career as a hacker (before realizing his technical skills were far too limited for that).

Francesco Giacomini, *IT Specialist, Italian National Institute of Nuclear Research*
Francesco Giacomini is an IT Specialist at the Italian National Institute of Nuclear Research, with 15 years of experience in software engineering, high-performance computing and large-scale distributed computing. His main interests cover the technologies at the base of security systems and how they could help in defining better policies for the governance of the Internet.

Chunmei Kang, *Associate Professor, China Academy of Engineering Physics*
Chunmei Kang earned her PhD degree in the field of nuclear materials and is currently Associate Professor with the China Academy of Engineering Physics. Dr Kang has worked in the field of Arms Control for more than ten years and her research fields include nuclear strategy, arms control verification technology and non-proliferation issues. Cyberspace is a new field that she interested in, as cyberspace security is becoming more and more important to national security strategy. She is a co-author of *Nuclear Capability of Countries and Areas around China* (published by Atomic Energy Press) and *English-Chinese Chinese-English Nuclear Security Glossary* (also by Atomic Energy Press).

Andreas Kuehn, *Fulbright Scholar, School of Information Studies at Syracuse University, New York*
Andreas Kuehn is a PhD candidate and Fulbright Scholar at the School of Information Studies at Syracuse University, Syracuse, New York. His research areas include Internet Governance, Information Policy, and Science and Technology Studies. His current work focuses on the use of deep packet inspection in online copyright enforcement, behavioural targeting and cyber-security and its effects on Internet governance. He has worked in various research and technology policy roles for the Austrian Ministry of Finance, the Swiss E-Government-Institute, the Swiss OFCOM, and the Malaysian National Advanced IPv6 Centre of Excellence. He holds an MSc in Information Systems from the University of Zurich.

Bruce D. Larkin, *Professor Emeritus, University of California at Santa Cruz*
Bruce D. Larkin is Professor Emeritus of Politics at the University of California at Santa Cruz, where he has lectured on war and disarmament, Chinese politics and foreign policy, and internet governance. He is author of *Nuclear Designs: Great Britain, France, and China in the Global Governance of Nuclear Arms* (1996), *War Stories* (2001), and *Designing Denuclearization: An Interpretive Encyclopedia* (2008). His current work on weapons denuclearization can be followed at www.gcdd.net. A more extensive résumé is available at www.brucelarkin.net.

Rossella Mattioli, *Security and Resilience of Communication Networks Officer at the European Union Agency for Network and Information Security (ENISA)*
Rossella Mattioli holds a MSc in Engineering specializing in Cybersecurity at the Tallinn University of Technology in Estonia and BA in Communications

Sciences at the University of Modena and Reggio Emilia, Italy. Before focusing on Internet security and resilience, she was the intranet manager of a major Italian financial group where she dealt with network governance on an enterprise level for nine years. Her independent research includes incident information exchange, transnational incident management, Internet global operational security and governance issues related to critical information infrastructures. She is now Security and Resilience of Communication Networks Officer at the European Network and Information Security Agency (ENISA).

Milton Mueller, *Professor, Syracuse University School of Information Studies, New York*
Milton Mueller is Professor at Syracuse University School of Information Studies. He has conducted research on the political economy of telecommunications and the Internet for 25 years. His widely read book *Ruling the Root: Internet Governance and the Taming of Cyberspace* (MIT Press, 2002) provided the first scholarly account of how the battles over domain names led to an institutional innovation known as ICANN. His newest book, *Networks and States: The Global Politics of Internet Governance* (MIT Press, 2010) is a historical and theoretical challenge to the territorial nation-state's control of communication-information policy. He has been active in ICANN, the regional Internet address registries, the World Summit on the Information Society, and the Internet Governance Forum. He received his PhD from the University of Pennsylvania, Annenberg School, in 1989. From 2008–11 he held the XS4All Chair on the Security and Privacy of Internet Users at the Technology University of Delft, the Netherlands.

Patryk Pawlak, *Senior Analyst, EU Institute for Security Studies in Paris*
Patryk Pawlak is a Senior Analyst at the EU Institute for Security Studies in Paris where he deals with internal security policies of the EU, including cyber-security. He holds a PhD in Political Science from the European University Institute in Florence. Prior to joining the EUISS, he was a visiting scholar at numerous research institutions in Europe and in the United States. Dr Pawlak has published extensively in numerous peer-reviewed journals and contributed to several collective research and publication projects on European foreign and security policies, including on transatlantic homeland security and data protection co-operation.

Maria Grazia Porcedda, *Research Assistant, European University Institute (Italy)*
Maria Grazia Porcedda is Research Assistant with the SURVEILLE and SurPRISE projects at the European University Institute (Italy), where she will complete her PhD thesis on the reconciliation of privacy and data protection with the prevention of cybercrime and the pursuit of cybersecurity. She holds an LLM. in Comparative European and International Law from the European University Institute and an MA in International Relations from the University of Bologna. She previously worked at the Centre de Recherche Informatique et Droit (Belgium) on privacy and cloud computing, and as a trainee on privacy issues at both the Organization for Economic Co-operation and Development (OECD) and the European Data Protection Supervisor (EDPS).

Judith V. Reppy, *Professor, Cornell University*
Judith V. Reppy, PhD, is Professor Emerita in the Department of Science and Technology and Studies and a Graduate School Professor at Cornell University. She is also a former Director and Associate Director of the Peace Studies Program (now the Judith Reppy Institute for Peace and Conflict Studies). She has been a visiting fellow at the Science Studies Unit (Edinburgh University), Science and Technology Studies (Manchester University), the Science Policy Research Unit (Sussex University), and the Center for International Studies (MIT). She was co-chair of US Pugwash from 1995–2000 and in 2002–3 served on the National Academy of Sciences' Committee on Research Standards and Practices to Prevent the Destructive Application of Biotechnology ('the Fink Committee'). Dr Reppy's current research interests include dual-use technology, export control policy, and the impact of WikiLeaks on journalism and on diplomatic practices. Her most recent book is *Getting to Zero: The Path to Nuclear Disarmament* (Stanford University Press, 2011), co-editor (with Catherine Kelleher) and author.

Andra Siibak, *Senior Research Fellow, Institute of Journalism and Communication, University of Tartu, Estonia*
Andra Siibak, is a Senior Research Fellow in Media Studies at the Institute of Journalism and Communication, University of Tartu, Estonia. Her present research interests include audience fragmentation in new media environments, perceptions and constructions of privacy on social media. Her articles have appeared in *Journal of Computer-Mediated Communication*, *Cyberpsychology*, *Young*, *Trames*, and others.

Introduction: Security in Cyberspace

Giampiero Giacomello

Cyberspace is catch-all term that identifies a (virtual) area where computer networks, the semantic Web, social media and other information and communication technologies (ICT) exist and function together. Originally made popular by sci-fi (science-fiction) author William Gibson in 1984, cyberspace has been recently defined by the US National Institute of Standards and Technology (NIST) as a 'global domain within the information environment consisting of the interdependent network of information systems infrastructures including the Internet, telecommunications networks, computer systems, and embedded processors and controllers' (Kissel, 2013: 58). The emphasis here is more on the infrastructure (networks and computers), but as such global domain is 'within the information environment', cyberspace clearly includes all information and data available in it. Cyberspace today is simply indispensable for modern societies to work and live. In fact, one of the most crucial elements of cyberspace is the 'nerves and blood' of those societies, namely the 'critical information infrastructure' (CII), without which there would be no distribution of energy, no services like banking or finance or communication, no air traffic control and so on.[1]

The concept of security has a long (and controversial) history (Rothschild, 1995; Giacomello and Nation, 2009). Predictably, the *security* of cyberspace (or cybersecurity for short) must be a top priority today for governments, companies and scientists, because if such critical infrastructure collapses or communications fail, social life would be disrupted and the world economy compromised. Again the NIST describes cybersecurity as 'The ability to protect or defend the use of cyberspace from cyber attacks' (Kissel, 2013: 58). Indeed, threats and actual attacks to cyberspace and its integrity abound; they may come from states against other states, from non-state groups (terrorists, 'hacktivists' and the like), from companies against competitors or even from individuals.

This volume explores what 'security in cyberspace' is today. In the past it existed only in science-fiction (sci-fi) literature and movies, which have always portrayed computers communicating with each other as well as with humans.

Inevitably, in every sci-fi plot, at some point, 'security fails', giving the opportunity to narrate the story. Reality has been more mundane and only toward the end of the twentieth century did it slowly begin to catch up with imagination. As early as the 1970s, it was known that the new technologies of information were likely to increase states' exposure to external threats.

A report to the Swedish government, the 'Tengelin Report' (Tengelin, 1981) clearly identified some of the risks that a networked, highly interconnected society would face, including the dependence on foreign vendors and the threat of hackers' raids. Back then, computer networks were proprietary, namely they linked together the US strategic command with its nuclear missile silos or a bank with its subsidiaries. Most importantly, they used protocols that authorized only the legitimate users to be in each network. Hence, they were expensive, so that a handful of organizations or institutions could afford them, and they were bulky and slow. Today a vast cyberspace (and the Internet, *in primis*) has so reduced the cost of networking that not only computers and mobile phones are connected, but so are cars and household appliances. Speed of communication and economic efficiency are at premium, not security. The price for this state of affairs is that criminals, wrongdoers or simply 'the enemy' may exploit the structural vulnerabilities of one's networks for their own ends.

In their first six decades of existence, computers and computer networks have evolved considerably, but their primary mission remains the same today. Computers have been built to perform routine activities more *efficiently* than humans – who are not too good at repetition – and computer networks have allowed remote control over such process over long distances. Based on empirical observation, we could summarize the main features of the early period of cyberspace as follows: (1) reliance on computer networks for all vital functions in even moderately advanced societies has continued to increase unabated; (2) the Web has become an information source that no country, nor company, nor most people in advanced economies can do without; and (3) risks to cybersecurity have, accordingly, grown.

Until recently, it was unthinkable that somebody might actually exploit the (inevitable) 'gap between theory and practice' (Libicki, 2009: xiv), that is, between what a system or software is designed to do and what it actually does, to fulfil goals quite diverse from those that developers and engineers originally had in mind. If everybody just wanted to go after his or her business in a more efficient manner, why bother with security? The latter would indeed make the system and processes *less* efficient. Only after the gap was acknowledged, did it become manifest and accepted by users and developers that while security checks and policies would make the individual process less efficient, they would make cyberspace, as a whole, more functional.

Examples of this state of affairs abound: from Google's clash with the Chinese government to security firms broken into by hackers;[2] from the role of Twitter and Facebook in the Arab Spring to Stuxnet;[3] from the ravening curse of identity theft to the blunt admission that cyber-crime has proven unstoppable. From the National Security Agency (NSA) attacking Web privacy (Perlroth and Shane, 2013) to whistleblowers as Edward Snowden and Private Bradley Manning. In fact, the military is far from being exempt. When announcing the Pentagon's modernization plan for the US Armed Forces of the future in 2011, President Obama made clear that one of the few areas that will not be cut, will be that of cybersecurity/cyberwarfare. Likewise, cybersecurity is now a central tenet of NATO's smart defence posture. This is a tiny sample of cases; given such conditions, it is hardly surprising that security in cyberspace is a rather problematic topic to address, as authors and readers alike would claim that (cyber)warfare, terrorism, social activism, social resilience, ownership of information, privacy and censorship and other issue areas are all affected.

Contrary to what many users think, the Internet and the Web are not the same. The distinction is not always neat, but the Internet is (part of) the 'infrastructure', the underlying bundle of cables, protocols and lines that supports the rest. The World Wide Web functions as the primary information source, followed by other communication technologies, such as email and social media. More precisely, Martin Libicki (2007: 236–40) suggests a three-layered structure, comprising the 'physical' (the hard physical infrastructure of computers, routers, and cables), the 'syntactic' (the software and protocols which control network flows), and the 'semantic' (the actual information and ideas exchanged in human language through the network).

Broadly speaking, sovereign states are first concerned about the physical level, next with the semantic one (how they are seen and perceived by other fellow states) and finally, with the syntactic level (software should be working flawlessly). With the exception of telecom companies, which provide the physical infrastructure, most businesses worry about only the syntactic (their communication and online services function well)[4] and the semantic (their public 'image'). Individuals are totally unconcerned about the first two levels, as long as the social function (via the Web and social media) of the network allows them to communicate and gather information.

The situation in cyberspace is a striking example of a typical 'principal-agent' theory (PAT). In the PAT, the principal has to delegate 'authority' to agents, usually via a 'contract', to achieve its goals, because the agent has informational advantage and greater technical expertise over the principal.[5] But the latter's actions have impact on both players 'utility' and the only way the former can make sure the agent will comply with the contract is through incentives and sanctions (Laffont and Martimort, 2002). The PAT originated in economics, in the insurance sector first (Spence and Zeckhauser, 1971) and was later applied in political science as well (Cook and Wood, 1989). In cyberspace, the government has to delegate the defence (or some of it) and maintenance of a large part of the infrastructures to the private sector and, to less extent, to users.[6] The interdependence and multiple ownership of cyberspace infra-structures make for complex principal-agent relationships and the incentives and sanctions that the state can recur to not infrequently fail to keep a unity of purpose, which should be the security of 'national' access to cyberspace. Overall, this approach may well become one of the most rewarding in future cybersecurity research.

A priority goal of cybersecurity is to protect the targeted victims of cyber-attacks. Hence, cybersecurity today is about the protection of information and control systems from malicious actors that try to compromise the system through malicious software, which is often capable of replicating and distributing itself while remaining undetected. As we noted earlier, the concept of 'cybersecurity' is larger than the purely technical concept of IT-security, because it involves actors, malicious or protective, policies, and their societal consequences. It would be next to impossible to address the many instances and aspects that now shape cybersecurity in just one volume, but here we hope to offer some food for thought and reflections on the most relevant issues. In planning this volume, we came to the conclusion that a better understanding of the risks, perceptions, and myths that surround cybersecurity would be possible if the matter in question were investigated from the viewpoint of the 'target-victim' of cyber-attacks. We identified three 'targets' (or levels of analysis) which are strictly linked to the network's structure itself and its principal stakeholders, as presented in the relevant literature (Giacomello, 2005a; Libicki, 2007; Choucri, 2012), namely (1) nation-states; (2) infrastructures (owners and stakeholders); and (3) individuals (users).[7]

Among nation-states, it is just a few years ago that the United States, then the 'most wired' country in the world, was concerned with cybersecurity; today a larger number of nation-states are increasingly interested in cyber-defence as well as cyber-offence. In addition to the United States, China, Russia, India, Brazil, and Israel, as well as the whole of the European Union and 'newcomers' like Iran and Saudi Arabia, have come to the realization that their survival and well-being are so dependent on the Internet and the Web that any serious threats to those infrastructures should be countered at the highest level, including, if necessary, the recourse to 'kinetic strikes' (that is, real, conventional weapons).[8] At the same time, the same group of states is investing in the development of cyber-weapons to be used against other adversaries, most likely in the opening stages of an inter-state conflict, much like, for example, electronic warfare was intended for use during the Cold War (Markoff, 2008).

Computer networks (including fibre optic cables, routers, etc.) and the specialized software to run them constitute the infrastructure of cyberspace. Such systems not only make it possible to communicate, entertain, and transfer information and money, but also to facilitate the operation of utilities and other essential public services (for instance, air traffic control). This infrastructure is jointly owned by public and private stakeholders, whose interests often overlap to the point that it is difficult to understand who owns what and, above all, whose responsibility it is to protect and defend certain parts of the infrastructure. And here arises the most serious consequence of this public-private 'partnership': the only viable way to protect the infrastructure is resilience and redundancy, that is, for each safety/security mechanism there should be another one, so in case the former fails, there is a back-up. This course of action, however, is expensive. To increase profits, companies look for ways to cut costs and, under normal conditions of operations, back-ups and redundancy are mostly seen as expensive luxuries, until normality ceases. The type of economic and organizational logic that requires hospitals to have back-ups in case of power failure (and thus avoid serious law suits after the crisis) still appears foreign to many managers of the infrastructure.

Finally, individuals, with their communication, personal and financial data and general information online all the time, have as much at stake as companies and states. At times it even seems that the 'super-individual', the 'lone wolf' terrorist with a laptop, could take down a whole country. Cyber-criminals and market researchers both consider the Web the best mine of information. Given this state of affairs, it is not surprising that so many data protection authorities exist in Europe and elsewhere and privacy NGO advocates are so numerous and active, especially within advanced democracies.

Of cyber space and security

On cybersecurity there have literally been 'volumes' published in the last decade and this is just a small sample. Most of the works cited here tend to focus narrowly on specific applications such as the educational or business sectors, presenting the viewpoint of computer scientists or engineers and are, in many cases, targeted to IT professionals. A typical example is *Cyber Security Essentials,* edited by Graham, Olson and Howard (2010), which focuses on the sophisticated methods used in recent high-profile cyber incidents. While useful to ICT professionals, volumes like *Cyber Security Essentials* are not accessible to more general readers who have an interest in how ICT influences their societies and way of life.

The same limitation applies to practical, 'hands-on' manuals such as the one by Perry Craft (2012) which focuses on business operations and long-term strategy for risk assessment and incident handling, or to the *Cyber Security Policy Guidebook* (Bayuk et al., 2012), which covers a plethora of issues, trying to explain what is meant by cyber security and cyber security policy and how cyber security policy goals are discussed. Quite comprehensive, the latter volume is policy-oriented. Thus, it does not try to establish links to disciplines other than policy analysis and computer sciences. Even when addressing broader areas affected by ICT, the emphasis of other recent works continues to be on (1) applied knowledge for (2) a very narrowly defined field. A typical example is *Cyber Security for Educational Leaders* (Phillips and Sianjina, 2013), in which the authors explain what cybersecurity is for 'educational leaders', but with narrow focus, because it is confined to a technical response and ignores the broader context.

Moving toward more general approaches to the study of cybersecurity, Shoemaker and Conklin (2011) provide a synthesis of the practices for assuring information security. Their book is based on cybersecurity practices of the Department of Homeland Security's 'Essential Body of Knowledge' for IT-security. The limitation of this book, however, is the same as the previous ones, as it, too, speaks to the technically proficient reader, without much consideration for the larger picture. Another title is *Cybersecurity: Public Sector Threats and Responses* (Andreasson, 2011), which, for example, offers practical guidance on the convergence of globalization, connectivity, and the migration of public sector functions online. Unlike other volumes on cybersecurity however,

Andreasson explores the current policy environment in the United States as well as in Europe and the challenges at all levels of government. While it is organized into three sections (Global Trends, National and Local policy approaches), it does not tackle the 'individual level' of target analysis in cybersecurity.

The individuals' level is considered, for instance, by Moeller (2011), who specifically analyses on the role of auditors in the areas of computer audit, control, and security, with the goal of providing guidance for them and by Migga Kizza (2011). Migga Kizza's volume is undoubtedly original, as it investigates cyber vandalism and identity theft made possible by the loopholes inherent in the cyberspace infrastructure. Dorothy Denning (2001) has been the 'first explorer' of this area of study and Kizza convincingly explores the nature and motives behind cyber-attacks. But, again, there is no examination the links between the 'infrastructure' and individual levels and the macro level of nation-states,

While research on the overlap of information technology with global affairs and security is some years old (Eriksson and Giacomello, 2007), chapters on cybersecurity and cyber-threats (Dunn, 2010, 2009) are now regularly included in more general publications on security, thus showing how quickly this topic has become an established field of 'security studies' and international relations. A recent addition to this field is *Cyberspaces and Global Affairs* (Costigan and Perry, 2012) in which editors and contributors specifically concentrated on the nexus between cyberspace, and the effects of new communication technologies. Various case-studies (from the Middle East and North Africa to the 'Colour Revolutions' of Eastern Europe and Central Asia, to terrorism and warfare and 'humanitarian ICT needs') and how these issues are affected by modern information technologies are examined. But in this specific domain, which is adjacent to cybersecurity, a more comprehensive work undoubtedly is *Cyberpolitics in International Relations* by Nazli Choucri (2012).

Finally, there is a large body of work on 'cyberwar and warfare', but we make a quick reference to only three examples here, as a thorough literature review would take up too much space. The first is *Cyberwar* by Clarke and Knake (2010), who argue that the United States has already lost the 'cyber battles' of the new millennium, economically and militarily, outlining how the country is vulnerable and how Americans, as individuals, are too exposed to the 'vast and looming web of cyber-criminals' and cyber warriors. While the book, as its authors claim, is 'about technology, government, and military strategy (as well as criminals, spies, soldiers, and hackers), it conveys such a powerful sense of conspiracy theory and of inevitable doom as to be hardly credible. Furthermore, although it does acknowledge the 'three levels', it fails to explore their linkages and there is no explanation of how the levels may affect each other.

Another volume is *Cyber Warfare* by Andress and Winterfeld (2011), who explore cyber conflicts in the forms of espionage, hacktivism, insider threats, and non-state actors like organized criminals and cyber terrorists, again the 'Denning' approach. The authors also provide concrete examples and guidance about ethics, laws and consequences of cyber war. Yet, there are the usual limits of narrow focus and no attempt at establishing links and providing explanations of the three levels of analysis, as this work too is aimed at professionals in the field.

Carr (2011)[9] convincingly provides details on how nations, groups, and individuals throughout the world use the Internet as an attack platform to gain military, political, and economic advantages over their adversaries. The author explicitly addresses the three levels, examining topics such as the US Cyber Command, the role of social networks in fomenting revolution in the Middle East and Northern Africa, the intellectual property wars and the use of Stuxnet, which are also at the centre of this volume. This (inevitably) short sample of the large literature on cybersecurity would be defective, if we did not mention the volume *Black Code*, by some of the most respected contemporary authors on cyberspace issues, namely Deibert, Rohozinski, and Hafner[10] (2011). In 2009, searching through that obscure area of computer communications spaces known as 'black code', of which average users are totally unaware of but where intelligence services as well as 'good and bad' hackers are a constant presence, Deibert and his colleagues uncovered a major Chinese cyber-espionage ring. They also discovered how the confidential information on several ministries of foreign affairs, international organization officials and private firm executives was quietly gathered and stolen.

Structure of the book

Relying on 'triads' of agents or concepts to analyse cyberspace and cyberse-curity is, *per se*, quite common (Herrera, 2002; Giacomello, 2005a; Libicki 2007, 2009). In this volume, we present a three-level target analysis (based on potential objects of attacks), which is a rather novel approach. We consider the three crucial objectives of (1) sovereign states (or nations), (2) the computer networks (and its stakeholders, both public and private) and, last but not least, (3) the individual. Hence the volume is divided into two parts, with the first of these parts addressing the national/state level of target analysis and the second concentrating on the infrastructure/individual.

Because of the nature of computer networks and of cybersecurity, it is difficult to draw clear lines between the different levels. Examples are abundant: a private company may own the power distribution grid, but since the grid provides a 'common good', national or state authorities are concerned that the grid works smoothly. Moreover, other companies, state authorities and individuals use the computer networks also utilized by that company to remotely control the grid and distribution mechanisms. If something, for chance or malfeasance, goes wrong, whose responsibility is it?[11] Individual case-studies will typically include elements of all three levels, and actors may move fluidly between the three levels. The focus on standpoints, however, allows us to embed our analyses of the competing interests at stake in their specific context, while still offering an opportunity for generalizing about those aspects of cybersecurity that are shared across stakeholders. The selection of cybersecurity issues here is intended to demonstrate that the three-layer structure is valid framework of analysis and it can foster a better comprehension of the whole realm of cybersecurity.

After the introduction, which outlines the scope of this volume and its structure and main conclusions, Part One (The Nation) opens with Rossella Mattioli's Chapter 1 on 'The "State(s)" of Cybersecurity', Mattioli argues that cybersecurity is a 'paradigm in progress' because it lies at the intersection of society and technology where concepts like space and security assume different meanings because of the interdependencies between nation, infrastructures, and individuals. Thus, the aim of her chapter is to provide an overview on where the security and cyberspace spheres cross these levels and become 'cybersecurity.' Using the dichotomy of offence and defence, the reader will be able to grasp the different aspects of the cybersecurity definition from national, infrastructure, and individual perspectives. Two cybersecurity policy approaches, those adopted by United States displayed by the European Union (EU), are also presented to show how even at the same level different players address such challenges.

In fact, Mattioli points out, the novelty in the cybersecurity debate is not only about the explicit and implicit consequences of its definition but also the roles of the actors involved in the process. Before the Internet, the borders of the security realm were relatively clear, but now, due to the nature of cyberspace, it is challenging to capture all the connected actors in the same frame. Clearly, cyberspace may encompass many different parties, including international intergovernmental organizations, states, academic and hacker communities, information technology corporations, cyber-criminals, non-state actors, and ultimately, individuals. Cybersecurity cannot but be directly related to the dependence of contemporary society – and all its stakeholders – on network technologies.

In Chapter 2, 'Reducing Uncertainties in Cyberspace through Confidence and Capacity Building Measures', Patryk Pawlak tackles the problems arising in the issue-area of cybersecurity because of the sheer size of cyber-authority and cyber-capabilities that non-governmental actors now have by focusing on two germane 'strata'. On the one hand, the European Union and many individual countries around the world deal with cybersecurity by focusing on improving their own resilience and building up their cyber-capabilities. This, however, may create uncertainties as to the peaceful nature of those efforts that in turn need to be accompanied by political initiatives like confidence building measures. On the other, because there is no physical border at which cyber-threats would stop, many actors acknowledge the need to deal with cyber-threats through political and capacity building measures. Pawlak concludes that there is also a widespread recognition among policymakers that capacity building is a global effort, which has to take place in cooperation with the other stakeholders of cyberspace, namely the private sector and civil society.

In Chapter 3, Judith Reppy addresses the controversial debate on 'WikiLeaks and State Control of Information in the Cyber Age'. Noting that, while we are a long way from the old definition of state sovereignty as 'the sovereign is obeyed and does not obey', Reppy acknowledges that even in today's globalized world 'the state' still retains significant powers of control, not least in the control of information. Her chapter moves from a brief history of WikiLeaks to illustrate both the challenges that the Internet poses to state power and the legal and extra-legal means at the state's disposal to exert control over the Internet. It raises questions of the trade-offs between the need for secrecy in matters touching on national security and the democratic values of transparency in government. The related implications of WikiLeaks for journalism and the protection of whistleblowers are also persuasively examined the author.

Following Judith Reppy's footsteps, in Chapter 4, 'Leaks: Securing Communications and Achieving Nuclear Zero', Bruce Larkin takes on the critical topic of communication and nuclear weapons. Modern societies are defined by transportation and energy grids, financial transfers, technically 'advanced' design and production, and daily more intensive collaborations. Although the current nuclear weapon inventory and delivery systems largely predate the impact of the Internet and Web, military capabilities and operational plans – and policy-making and decisions – are now inextricably reliant on computing and telecommunications. Concurrently, there is a growing consensus among policymakers that nuclear weapons are unusable (except to deter others' nuclear weapon use) and that the ongoing risk of their use mandates elimination. The political process of agreeing to global zero and then maintaining it will, however, be multiply dependent on reliable and secure communications. This chapter explores the cyber requirements of nuclear disarmament, illustrating vulnerabilities in part by querying prior breaches of 'reliability' and 'security', and extrapolates to the conditions and capabilities that will be required.

Larkin concludes that future breaches are simply 'certain', that prudent planning for breach should be built into the new 'zero nuclear weapons' regime, and that operating in daylight is the best preventive of harm through breach. This orientation favours ongoing mutual reassurance, public access to evidence and its assessment, and full disclosure, while acknowledging that negotiations are often more fruitful when preliminary discussion can take place in private. The burden of justifying secrecy should lie on the party that actually proposes it. From a technical viewpoint this orientation favours ongoing refinement and prudent use of standard practices, including encryption, redundancy, ready access to disputed sites, and shared assessment.

The closing chapter of Part One is dedicated to the 'rising nation' of cyber-power, namely China. North America, along with Europe, Japan, and Australia, are still the dominant players for technology and content production in cyber-space, but China has a fast growing (and young) online population and Chinese may well become the cyberspace's dominant language.[12] Cyber-attacks – in the form of distributed denial-of-service (DDoS), hacking of email accounts, or even cyber-espionage *tout court* – against (mostly but not exclusively) the United States that are said to be originating from China are now a monthly occurrence (for example, Barboza, 2010; Shane, 2012; Sanger, Barboza and Peroth, 2013.) Often the Chinese government, and particularly the military, is accused of being linked to – if not the instigator – of the attacks (Fritz, 2008; Markoff and Barboza, 2010.) Simultaneously, Chinese officials consistently deny any connection to such assaults, asserting that the Chinese government attaches great importance to cybersecurity and opposes cyber-crime and that China too is a 'victim' in cyberspace (LaFranerie and Ansfield, 2010; Sanger, 2013).

As it is often the case, the truth lies somewhere in the middle, with elements of the Chinese state being culpable in some cases, but not necessarily responsible for all such attacks. All victims of attacks should conduct thorough investigations to identify culprits. Thus, the Chinese government should show good faith by prosecuting attackers when such investigations reveal that the individuals responsible are indeed operating from within Chinese territory. Such a good faith attitude would help foster international cooperation on cybercrime and terrorism and even cyberwarfare. Chunmei Kang and her colleagues in Chapter 5, 'Establishing Norms of Behaviour in Cyberspace: The Chinese Viewpoint', offer a view from 'other side of the hill'. Kang observes that, unsurprisingly, cyberspace is now embedded into such an increasing number of capabilities that states and people cannot help but heavily rely on cyber-technologies to work, function and 'live'. Yet, precisely because of the global nature of cyberspace, the vulnerabilities that exist are open to the world. According to Kang, China as a developing country is far less capable of maintaining Internet security than the developed counties, which face a much bigger threat of online attacks. For promoting the use of information and cyber technology in advancing economic and social development and people's welfare, behavioural norms and related law should be established.

If the issue of cyberspace is now beyond the 'simple' technical dimension, as Kang writes, it has now become a social, political, economic and cultural phenomenon, affecting every country, China even more so. Such conditions make it a concern not just for the Chinese. Given that different countries have different historical and cultural traditions and economic and social development levels, cyber behaviour norms should first be established nationally. International cooperation could first be developed in those areas that facilitate a common view and common laws, such as anti-terrorism and inhibiting criminal behaviour. The author convincingly concludes that, while there are other countries particularly prominent in cyberspace, such as North Korea, with its cyber warriors or Russia with its hackers and cyber-criminals or the cases of some European countries cited in other chapters, nevertheless, there is little doubt that, if there is only one other country apart from the United States that will gain prominence in cyberspace (as competitor or possibly partner), that country could only be China.

Part Two concentrates on the other two levels of 'targeting' in cyberspace, namely the infrastructures of computer networks, with their stakeholders, and individuals. These levels of target analysis are, perhaps, even more complex, as property rights and commercial-public interests and individuals' privacy and freedom of speech overlap but not always coincide, thus making this a very 'grey area'.

Chapter 6, 'Einstein on the Breach: Surveillance Technology, Cybersecurity and Organizational Change', by Andreas Kuehn and Milton Mueller opens this section. The authors explore the way cybersecurity technology alters organizational relationships. The chapter is a detailed case study of the implementation of intrusion detection and prevention technology (IDS/IPS) in US government agencies, including the Einstein program and the Defense Industrial Base (DIB) Enhanced Cybersecurity Services (DIB/ECS) program. IDS/IPS employs deep packet inspection (DPI) capabilities to scan data packets in real-time and make decisions about how to handle incoming and outgoing network traffic based on automated recognition of threats. Drawing on the theory of the firm, Kuehn and Mueller ask whether these cybersecurity initiatives lead to more centralized, hierarchical control of Internet services and/or the internalization of functions and operations formerly provided by the private sector. In the end, the authors find that DPI implementations do lead to significant organizational changes in government agencies and threatens to blur the boundary between cybersecurity efforts confined to US government agencies and private sector ISPs, defence contractors and ISPs.

Shifting to the technical-legal side of cybersecurity, in Chapter 7, 'Artificial or "Legitimate" Barriers to Internet Governance?', Francesco Giacomini and Laura Cordani outline some of the key elements that may facilitate a viable distinction between online practices that are truly legitimate and those that are not. The Internet has certainly fostered the diffusion of information and technical knowledge without many of the 'natural' (that is, structural) impediments typical of past innovations. But like all novelties, the authors argue, the benefits that the Internet offers to most of society may constitute a danger (or be perceived as such) to stakeholders with vested interest, generating resistance by a number of players. Moreover, the novelty of the technology and the lack of uniform governance of the virtual space have opened the door to practices that risk undermining human rights.

Content providers are often bound to classical business models (those rooted in the analogue world) and still tend to be cautious regarding new alternatives, while service providers heavily profile all their users, collecting personal information, for marketing purposes. Law-enforcement agencies have the same urge to gather information about citizens, ostensibly with the goal to protect them, but with the consequence of creating a tool for political control.[13] Militaries are worried about attacks on national critical infrastructures, which are more and more integrated with general-purpose cyberspace. The authors use the telling example of the Stuxnet worm to prove their point here. Giacomini and Cordani conclude that the solutions devised thus far to address the above concerns will converge towards a strictly controlled model of Internet governance, where those losing the most will be, inevitably, the individuals.

As the third contribution to this section, Maria Grazia Porcedda's Chapter 8, 'Public-Private Partnerships: A "Soft" Approach to Cybersecurity? Views from the European Union', investigates the importance of the CII in today's economy and national security. Cybersecurity policies are therefore being developed ubiquitously, and collaborations across the globe are emerging, one example being the Working Group on Cybersecurity and Cyber-crime, created by the EU/US Summit. Since, however, key resources are shared between the public and the private sectors, governmental initiatives alone seem insufficient to address the growing demand for cybersecurity. Therefore, as the author observes, the so-called private-public partnerships (PPPs) – whereby the government and the foremost ICT operators pool their resources and know-how to tackle protection of the CII and cyber-crime prosecution – have proliferated.

The landscape is varied. Some PPPs are strictly national, such as the 'Enduring Security Framework' (made up of the CEOs of ICT and defence companies, and the heads of the most important departments of the United States), and the partnership between Google and the National Security Agency, negotiated after the attacks suffered by gmail, to share information with a view to improving Google's (privately-owned) network's security. Other PPPs are bilateral, such as the one established by the EU-US Working Group on Cybersecurity and Cyber-crime, and still others are multinational, such as the many partnerships created to address child pornography, often sponsored by an international organization such as Interpol. Regardless of their nature, though, PPPs are developing outside clear, binding legal frameworks.

Under these conditions, Porcedda explores examples of each of the three types (national, bilateral, multilateral) of the existing partnerships to address such questions as: are PPPs keeping up with their promise of better addressing cyber-challenges? Is the lack of a binding legal framework necessary to allow for flexibility or, rather, is it shielding collusion? Is the lack of a legal framework facilitating the violation of citizens' rights, and exposing companies to liabilities? She also provides some preliminary answers.

Andra Siibak's Chapter 9, 'Being Publicly Private: Extreme Nationalist User Practices on Social Networks', closes the volume by specifically addressing individuals as targets. In her contribution, Siibak describes the changes that have occurred in the self-presentation practices of extreme nationalist users of the Estonian-language social networking site between 2007 and 2011. According to Siibak, the analysis of the user profiles in 2011 indicates that, in comparison to the results of the content analysis carried out in 2007, the extreme nationalist users on Rate started to use more complex strategies for introducing their ideology.

In the profiles, the author finds examples of Padonki and Leet-speak (the counter-culture versions of 'netspeak'), computer text symbols, and computer text art, as well as a privacy technique known as social steganography. Furthermore, compared to the acronyms and secret number combinations used in the 2007 profiles, their variety has grown remarkably. Siibak discovers that, in comparison to the findings of 2007, users with extremist worldviews have also broadened the scale and genres of their posts. These multimodal profiles now combine various texts (that is, song lyrics, poems, slogans, short fictions, and personal diary entries), as well as various YouTube videos and images. All the above-mentioned changes in the user practices indicate that, on social media sites where multiple audiences are blended into one, the profiles and posts made by the extreme nationalist users are mainly targeted to their 'ideal readers', that is, the individuals who share and hence are able to interpret their worldviews.

In an 'old' (at least by ICT standards) article, the volume's editor suggested that scholars approaching the field of cybersecurity should look to the experience of the early peace and disarmament researchers who, during the Cold War, did not have accessed to classified information, but through various innovative methods could amass considerable amount of reliable data on conventional forces or nuclear, biological and chemical (NBC) warfare (Giacomello, 2005b). At first, it appeared an almost impossible task to those independent researchers who did not have access to classified information. They were also well aware that their work would be the main reference point for debates on disarmament and arms control by some of the actors involved in those debates, such as peace movements or opposition parties. The range and proficiency of many studies on conventional and NBC warfare that resulted from that effort is an unquestioned tribute to the insight and determination of those scholars as well as to such independent organizations like ISODARCO that, as Carlo Schaerf notes in this volume's Foreword, have been invaluable to ensure that that knowledge would be diffused. Today, scholars who do not have access to classified information on cybersecurity are, to some extent, in a similar situation as arms control and peace researchers were at the onset of the Cold War. Will they then match the quality and insight that their colleagues of that earlier period were nonetheless capable of? The reader will be the ultimate judge, but the contributors and editor of this volume are quite confident that they will indeed.

Notes

1 As of May 2013, the NIST considers as 'critical infrastructures' those 'system and assets, whether physical or virtual, so vital to the United States that the incapacity or destruction of such systems and assets would have a debilitating impact on security, national economic security, national public health or safety, or any combination of those matters' (Kissel, 2013: 51).

2 As was the case, for instance, of Stratfor, a Washington-based security company that was 'hacked' in 2011.

3 Stuxnet was a particularly advanced 'worm' (a self-replicating piece of software) that contributed to delaying the Iranian nuclear program in 2009–10. For more details, see Chapter 4.

4 It is not only that businesses groom their Web images for their sales and so on, but many companies use the Internet for remote control via SCADA (Supervisory Control and Data Acquisition). The US NIST define SCADA as 'networks or systems generally used for industrial controls or to manage infrastructure such as pipelines and power systems' (Kissel, 2013: 191).

5 I am in debt to Francesco Giumelli, who works on the PAT applied to economic sanctions, for giving me the idea of 'exporting' this theory to cyberspace.

6 In a sense, users are agents too. They have a personal interest in keeping their computers malware free and updated. But they also have a 'public' interest to do so, because if they do not follow minimal security precautions, more computers will become malware victims and be turned into 'bots', namely machines that unbeknownst to their owners can be remotely used by unauthorized users, or 'insecurity gates' through which more critical or classified computers and networks could be accessed.

7 For a more extensive discussion on the several levels in cyberspace see Choucri (2012).

8 For more details on what the relationships among these countries in cyberspace are see for instance Sanger (2010), Perlroth (2012) and Shane (2012).

9 Carr's volume was originally published in 2009.

10   Katie Hafner is the co-author, with Matthew Lyon, of *Where Wizards Stay Up Late* (1996), one of the earliest and best accounts of how the Internet was born. Incidentally, she was also a guest-speaker at the first ISODARCO (Summer) Course dedicated to computer networks in August 1999.

11   For a broader discussion (and examples) on these issues see Saadawi and Jordan (2011), Bygrave, and Bing (2009), Personick and Patterson (2003) as well as Chapter 5 in Fischer (2009).

12   For more details on these topics see, for example, Damm, and Thomas (2006), LaFranerie and Ansfield (2010) and So and Westland (2010).

13   It is an issue not limited to dictatorial or undemocratic regimes, if one thinks of the debate over domestic drones and camera surveillance in the United States and the United Kingdom. For a survey of countries and privacy and control issues, see Deibert et al. (2010) and Giacomello (2005a). For the reactions to the revelation of the National Security Agency (NSA) eavesdropping on domestic phone calls in the United States, see Nagourney (2013).

References

Andreasson, K. J. (ed.) (2011), *Cybersecurity: Public Sector Threats and Responses*, Boca Raton, FL: CRC Press.

Andress, J. and S. Winterfeld (2011), *Cyber Warfare: Techniques, Tactics and Tools for Security Practitioners*, Waltham, MA: Syngress-Elsevier.

Barboza, D. (2010), 'Hacking for Fun and Profit in China's Underworld', *The New York Times*, 2 February 2010, B1.

Bayuk, J. L., J. Healey, P. Rohmeyer, M. Sachs, J. Schmidt and J. Weiss (2012), *Cyber Security Policy Guidebook*, Hoboken, NJ: John Wiley & Sons, Inc.

Bygrave, L. A. and J. Bing (eds) (2009), *Internet Governance: Infrastructure and Institutions*, Oxford: Oxford University Press.

Carr, J. (2011), *Inside Cyber Warfare: Mapping the Cyber Underworld*, 2nd edn, Sebastopol, CA: O'Reilly Media.

Choucri, N. (2012), *Cyberpolitics in International Relations*, Cambridge, MA: MIT Press.

Clarke, R. A. and R. K. Knake (2010), *Cyberwar: The Next Threat to National Security and What to Do About It*, New York: HarperCollins.

Cook, B. and B. Wood (1989), 'Principal-Agent Models of Political Control of Bureaucracy', *American Political Science Review*, 83: 965–78.

Costigan, S. S. and J. Perry (eds) (2012), *Cyberspaces and Global Affairs*, Aldershot: Ashgate.

Craft, J. P. (2012), *Leading a Cyber-Security Program: A Guide for Information Security Professionals*, New York: Auerbach Publications-Taylor and Francis.

Damm, J. and S. Thomas (eds) (2006), *Chinese Cyberspaces: Technological Changes and Political Effects*, London: Routledge.

Deibert, R., J. Palfrey, R. Rohozinski and J. Zittrain (eds) (2010), *Access Controlled: The Shaping of Power, Rights, and Rule in Cyberspace*, Cambridge, MA: MIT Press.

Deibert, R., R. Rohozinski and K. Hafner (2011), *Black Code: The Battle for the Future of Cyberspace*, Toronto: McClelland & Stewart.

Denning, D. E. (2001), 'Activism, Hacktivism, and Cyberterrorism: The Internet as a Tool for Influencing Foreign Policy', in J. Arquilla and D. Ronfeldt (eds) (2001) *Networks and Netwars: The Future of Terror, Crime, and Militancy*, Santa Monica, CA: RAND.

Dunn Cavelty, M. (2009), 'Cyberwar', in G. Kassimeris and J. Buckley (eds), *The Ashgate Research Companion to Modern Warfare*, Aldershot: Ashgate.

—(2010), 'Cyber-security', in P. Burgess (ed.), *The Routledge Companion to New Security Studies*, London: Routledge.

Eriksson, J. and G. Giacomello (eds) (2007), *International Relations and Security in the Digital Age*, London: Routledge.

Fischer, E. A. (2009), *Creating a National Framework for Cybersecurity: An Analysis of Issues and Options*, New York: Nova Science Publishers.

Fritz, J. (2008), 'How China will use cyber warfare to leapfrog in military competitiveness', *Culture Mandala*, 8: 28–80.

Giacomello, G. (2005a), *National Governments and Control of the Internet: A Digital Challenge*, London: Routledge.

—(2005b), 'The critical role of peace research in assessing cyberthreats', *Peace Review*, 17: 239–46.

Giacomello, G. and R. Craig Nation (eds) (2009), *Security in the West: Evolution of a Concept*, Milan: Vita e Pensiero.

Graham, J., R. Olson and R. Howard (eds) (2010), *Cyber Security Essentials,* New York: Auerbach Publications-Taylor and Francis.

Herrera, G. (2002), 'The politics of bandwidth: international political implications of a global digital information network', *Review of International Studies*, 28: 93–122.

Kissel, R. (ed.) (2013), 'Glossary of Key Information Security Terms', NIST IR 7298 Revision 2, National Institute of Standards and Technology, US Department of Commerce, http://csrc.nist.gov/publications (accessed 31 August 2013).

Laffont, J. and D. Martimort (2002), *The Theory of Incentives: The Principal-Agent Model*, Princeton, NJ: Princeton University Press.

LaFranerie, S. and J. Ansfield (2010), 'China Alarmed by Security Threat From Internet', *The New York Times*, 11 February 2010, A1.

Libicki, M. (2007), *Conquest in Cyberspace: National Security and Information Warfare*, Cambridge: Cambridge University Press.

—(2009), *Cyberdeterrence and Cyberwar*, Santa Monica, CA: Rand Corporation.

Markoff, J. (2008), 'Before the Gunfire, Cyberattacks', *The New York Times*, 13 August 2008, www.nytimes.com/2008/08/13/technology/13cyber.html?hp=&p (accessed 11 January 2013).

Markoff, J. and D. Barboza (2010), 'Academic Paper in China Sets Off Alarms in US', *The New York Times*, 21 March 2010, A11.

Migga Kizza, J. (2011), *Computer Network Security and Cyber Ethics*, 3rd edn, Jefferson, NC: McFarland.

Moeller, R. R. (2011), *Cyber Security and Privacy Control*, Hoboken, NJ: John Wiley & Sons, Inc.

Nagourney, A. (2013), 'In US, News of Surveillance Effort Is Met With Some Concern but Little Surprise', *The New York Times*, 8 June, A12.

Perlroth, N. (2012), 'Cyberattack On Saudi Firm Disquiets US', *The New York Times*, 24 October 2012, A1.

Perlroth, N. and S. Shane (2013), 'N.S.A. Able to Foil Basic Safeguards of Privacy on Web', *The New York Times*, 6 September 2013, A1.

Personick, S. D. and C. A. Patterson (eds) (2003), 'Critical Information Infrastructure Protection and the Law: An Overview of Key Issues', Committee on Critical Information Infrastructure Protection and the Law, National Research Council, www.nap.edu/catalog/10685.html (accessed 8 September 2013).

Phillips, R. and R. R. Sianjina (2013), *Cyber Security for Educational Leaders*, London: Routledge.

Rothschild, E. (1995), 'What is security?', *Daedalus*, 124: 53–98.

Saadawi, T. and L. Jordan (eds) (2011), 'Cyber Infrastructure Protection', Strategic Studies Institute, Carlisle, PA: US Army War College.

Sanger, D. E. (2010), 'Iran Fights Malware Attacking Computers', *The New York Times*, 26 September 2010, A4.

—(2013), 'In Cyberspace, New Cold War', *The New York Times*, 25 February 2013, A1.

Sanger, D., D. Barboza and N. Peroth (2013), 'Chinese Army Unit Is Seen as Tied to Hacking Against US', *The New York Times*, 19 February 2013, A1.✓

Shane, S. (2012), 'Cyberwarfare Emerges From Shadows for Public Discussion by US Officials', *The New York Times*, 27 September 2012, A10.

Shoemaker, D. and W. Conklin (2011), *Cybersecurity: The Essential Body of Knowledge*, Boston, MA: Cengage Learning.

So, S. and J. C. Westland (2010), *Red Wired: China's Internet Revolution*, London: Marshall Cavendish Business.

Spence, M. and R. Zeckhauser (1971), 'Insurance, information, and individual action', *American Economic Review*, 61: 380–7.

Tengelin, V. (1981), 'The Vulnerability of the Computerized Society', in H. Gassmann (ed.) *Information, Computer and Communication Policies for the '80s*, Amsterdam: North Holland Publishing Company, 205–13.

Part One

The Nation

1

The 'State(s)' of Cybersecurity

Rossella Mattioli[1]

Cybersecurity is a recurring term of the first decades of the twenty-first century. Yet, a single definition of cybersecurity, agreed upon by all parties involved, is absent from both the existing academic and policy literature. As in every field, the formulation of a common baseline is part of the beginning. Moreover, due to the increasing importance of this topic, a definition of cybersecurity is every day more necessary, especially considering the current multidisciplinary debate regarding security issues related to the use of ICT. This chapter aims to depict the different actors and variables involved and to provide examples of the complexity of this task.

Cybersecurity emerged from the intersection of technological, political, organizational and social variables and thus it transcends the usual territorial nation-state perspective to occupy the continuum between cyberspace and physical space (Marvin, 1988; Shapiro, 1998). After a brief introduction of the nature of cyberspace, this chapter will present examples of how the term cybersecurity is used. The aim is to provide an excursus on how this field may be broadly approached in all its aspects. In addition, a brief presentation of the various layers and actors involved will be sketched, in order to propose a comprehensive overview of the structure of the field.

The problem of cybersecurity definitions is directly related to the multidisciplinary nature of its issues. This does not depend on the fact that large-scale cybersecurity incidents have not been experienced yet, but on the fact that, when we think about security, we usually apply a territorial approach due to the nation-state environment, which characterized the international system from the Peace of Westphalia up to the creation of the Internet. Before the Internet, ethnic groups or political entities waged war in order to persuade one another or conquer a physical territory. Cyberspace has brought a paradigm shift. First, the actors on stage are no longer only nation-states, but also non-state actors

(NSA) and can even be just individuals. Second, cyberspace is a territory by itself, one that can have repercussions on physical space but at the same time has a dimension that it is not determined by its borders, which are not the same as those of the nation-states. Third, since cybersecurity encompasses different actors that do not fall into the usual dichotomy of nation-state vs. nation-state but range from businesses to policymakers, from militaries to cybercriminals, from academics to security researchers or white (and in some case also grey and black) hat hackers, developing a proper and common terminology is hampered by the different terms used by these entities. In addition, at this moment there is great debate about the domain of cybersecurity, inflamed also by the media hype. Just think about how many times you see the term 'cyberwar' in the newspapers.

To add complexity to an already multifaceted problem, cyberspace relies on global critical information infrastructures such as the domain name system (DNS), border gateway protocol (BGP) and telecommunication infrastructures, and there is discussion among all parties involved regarding who has jurisdiction to coordinate efforts to provide security and resilience of these components. Cyberspace is a territory of its own and the interest in fostering its evolution and define a proper governance model is emerging from different actors; for example, at the last Internet Governance Forum (IGF) in November 2012 in Baku the main theme was 'Internet Governance for Sustainable Human, Economic and Social Development'. Clearly such a multi-lateral approach requires nation-states to become completely aware of prospective changes in governance and their implications. Whereas national governments should try to protect the interests interconnected with the growth of the information society, they also need to protect themselves in cyberspace. Thus cybersecurity is going to acquire more importance in the coming years.

The nature of cyberspace

Defining cyberspace is a complex task. According to the 2009 United States Cyberspace Policy Review (Executive Office of the President of the United States 2009) it is defined as:

> the interdependent network of information technology infrastructures, and
> includes the Internet, telecommunications networks, computer systems, and
> embedded processors and controllers in critical industries. Common usage of

the term also refers to the virtual environment of information and interactions between people. (p. 1)

This description does not assume that cyberspace coincides solely with the Internet defined by as the transmission control protocol (TCP) and internet protocol (IP) or TCP/IP network since the request for comment (RFC) 801. Instead, it also includes other types of networks. Although the original definition of cyberspace is usually attributed to William Gibson in the *Neuromancer* (1984)[2] to give the reader a full overview of all its different meanings, here is a description from Bruce Sterling in *The Hacker Crackdown* (1992):

> Cyberspace is the 'place' where a telephone conversation appears to occur. Not inside your actual phone, the plastic device on your desk. Not inside the other person's phone, in some other city. The place between the phones. The indefinite place out there, where the two of you, two human beings, actually meet and communicate … Since the 1960s, the world of the telephone has cross-bred itself with computers and television, and though there is still no substance to Cyberspace, nothing you can handle, it has a strange kind of physicality now. It makes good sense today to talk of Cyberspace as a place all its own. (p. 10)

The US government and Sterling definitions represent different approaches to defining cyberspace, and they perfectly represent the obstacles to a unique definition of this global new space where 2,405,510,036 users communicate and share experiences every day, according to the latest calculation of the Internet World Statistics website. Without delving further into the origin of the term 'cyber', which was coined by Norbert Weiner in 1948, I will use from now on the definition of cyberspace suggested by Ottis and Lorents in 2010 (p. 1): 'cyberspace is a time- dependent set of interconnected information systems and the human users that interact with these systems'. Paying particular attention to the human and information systems components in order to underline their interactions, the next section gives a brief overview of the definition of cybersecurity in order to fully cover the spectrum of different meanings and constituencies of this domain.

Defining cybersecurity

As was underlined at the beginning of this chapter, just as there are multiple proposed definitions of cyberspace, there are different usages of the term cybersecurity with no unique and agreed characterization. Before proposing the main components of a single definition, a brief overview of the more popular usages is in order. Cybersecurity is a term used in several resolutions from different prominent actors, such as the UN resolution 57/239 'Creation of a global culture of cybersecurity'; UN resolution 58/199 'Creation of a global culture of cybersecurity and the protection of critical information infrastructures'; the Organization for Economic Cooperation and Development (OECD) 'Recommendation of the Council on the Protection of Critical Information Infrastructure'; and EU commission 'Achievements and next steps: towards global cybersecurity'.

In order to understand the different characterizations of cybersecurity, we propose here the definition of cybersecurity contained in the Cybersecurity Strategy of the European Union (European Commission High Representative, 2012):

> Cybersecurity commonly refers to the safeguards and actions that can be used to protect the cyber domain, both in the civilian and military fields, from those threats that are associated with or that may harm its interdependent networks and information infrastructure. Cyber-security strives to preserve the availability and integrity of the networks and infrastructure and the confidentiality of the information contained therein.

and the one contained in American Cybersecurity Enhancement Act of 2005 (US Department of Homeland Security):

> the prevention of damage to, the protection of, and the restoration of computers, electronic communications systems, electronic communication services, wire communication, and electronic communication, including information contained therein, to ensure its availability, integrity, authentication, confidentiality, and no repudiation.

In a brief overview, it is not possible to offer a comprehensive definition, but to pinpoint only some main characteristics. Collecting the inputs from the presented definitions, a comprehensive description of cybersecurity should contain a human and information systems component, the underlying interconnection, and the aim to preserve availability, integrity, authentication, confidentiality and non-repudiation. As Rowe and Lunt (2012) underlined in 'Mapping the Cybersecurity Terrain in a Research Context', 'the term cybersecurity reflects the relationships and interconnections between cyberspace and the physical world'.

For these reasons framing cybersecurity encompasses technical and organizational problems involving policy matters at different levels, starting from the global infrastructure and arriving at the end-user while passing throughout the interaction between transnational organizations, governments, enterprises and techno-scientific communities like academia and the hacker community. As Agresti (2010) underlined, to approach cybersecurity one must work on four different levels: personal, organizational, national, and global.

The state(s) of cybersecurity

As the previous section makes clear, it is as difficult to depict clear boundaries for cybersecurity as for cyberspace. This issue is probably connected with the paradigm shift that cyberspace is bringing with its evolution, as described by Thomas Kuhn in *The Structure of Scientific Revolutions* (1970) regarding other paradigm shifts. One main difficulty of proposing a clear statement regarding cybersecurity is that it exceeds the current territorial approach. Cyberspace is flat, has no centre, is interconnected and worldwide, and classical territorial measures cannot be used. Moreover, for the first time in history, non-state actors could have an unexpected impact on the global scenario such as compromising CIIs or disrupting or hijacking large portions of the Internet. As Gady and Austin state in *Russia, the United States, and Cyber Diplomacy* (2010), 'cybersecurity is a global problem, transcending national boundaries. Traditional concepts of national power based on conventional economic, political and military factors are of little consequence in the cyber world'. For these reasons, examples of the complexity of cybersecurity issues will be analysed, starting from the global perspective and arriving to the individual one, with particular attention to the human and information systems components. They will be analysed in order to give the reader a clear overview of the different levels and interactions at which cybersecurity operates.

Cybersecurity at the global level

Cyberspace is constituted by electromagnetic signals and is regulated by international organizations. This is a brutal but clear definition of the cyberspace.

Cyberspace is not made by unregulated interconnections of networks or free exchange of information. Every single packet is transmitted from one point to another thanks to different technologies and via electromagnetic signals, which can be transmitted via cables or air, from organizations that pay or are paid to enable this. The internet protocol suite, which enables this interaction, encompasses the following four layers:

- the *link layer*, which covers the local network where a device resides;
- the *Internet layer*, which connects different local networks and enables the inter-networking;
- the *transport layer*, which activates the host-to-host communication;
- and the *application layer*, which is represented by all the protocols that allow the end-user to experience the different communication services, such as web browsing, e-mail, File transfer protocol (FTP) and Internet relay chat (IRC).

These interactions involve several different transnational organizations and companies and this is another place where the clear definition of boundaries is under debate. Since the Internet emerged from interconnections at the bottom and not with the usual top-down approach (as in telephone and TV, for example), the current situation is highly variegated. From a technical point of view the interconnection is now provided by network centres, which can belong to private companies, educational institutions, not-for-profit organizations or government bodies. The communications within these entities is based on two core protocols: the border gateway protocol (BGP) for routing traffic among different autonomous systems (AS) and the domain name system (DNS) for matching between IP addresses and domain names.

The not-for-profit organization, Internet Corporation for Assigned Names and Numbers (ICANN), coordinates the allocation and assignment of domain names, IP addresses and AS numbers. Considering the rapid and constantly growing importance of the Internet and due to complexity of all these interactions and different interested parties, this organization, which is responsible of the multi-stakeholder model, is in constant evolution, as underlined by ICANN's president, Fadi Chehadé, during his presentation speech at the ICANN meeting in Prague in June 2012. Other bodies and institutions are also part of this ecosystem as the Internet Governance Forum where discussion is open on how to preserve the main characteristics of the Internet while fostering security, free movement of information and market growth.

Other actors include the Internet Society (ISOC), International Organization for Standardization (ISO), regional Internet registries (RIRs), World Wide Web Consortium (W3C), Internet Network Operators' Groups (NOGs), International Telecommunication Union (ITU) and governments and intergovernmental organizations.

As it emerged during the World Conference on International Telecommunications (WCIT) in Dubai in December 2012 the cybersecurity debate is now focusing about who should be in charge of global cybersecurity issues and Internet governance. Cybersecurity or security in cyberspace is the hot item on the agenda, not only because of the current media hype but also because being in charge of this governance problem will allow impacting the future of the information society. The outcome of this debate will include not only the regulation of the telecommunications capabilities, regulation of the online market and freedom of expression, but will also set the direction of the evolution of the information-based society. Currently, because these threats are relatively new and the borderless nature of the cyberspace represents a governance challenge, as discussed above, the right to coordinate the Internet and specifically cybersecurity efforts is still under vigorous discussion. Several transnational agreements are in place, for example, the Council of Europe 'Convention on Cybercrime' signed in 2001, but they do not cover all the different aspects.

The multi-stakeholder approach that characterizes ICANN and the IGF, is under discussion regarding the interaction with major and more institutionalized organizations such as the UN and OECD. Being in a conjuncture moment, where we have the transition from a territorial/market to the information-based society, this diversity of approaches is understandable, but from a security point of view it also represents a key issue regarding the direction of global cybersecurity efforts. If the current Internet governance debate fails its multi-stakeholder model, which is the same that enabled the growth of the Internet, chances are that a more conservative and border-based top-down approach will replace the benefits and the information society principles that the Internet brought with itself.

As stated at the beginning of this section, the Internet is made by every single packet transmitted from one point to another, thanks to different technologies and via electromagnetic signals that can be transmitted via cables or through the air from organizations that pay or paid to enable this. A deeper examination of the technological aspects is not the aim of this chapter, and therefore only examples of the three main items in the global infrastructure cybersecurity cluster will be discussed: submarine cable and physical infrastructure resilience, the physical backbones and infrastructures that allow packets to be routed; the BGP, which is the software protocol that define the routes; and the DNS, which allow us not to have to remember IP addresses but simply domain names.

Major natural events, like the 'superstorm' Sandy in 2012 and Japan's earthquake in 2011, showed that the Internet is more resilient than organizations. James Cowie (2011) argues that there is a close connection between geopolitics, markets, and the availability of the Internet technologies. Submarine cables, continuity in data centres, and the possibility of energy outages represent critical vulnerabilities to the connections and therefore of the Internet. What if a major disruption happens and large portions of a nation are disconnected? The underlying infrastructure of the Internet is very delicate as was shown by the recent cable cut in Egypt or by the Georgian women who accidentally cut Armenia and Georgia off the Internet for several hours. On the otherhand, if we want to use Nicholas Negroponte's (1995) bit vs. atom dichotomy, the border gateway protocol is the technology that allows a packet to be routed from one autonomous system in the world to another. It is represented by the federation of autonomous systems and while this protocol is mostly unknown to the public, it represents the core of the Internet's functions. Blocking or misusing this routing protocol can cut off one country or large portions of networks from the Internet as, for example, during the Arab Spring when Egypt was cut out of the Internet for several days; the YouTube accident in 2008, when YouTube traffic was accidentally hijacked by Pakistan Telecom; and more recently in 2012 when an erroneous routing message broadcast by an Indonesian telecommunications company caused a blackout for Google. What if a router's vulnerability is exploited causing a major disruption in route announcements and the cascading effects affect hundreds of ISPs which provide connection to millions of users?

DNS is another critical component to the functioning of the Internet and hampering its functionality could cause a domino effect that could disable the capacity of the main Internet services. Better known than BGP, it has gained attention in recent years with the debate in the United States and also around the world regarding the PROTECT IP Act of 2011 and the Stop Online Piracy Act in 2012. An incident compromising DNS core functionalities or an attempt to wrongly regulate it could hamper its operations and have repercussions on the Internet as a whole, as underlined in the 'Security and Other Technical Concerns Raised by the DNS Filtering Requirements in the PROTECT IP Bill'. Several scenarios are possible, as the different reports have emphasized, and the involved parties are trying to set up a comprehensive risk assessment framework and also a defined perimeter of technical and policy actions for ICANN and other actors involved. In the case of another and more advanced worm, Conficker, that infected millions of computers over 200 countries using an automatically generated list of domain names and was faced by an informal and voluntary working group, who will be in charge of coordinating all efforts in securing the DNS or, more generally, the Internet?

Cybersecurity at the national level

> The Internet has become the public space of the 21st century…We all shape and are shaped by what happens there, all 2 billion of us and counting. And that presents a challenge. To maintain an Internet that delivers the greatest possible benefits to the world, we need to have a serious conversation about the principles that will guide us …
>
> (Secretary of State Hillary Rodham Clinton, 15 February 2011)

With these words, Secretary Clinton envisioned the American approach to the cyberspace and defined the line of the American foreign policy. In the same remarks she also announced the creation of the Office of the Coordinator for Cyber Issues within the State Department and paved the way for the release of the first US International Strategy for Cyberspace. For the first time in history, a government was including cybersecurity as a key issue in its diplomatic agenda and was defining a wide framework to address it not only within the national borders but also in the international arena.

As Adam Watson (1982) said 'Diplomacy is a dialogue between states', and this dialogue has now a new and hot topic on the agenda: cybersecurity. Several big players[3] in the current geopolitics system have already developed national cybersecurity strategies and other countries are working on them. Cybersecurity has not reached yet a definitive place in every national political agenda but the growth of threats and the rising dependence on the information and communications technology in every market are focusing more attention on this. The growing reliance on interconnected networks paves the way for several security concerns, and even nations where the debate has a long track record are conscious that it will take at least 30 years to create the policy and military personnel with a comprehensive knowledge and background of all the different technical and organizational aspects needed. At the same time, several efforts are made to secure critical infrastructures, both at national and international levels, which are deeply connected to the use of communication networks, and represent those clear connections between the physical and the virtual world.

It is important to underline that these issues affect not only the core capabilities of a nation but also represent the passage between online and offline impact which is so important in the computer network operations (CNO) and which is perfectly described by the famous statement that cyberspace is the fifth warfare domain after land, sea, air and space. Malware like Stuxnet, Duqu, Flame and Gauss are the most famous and popular examples of new, upcoming threats. Nation-states are becoming aware of the power of cyberspace and the benefit of using offensive capabilities to exploit adverse nation-states without the risk of confirmed attribution. Hacking communities, which in the past were depicted as the realm of extremely intelligent teenagers who wanted to learn and show off their expertise, as in movies such as 'Wargames' or 'Hackers', have become a natural recruiting ground for governments. Described by Steven Levy (1984) as an art for the art's sake, hacking is now another possibility for governments to undertake covert operations by using avant-garde network and information technologies. And most of all, governments are now one of the most important customers of the multimillion dollar black market where it is possible to buy exploits that are unknown to the hardware and software vendors and allow a nation to perform an attack that is impossible to detect with usual antivirus or other defensive resources (Greenberg, 2012).

Cybersecurity at the organizational level

Cybersecurity risk management is rising as a key issue also in the private sector agenda where there is a fervent debate on how to face threats and what kind of methodologies to introduce. Efforts have been made to align the different approaches, for example in the energy sector, or to widen awareness in public and private organizations. For example, a service about national cyber response has been launched in United Kingdom by the Communications-Electronics Security Group (CESG), while the European Network and Information Security

Agency (ENISA) is working to fill the gap at the European level. The economic side of cybersecurity is yet to be completely understood by businesses. Although attention to cybersecurity is already a core capability for markets driven by the need for confidentiality, such as finance, military and the government, it is usually underestimated in other sectors that do not consider themselves as affected by cybersecurity concerns. This is actually a sign of the change which is taking place, and as in the military environment, it is possible to apply a long-term horizon, for the development of a generation of experts who are fully aware not only of the technical impacts of an incident but are also able to deal with policy issues concerning data protection, privacy, compliance and interaction with national and transnational legislation regarding information exchange and security awareness.

Clearer directives provided by national and transnational organizations, such as the EU's recently proposed directive, can only be a benefit in this respect, where enterprises find themselves facing issues that have never been considered in the past, a lack of specialized personnel and impressive media repercussions, as will be discussed in the next section. Like governments, which are gradually becoming aware of cybersecurity risks and possibilities, enterprises are also facing the need to change and it is clear that due to the interdependence of businesses and ICT, it is necessary to insert and enhance cybersecurity capabilities and expertise at the organizational level. While methodologies regarding cybersecurity risk assessments are under development, companies' systems keep on being breached. This is an example of the room for improvement that can have a comprehensive cybersecurity approach.

It is not the evolution of the breaches but the need for common and agreed minimum security requirements that is underlined in examples like the June 2012 LinkedIn breach (Perlroth, 2012), when attackers stole more than 6 million passwords and it was possible to understand that an online company, which claims to have more than 175 million of users, did not have basic security countermeasures to protect its users' passwords. Another example is the case of the Yahoo breaches in July 2012, when 453,000 login credentials were published online. It is clear that companies need to be guided to address cybersecurity risks and impacts when such incidents continue, even in major companies like Sony, which hired a Chief Security Officer (CSO) only after several data breaches that compromised millions of accounts (Higgins, 2011), or Adobe, which although it produces a widely popular technology Flash, is still suffering important incidents like the one in September 2012, when its own code signing certificates (which should allow the certification of genuine Adobe software) were compromised and certified two malicious utilities as genuine (Arkin, 2012).

The heterogeneity of approaches in private businesses regarding cybersecurity threats allows attackers to move from very simple to more sophisticated attacks and to lurk unnoticed for months. It is clear that a serious concern for this kind of attacks should be not underestimated by any organization, first in the ICT life chain, but also those that are not directly involved in ICT but can be subjected of a domino effect or be targeted due to their CII interdependency or as a means in a broader attack. As can be noticed, the end-user must be both a concern for the company first, regarding the compliance and data retention legislation and second as he/she is mostly the ultimate target of an attack and data compromise.

Cybersecurity at the individual level

Introducing the individual point of view of cybersecurity has several impacts. First of all, individuals are the prime users of the Internet and by exercising their use of the network and its services they constitute the network itself. Without the end-user, cyber space would not exist. The end-user is affected in various ways by the interaction at the global, national, and organizational level. From a global point of view, Internet regulation and the ability of states to limit access to Internet infrastructure, as in the Arab Spring example, can hamper individual's Internet usage and freedom of expression. From a national point of view the individual's right to freely view content online can be limited as in China (Zuckerman, 2012) or, on the other hand, be considered a legal right, as in Finland. From an organizational point of view, the individual is the recipient and the ultimate target of an attack or an incident. There are, moreover, several issues regarding the privacy and freedom of usage of the individual which intersect at various levels of national and international legislation. Due to the borderless nature of the Internet, various transnational copyright issues and security violations can be considered legitimate in one country, while forbidden and persecuted in another.

It is clear that cybersecurity at the individual level involves several different interdependencies and factors. An individual can have his/her credentials stolen and become, without knowing it, the owner of a compromised computer that is part of broader attack. From there the computer can be traced, the person's Internet connection analysed, spoofed or hijacked and what he/she shares online can be used for profiling for criminal intents. Considering the intersection of the global, national and organizational variables all the presented examples represent a part of the problem in the cybersecurity domain. Several are the cybersecurity implication and while it is not in the aim of this chapter to list them all, it is goal of the writer to help the reader to understand the complexity of this discipline. Regarding the technical component is, on the other side.

From a technical perspective, the impact of malware and data leaks on the individual are clear. Malware has different forms and the chances of data compromise and effects that can result from online and offline exploitation are infinite. Malware can take advantage of infrastructure components as DNS, as in the DNS Changer case in which about 4 million computers were infected and the estimated revenue of the hijack and advertisement replacement fraud was around $14 million dollars or Conficker, where millions of computers were infected and it is still unknown what was the final goal of this worm. Personal data can be exposed through one of the big governments or businesses data leaks or can be traded on the black market or be used for abusive transactions. As it can be noticed several are the technical implications that can emerge from a cybersecurity perspective. It is important to underline the vulnerability of the individual to becoming an unknowing part of a cybersecurity attack merely by the use of ICT tools, but also if only subjected to a social engineering attack. Individuals represent the ultimate attack surface for a criminal and thus also the ultimate concern in every cybersecurity effort. It is clear that no consideration in this discipline should avoid the central importance of this actor, at each level of interoperability with the other variables and most of all in considering the impact of every policy on the individual user.

The way ahead

Cybersecurity is the intersection of international, national, organizational and individual issues which have a human and information system component in preserving security and resilience of cyberspace. From critical information infrastructures via national and private sector infrastructures to the computer of the citizen, it encompasses the whole continuum between the borderless nature of cyberspace to the territorial perspective of the nation-state. Cybersecurity is not information assurance or information security nor should it concern only the fifth domain of warfare. Cybersecurity is a new global and interdisciplinary paradigm that is concerned with the security and resilience of a new dimension of the social interaction. It represents a governance challenge since it requires having technical, policy and organizational knowledge to address a comprehensive answer. Moreover, due to its political, technological and economic repercussions, it represents an important effort in applying the network model to the mind-set of all the parties involved. For these reasons it is important to consider all the variables and foster research and debate about its different aspects. It is clear that this discipline is going to play an important role in the definition of the future geopolitics scenarios and in the development of the future shape of human society.

Notes

1   The views expressed here are solely those of the author in her private capacity and do not in any way represent the views of her current employer.

2   Gibson, however, first coined the term in 1982 for the short novel *Burning Chrome* on page 64.

3   The full list of countries is available at www.enisa.europa.eu/activities/ Resilience-and-CIIP/national-cyber-security-strategies-ncsss/national-cyber-security-strategies-in-the-world (accessed 14 September 2013).

References

Agresti, W. W. (2010), 'The four forces shaping cybersecurity', *Computer,* 43: 101–4.

Arkin, B. (2012), 'Adobe Secure Software Engineering Team (ASSET) Blog – Inappropriate Use of Adobe Code Signing Certificate', http://blogs.adobe.com/asset/2012/09/ inappropriate-use-of-adobe-code-signing-certificate.html (accessed 1 December 2012).

Council of Europe (2001), 'Convention on Cybercrime', Budapest. http://conventions. coe.int/Treaty/en/Treaties/Html/185.htm (accessed 1 December 2012).

Cowie, J. (2011), 'Geopolitics of Internet Infrastructure', Cyber Law, http://cyber.law. harvard.edu/events/luncheon/2011/11/cowie (accessed 1 December 2012).

Department of Homeland Security, (2009) *Cyberspace Policy Review,* www.dhs.gov/ publication/2009-cyberspace-policy-review (accessed 4 May 2014).

European Commission High Representative for Foreign Affairs and Security Policy (2012), 'Joint Communication to European Parliament, Council, European

Economic and Social Committee, Committee of The Regions, Cybersecurity Strategy of the European Union: An Open, Safe and Secure Cyberspace', JOIN(2013) 1 final, Brussels, 7 February 2012, http://eeas.europa.eu/policies/eu-cyber-security/cybsec_comm_en.pdf (accessed 14 September 2013).

Gady, F. S. and G. Austin (2010), *Russia, the United States, and Cyber Diplomacy: Opening the Doors*, New York: EastWest Institute, www.ewi.info/system/files/USRussiaCyber_WEB.pdf (accessed 14 September 2013).

Greenberg, A. (2012), 'Shopping For Zero-Days: A Price List For Hackers' Secret Software Exploits', *Forbes*, Online Edition, www.forbes.com/sites/andygreenberg/2012/03/23/shopping-for-zero-days-an-price-list-for-hackers-secret-software-exploits/ (accessed 1 December 2012).

Higgins, K. J. (2011), 'Sony Names Ex-DHS Official As Its CSO', *Dark Reading*, Online Edition, www.darkreading.com/database-security/167901020/security/security-management/231600854/sony-names-ex-dhs-official-as-its-cso.html (accessed 1 December 2012).

ICANN Joint DNS Security and Stability Analysis Working Group (2012), 'Phase 1 Final Report', https://community.icann.org/display/AW/Phase+1+Final+Report (accessed 1 December 2012).

Kuhn, T. S. (1970), *The Structure of Scientific Revolutions*, Chicago: University of Chicago Press.

Levy, S. (1984 [2001]), *Hackers: Heroes of the Computer Revolution*, New York: Penguin Books.

Marvin, C. (1988), *When Old Technologies Were New*. New York: Oxford University Press.

Negroponte, N. (1995), *Being Digital*, New York: Alfred A. Knopf Inc.

OECD (2012), 'Recommendation of the Council on the Protection of Critical Information', *Infrastructures*, www.oecd.org/internet/interneteconomy/40825404.pdf (accessed 1 December 2012).

Ottis, R. and P. Lorents (2010), 'Cyberspace: Definition and Implications', *Proceedings of the 5th International Conference on Information Warfare and Security,* ICIW, http://dumitrudumbrava.files.wordpress.com/2012/01/cyberspace-definition-and-implications.pdf (accessed 14 September 2013).

Perlroth, N. (2012), 'Lax Security at LinkedIn Is Laid Bar', *The New York Times*, Online Edition, www.nytimes.com/2012/06/11/technology/linkedin-breach-exposes-light-security-even-at-data-companies.html?pagewanted=all (accessed 1 December 2012).

Rendon Group (2011), 'The Conficker Working Group – Lessons Learned Document', www.confickerworkinggroup.org/wiki/ (accessed 1 December 2012).

Rowe, D. C. and B. Lunt (2012), 'Mapping the Cyber Security Terrain in a Research Context', http://sigite2012.sigite.org/wp-content/uploads/2012/08/session06-paper02.pdf (accessed 14 September 2013).

Senate of the United States (2011a), 'PROTECT IP Act of 2011', Washington, DC,
    www.gpo.gov/fdsys/pkg/BILLS-112s968rs/pdf/BILLS-112s968rs.pdf (accessed 1
    December 2012).
—(2011b), 'Stop Online Piracy Act H.R.3261', Washington, DC. http://thomas.loc.gov/
    cgi-bin/query/z?c112:H.R.3261 (accessed 1 December 2012).
Shapiro, S. (1998), 'Places and Spaces: The Historical Interaction of Technology, Home,
    and Privacy', *Information Society*, 14: 275–284.
Sterling, B. (1992), *The Hacker Crackdown*, New York: Bantam Books.
Telegraph, The, 'Woman Who Cut Internet to Georgia and Armenia "Had Never Heard
    of Web"', Online Edition, 11 April 2011, www.telegraph.co.uk/news/worldnews/
    europe/georgia/8442056/Woman-who-cut-internet-to-Georgia-and-Armenia-had-
    never-heard-of-web.html (accessed 1 December 2012).
United Nations General Assembly (2003), 'Resolution 57/239 Creation of a Global
    Culture of Cybersecurity', New York, United Nations, www.itu.int/ITU-D/cyb/
    cybersecurity/docs/UN_resolution_57_239.pdf (accessed 1 December 2012).
—(2004), 'Resolution 58/199. Creation of a Global Culture of Cybersecurity and the
    Protection of Critical information Infrastructures', New York, United Nations, www.
    itu.int/ITU-D/cyb/cybersecurity/docs/UN_resolution_58_199.pdf (accessed 1
    December 2012).
Watson, A. (1982), *Diplomacy: The Dialogue Between States*, London: Routledge.
White House (2009), 'Cyberspace Policy Review: Assuring a Trusted and Resilient
    Information and Communications Infrastructure', Washington, DC: White House,
    http://energy.gov/oe/services/cybersecurity/cybersecurity-risk-management-
    process-rmp (accessed 1 December 2012).
Wiener, N. (1948), *Cybernetics: Or Control and Communication in the Animal and the
    Machine*, Cambridge, MA: MIT Press.
Zetter, K. (2012), 'Report: Half a Million Yahoo User Accounts Exposed in Breach',
    Wired, Online Edition, 12 July 2012, www.wired.com/threatlevel/2012/07/yahoo-
    breach/ (accessed 1 December 2012).

2

Reducing Uncertainties in Cyberspace through Confidence and Capacity-Building Measures

Patryk Pawlak[1]

Technological progress has been usually accompanied by periods of uncertainty stemming from political, societal or economic implications of new inventions. After debates about the use of nuclear weapons in the 1950s or the emergence of unmanned aircraft like drones in the 2000s, the pressure on international community is mounting to address the challenges in the cyberspace. There are two aspects to this debate.

First, uncertainty and mistrust between major actors emerge from limited information about cyber-capabilities (both offensive and defensive) and their potential use in the absence of a broader international agreement on the norms governing cyberspace. Several reports by private companies, organizations and in the press provide abundant data concerning the extent to which various countries resort to cyber-espionage or offensive cyber-operations. For instance, a report issued by a US cybersecurity firm Mandiant claims that hackers related to the Chinese military performed continued attacks on US websites, including the governmental ones (Mandiant, 2013). China, on the other hand, claims to be a victim of an increasing number of cyber-attacks which according to a report by the National Computer Network Emergency Technical Team Coordination Centre (CNCERT) originate primarily from foreign servers (96.2 per cent) with 83.2 per cent of them coming from the United States (Xinhua, 2013).[2] Indeed, several press reports suggest that only in 2011 that US intelligence services carried out 231 offensive cyber-operations, with China, Iran and Russia as primary targets (Gellman and Nakashima, 2013).

Second, international actions aiming at preparedness, prevention, response and recovery in case of cyber-attacks can be only as strong as the weakest link within the international system. Improving the access to broadband communication in the developing world is necessary for achieving the economic and social benefits which cyberspace brings, including an improved access to education, healthcare, and in the longer term reducing poverty. This, however, cannot be achieved without concurrent efforts to build-up their cyber capacities. At the same time, where the state structures and capacities are weak, there is a possibility of a country becoming – willingly or not – a safe haven from which cyber-attacks can be performed. For this reason High Representative and Vice President of the European Commission Catherine Ashton highlighted at the cybersecurity conference in Budapest in 2011 the need for new cyber capacity programmes and called for a better coordination of existing initiatives.[3]

This chapter argues that because of the conflicts over the governance of cyberspace – based on values, approaches to privacy or the application of the existing international laws – and the absence of an overarching cyber governance framework, the focus on capacity and confidence-building measures is a viable (if not the only) alternative. It starts with the discussion about the sources of uncertainty in cyberspace that provide the basis for strengthening the efforts at improving the existing capacity and confidence-building efforts. The chapter then proceeds to present efforts undertaken by the European Union to diminish those uncertainties, only to argue that unilateral efforts – while necessary – are not sufficient and international cooperation efforts are needed. The following sections present various confidence and capacity-building measures undertaken at the international level, however because of their relatively recent timing drawing any conclusions about their effectiveness is difficult at this stage.

Uncertainty in cyberspace

At least three concurrent debates about the global governance of cyberspace set the tone for the discussion about dealing with uncertainties in this dynamically developing field. The issues that will need to be addressed (and resolved) in the coming years regard the freedom of and in the Internet, ensuring the protection of privacy while ensuring security online, and regulating the international community in times of conflicts.

First, the growing relevance of digital communication networks for trade, politics or even warfare brings to the fore the conflicting visions about the future openness of the Internet. A group composed primarily of the advanced liberal democracies argues that the multi-stakeholder approach bringing together governments, the private sector, civil society and technical experts should continue to provide the basis for Internet governance. This position is opposed by a group of 'cyber-sovereignty advocates' (including China and Russia) who wish to see more governmental control of cyberspace. The World Conference on International Telecommunications in Dubai in December 2012 provided a space where these two visions have openly clashed. The aim of the conference was to review the current International Telecommunications Regulations – a UN treaty dealing with issues like roaming charges or the costs of wireless services. Instead, the discussions revolved around the future of Internet governance.

The most thorny issues that emerged between the coalition led by the United States (supported by the European Union Member States and a group of developed countries) and a group led by Russia (including also China, the United Arab Emirates, Bahrain and others) concerned: (1) bringing the governance of the Internet under the regulatory framework of the telecommunication union (*de facto* taking the control away from the private sector and putting it in hands of the governments); (2) network security and spam (giving the states authority to use spam as a pretext to curb free speech); and (3) the reference to human rights in the preamble of the treaty (a notion pushed forward by the EU Member States and supported by the United States, Tunisia Kenya and others). This divergence demonstrated that the discussion about defending values in cyberspace is not purely theoretical but one that requires concrete steps at the international level. The recent controversies surrounding the US surveillance programs and a clear abuse of the privileged access to the Internet's infrastructure (most of which is based in the United States) undermine US credibility in this respect and create the leadership vacuum which the EU is competent to fill. Establishing a credible leadership in the 'Western' camp is of particular importance ahead of the World Summit on the Information Society in 2015.

Second, the debate about security in cyberspace is closely linked to future data protection regimes. The EU's leadership and authority on data protection has remained unquestioned since 1995 when the EU's Data Protection Directive (DPD) was adopted. The Directive – currently under revision – provides a legal framework regulating transnational data exchanges between public and private authorities and for almost a decade constitutes a benchmark for international data flows. After the 9/11 terrorist attacks, the provisions of the DPD ensured that security considerations that drove most of the counterterrorism policies did not undermine civil liberties and in particular the citizens' right to privacy.

With several new regulations adopted over the past ten years – especially those addressing the use of personal information for security purposes – the European data protection regime (both laws and their implementation) remains the most robust in the world. This strong commitment has been often seen as detrimental to national security resulting in conflicts even on the same side of the barricade, most notably across the Atlantic. Such assessment, however, is only partly correct given that some of the basic concepts like 'privacy by design' or what is considered as 'hygiene' on the Internet have very often the same objectives as cybersecurity. Indeed, some privacy provisions (like the right to be forgotten) may create obstacles in the fight against cybercrime but they should not hijack the debate. On the other hand, the revelations about NSA surveillance programs only strengthen the arguments of the privacy-oriented camp and open the way for the European leadership.

The final element in the unfolding debate regards the application of the existing international law to cyber conflicts. The EU's engagement towards building international consensus in this respect is necessary for two major reasons. Most importantly, the EU and its Member States can be a target as well as the origin of cyber-attacks which will require a great deal of cross-border coordination of diplomacy, law enforcement and technological expertise. In addition, the uncertainty related to cyber-attacks – as to what constitutes an attack, the identity of the attacker and their links with the state structures – can be resolved only through joint efforts of international community towards developing common understandings and situational awareness.

Several international organizations have undertaken the task of developing confidence-building measures but so far bringing all members of international community on board has failed and the patchwork of efforts persists. The most prominent attempt undertaken by the UN Group of Governmental Experts (GGE) in 2010 resulted in the publication of a report on the application of international law and standards to cyberspace. A year later the Shanghai Cooperation Organization (in particular China, Russia, Uzbekistan and Tajikistan) made its own submission with the aim of stimulating the discussion about the international norms and rules regulating the conduct of states in cyberspace. The initiative undertaken in 2012 under the auspices of the Organization for Security Co-operation in Europe (OSCE) – a package aimed at preventing a cyber war and including, among others, advance warning of government cyber-operations that might otherwise spark unintentional conflict – has also collapsed after Russia refused to sign the conclusions. Instead, Russia advances an idea of a universal cyber-convention that codifies reasonable standards of state behaviour.

In conclusion, it needs to be stressed that most of the existing international norms are based on the Westphalian order prescribed by the principle of sovereignty and state monopoly over violence whereas the rules regulating the cyberspace have been so far based on the bottom-up approach. Some authors refer to the push to subject the virtual world to more government control as a rise of the 'cybered Westphalian age' (Demchak and Dombrowski, 2011). However, virtual borders do not provide the same protection as the physical ones and are therefore much more difficult to secure.

The creation of 'cyber fortress Europe' would therefore be difficult to implement without broader international cooperation. At the same time, cyber violence is not an exclusive attribute of a state anymore – with criminals operating through many jurisdictions, the principle of attribution applied in times of conflict is very difficult to implement. In practical terms, it means that the existing doctrines cannot be directly translated into cyber space. The additional difficulty comes from the fact that the current system is very fragmented (several international actors are involved, including OECD, UN, OSCE, the Council of Europe and NATO) with certain regulations having a binding nature (hence strengthening the compliance) and others taking the shape of non-binding guidelines or recommendations. Moving from the *status quo* towards changes in the existing rules or the adoption of new regulations is necessary to limit the existing uncertainty which impairs state and non-state actors alike.

Cyber fortress Europe: Are domestic efforts enough?

One of the ways to deal with the uncertainties resulting from the debates mentioned earlier is to focus on strengthening the protection of cyberspace and improving one's own capacities. To that end, the European Union Cyberstrategy endorsed by Member States (Council of the European Union, 2013) on 25 June 2013 sets out five strategic priorities: achieving cyber resilience, drastically reducing cybercrime, developing cyber defence policy and capabilities related to the Common Security and Defence Policy (CSDP), developing the industrial and technological resources for cybersecurity and establishing a coherent international cyberspace policy for the EU and promote core EU values (European Commission, 2013).

The Cyberstrategy also reiterates the EU's commitment to existing international laws regulating cyberspace, including International Convention on Civil and Political Rights, the Geneva conventions, the principles enshrined in the Budapest Convention on Cybercrime. All these goals require the EU to engage in meaningful international partnerships and offer an opportunity to increase the EU's standing on cyber space. Fighting cybercrime cannot be done effectively without the cooperation between key international partners. Promoting freedom of speech on Internet and other core values cannot be achieved without the engagement at the global and regional level. The build-up of cyber-capabilities for defence and resilience is in turn closely linked to establishing the EU's international credibility on cyber issues. The European External Action Service, in particular, is tasked to ensure the preservation of freedom and human rights in the digital world, to coordinate the capacity-building assistance, strengthen the accountability and stability of the Internet and maintaining relations with partners and international organization. It has also been a staunch supporter of the multi-stakeholder model for the governance of cyberspace, which brings together private actors, civil society, governments and international organizations.

The EU has also been at the forefront of the international harmonization and standard setting in the digital communication and eradicating safe havens where law enforcement and regulatory framework is weak or non-existent. Part of that endeavour is implemented through the constant support for the multi-stakeholder processes that – while recognizing the central role of governments in delivering the security and resilience of cyberspace – provide the means for contribution from all stakeholders, including the private sector and civil society. The benefits of this approach are clearly visible if one compares the availability of resources in public and private sector. According to a 2012 survey conducted by the Ponemon Institute and Bloomberg, achieving the highest possible level of IT security (i.e. capable of repelling 95 per cent of attacks) would mean nearly a nine-fold increase in company spending from the current €4 billion. To match these efforts, the EU committed in 2012 to a (modest) 14 per cent increase for cybersecurity programs in its long-term budget up to 2020 and an additional €450 million were assigned to the EU's Secure Societies Research program (which includes aspects of cybersecurity).

The EU is also making simultaneous efforts to build-up its own internal capacities (Table 2.2) and to demonstrate that the EU's model works for its citizens. Meanwhile, a Eurobarometer survey of 2012 revealed that almost one-third of European citizens do not feel confident using the Internet (European Commission, 2012a). One of the steps aiming at improving this situation is the Directive on network and information security foreseeing

Table 2.1 Cyber alphabet soup: Who does what?

	Regional and global level	EU level		
		European Commission	EEAS	Member States, EU agencies and other institutions
Cybercrime and justice	UN, Interpol, Council of Europe	DG Home, DG Justice	Conflict Prevention and Security Policy Division	Europol, Eurojust, FRA, EDPS, MS, Council (Friends of Presidency), EP
Cyber resilience	OECD, ITU, UNIDIR, UNICRI	DG Connect, DG Enterprise, DG Research	EUMC, EUMS, CMPD	ENISA, EU-CERT, MS (CERTs), Council (Friends of Presidency, PSC), EP
Cyber diplomacy	Council of Europe, NATO, OSCE	DG Devco EuropeAid	Conflict Prevention and Security Policy Division	MS, Council (Friends of Presidency)
Cyber conflicts	ITU, UNODC, NATO, OSCE	DG Enterprise, DG Research	EUMC, EUMS, CMPD	EDA, MS, Council (Friends of Presidency, PSC)

Source: Author's compilation on the basis of official documents.

that Member States will establish network and information security (NIS) national competent authorities, set up Computer Emergency Response Teams (CERTs) and adopt national NIS strategies and national NIS cooperation plans. Furthermore, public administrations, operators of critical infrastructure (such as energy, transport or banking) and key Internet enablers (e-commerce platforms, social networks etc.) will be responsible for performing risk assessment and adopting appropriate measures. Contrary to the position preferred by some members of the cyber community, the EU puts forward its own model for transparency that obliges these entities to report to competent authorities any incidents with a significant impact on core services provided.

In addition to efforts mentioned earlier, the EU has established the European Cybercrime Centre (EC3), developed the EU network of national centres of excellence for cybercrime training, research and education (already operational in seven Member States and under development in other three), and designed cybercrime training materials for law enforcement under the auspices of the European Cybercrime Training and Education Group hosted by Europol. The EU has also established the network of law enforcement contact points operational 24/7 and bringing together officials with cyber expertise capable of ensuring urgent assistance. In terms of legislative initiatives, the Foreign Affairs Council of 23 July 2013 approved a new directive on attacks against information systems. The Directive defines what constitutes a criminal offence in the area of cybersecurity and establishes criminal sanctions for basic offences or attacks against critical infrastructure information systems.

The EU's external action would be seriously impaired without the capabilities to effectively secure the conduct of CSDP missions and operations. A stocktaking study to assess the cyber defence capabilities of Member States conducted by the European Defence Agency concluded that the EU's cyber-intelligence gathering capabilities are only emerging while incident response capabilities and developing good practices could be further developed. The same study found a rather mixed picture among Member States. Several efforts are already underway (for instance to develop Cyber Defence Situational Awareness for CSDP operations or Cyber Defence Training Need Analysis). The European Council debate on security and defence in December 2013 provided an opportunity to elaborate some of the concepts outlined in the EU Cyber Strategy, in particular the need to integrate cyber defence into planning and conduct of CSDP missions, training and exercises or strengthening resilience at the national level. There is

Table 2.2 Performances of EU Member States on cybersecurity

Member State	Cyber security strategy	Ratification of the Budapest Convention (as of 11/7/2013)	National / governmental CERT
Austria	Yes (2013)	1/10/2012 (F)	Yes (2008)
Belgium	Yes (2013)	1/12/2012 (F)	Yes (2004)
Bulgaria	In progress (info as of September 2013)	1/8/2005 (F)	Yes (2008)
Croatia	No (info as of 2011)	1/7/2004 (F)	Yes (2009)
Cyprus	No (info as of June 2012)	1/5/2005 (F)	Yes (2002)
Czech Republic	Yes (2011)	9/2/2005 (S)	Yes (2012)
Denmark	No (info as of 2013)	1/10/2005	Yes (2009)
Estonia	Yes (2008)	1/7/2004	Yes (2006)
Finland	Yes (2013)	1/9/2007	Yes (2002)
France	Yes (2011)	1/5/2006	Yes (1999)
Germany	Yes (2011)	1/7/2009	Yes (2001)
Greece	No (info as of March 2012)	23/11/2001 (S)	Yes (n/a)
Hungary	Yes (2013)	1/7/2004	Yes (2005)
Ireland	In progress (info as of May 2012)	28/2/2002 (S)	Yes (n/a)
Italy	In progress (info as of April 2013)	1/10/2008	Research and Education (1994)
Latvia	In progress (info as of 2011)	1/6/2007	Yes (2006)
Lithuania	Yes (2011)	1/7/2004	Yes (2006)
Luxembourg	Yes (2011)	28/1/2003 (S)	Yes (2011)
Malta	No (info as of May 2011)	1/8/2012	Governmental (2002)
Netherlands	Yes (2011)	1/3/2007	Yes (2002)
Poland	Yes (2011)	23/11/2001 (S)	Yes (1996)
Portugal	In progress (info as of March 2013)	1/7/2010	Yes (2006)
Romania	Yes (2011)	1/9/2004	Yes (2011)
Slovakia	Yes (2008)	1/5/2008	Yes (2009)
Slovenia	In progress (info as of August 2013)	1/1/2005	Yes (1994)
Spain	Yes (2012)	1/10/2010	Yes (2006)
Sweden	In progress (info as of February 2013)	23/11/2001 (S)	Yes (2005)
United Kingdom	Yes (2011)	1/9/2011	Yes (2007)

(S – signed on, F – in force since)

Source: Author's compilation on the basis of government documents and official EU sources.

also a clear need to improve coordination between military and civilian actors, including law enforcement, competent cybersecurity authorities and the private sector.

It needs to be highlighted however that given the global nature of the challenges in cyberspace, the efforts at improving internal EU capabilities need to be accompanied by actions at the international level. As it is often underlined by cybersecurity experts, 'the core problem is that the cyber-criminal has greater agility, large funding streams and no legal boundaries to sharing information, and can thus choreograph well-orchestrated attacks into systems. The good guys have to attend meetings and publish reports to enable even minimal data sharing to track their opponents' (Security and Defence Agenda, 2012). The following sections discuss in more detail two specific approaches: confidence building and capacity-building measures.

Confidence-building measures: Diffusing conflicts and enhancing trust

Traditionally, confidence-building measures have been used as one of the instruments to build trust between nations by changing their perception of their respective approaches and by building shared understandings diminishing the chances of conflicts.[4] They can be of different nature: political (for instance power sharing), economic (e.g. cross-border trade), environmental (e.g. training in responding to natural disasters), societal (e.g. people-to-people dialogues) or cultural (e.g. multilingual regimes where ethnic minorities exist) (Organization for Security Cooperation in Europe, 2012). Confidence-building measures had their golden age during the Cold War, especially after the 1962 Cuban Missile Crisis. In 1988, the United Nations Disarmament Commission presented guidelines for CBMs whereby the objective was to prevent military confrontation (intended or by accident) through reducing or even eliminating 'the causes of mistrust, fear, misunderstanding and miscalculation with regard to relevant military activities and intentions of other States' (United Nations, 1988: para. 2.2.6). CBMs are usually codified in treaties and their verification is ensured by specially established entities like the International Atomic Energy Agency that checks the compliance with the 1968 Treaty on the Non-Proliferation of Nuclear Weapons.

Although some authors underline the limited usefulness of traditional mechanisms like effective verification or the establishment of demilitarized zones (Lewis, 2013; Neuneck, 2013b) – due to their focus on weapons, military forces, government/military controlled assets and facilities – the primary premise of CBMs as de-escalation mechanisms remains the same for cyberspace where the risks of miscalculations or misattribution remain high. A report by the UN Group of Governmental Experts presented in 2010 recommended 'further dialogue among states to discuss norms pertaining to state use of ICTs, to reduce collective risk and protect critical national and international infrastructure' and 'confidence-building, stability and risk reduction measures to address the implications of state use of OCTs, including exchanges of national views on the use of ICTs in conflict' (United Nations, 2010: para. 18). Despite this and other attempts by regional and international organizations (for example, OSCE, NATO), common approaches to cyber confidence-building measures are still missing and the debate on CBMs is underdeveloped due to competing and often contradictory views about legal obligations or threats (Neuneck, 2013c). For instance, the Russian position favours the development of a cyber peace treaty or alternative measures like guidelines and memoranda of intention.

The United States and some European countries, on the other hand, argue that in a quickly evolving environment like cyberspace a binding international treaty would not allow for a flexible and timely response needed to deal with most of the malicious cyber activities. James Lewis argues that 'Cyberconflict is shaped by covertness, ease of acquisition and uncertainty, and a legally binding convention that depends upon renouncing use, restricting technology, or upon verification of compliance is an unworkable approach for reducing the risk to international security from cyber-attacks' and consequently 'an effort to secure an overarching cybersecurity agreement or treaty […] would be impractical' (Lewis, 2011: 58).

In the absence of an overarching legal framework for cyberspace and the existing differences between major players, the challenge of designing CBMs for cyberspace gains in importance. The political context gets even thicker given that the US government has become more vocal on threats posed by Chinese and Russian computers as essential origins for espionage attacks on US businesses and government agencies (Fryer-Biggs, 2013). Two issues in particular need to be addressed at the outset: attribution and intentionality. The uncertainty about the attacker's identity creates the dilemma related to attributing an attack to a specific state actor while knowing that countries can be used as proxies for a cyber-attack.

It is not clear to what extent states from which an attack originates can be liable for attack conducted from their territories, although the tendency is to extend the principles applied to safe havens for terrorist activities. In fact, Chinese authorities have notoriously declined any connection to cyber-attacks against the United States. However, Baseley-Walker argues that 'even if the perpetrator is identified in a timely fashion with high degree of confidence, proving an act was state-sponsored is extremely challenging and often impossible' (2011: 33). This is a particularly pertinent issue given the possibility that conflicts may spill over from cyberspace and trigger a retaliatory action outside the cyber domain. Although in line with the 2010 UN report on cybersecurity there is a general recognition that the law of armed conflict applies to cyber-attacks, the ambiguity remains regarding the crossing of a red line which could be regarded as a military aggression. This is why the creation of a common vocabulary with internationally recognizable definitions for grades of attacks and potential targets is viewed as a priority.

Given the difficulties with elaborating a generally acceptable catalogue of CBMs, some countries have opted for establishing bilateral channels. One of the most prominent examples is the US-China civilian-military Cyber Working Group where the two sides 'committed to work together on cooperative activities and further discussions on international norms of state behaviour in cyberspace' (Department of State, 2013c). The first meeting of this group took place in the margins of the US-China Strategic and Economic Dialogue on 9 July 2013 which has as an objective to 'promote an open, cooperative, secure, and reliable cyber space' (Department of State 2013c). The militaries of two countries agreed 'to actively explore a notification mechanism for major military activities and continue to discuss the rules of behaviour' (Department of State, 2013c). The United States is also engaged into developing cyber partnerships with ASEAN countries in order to develop confidence-building measures for the whole region that would increase transparency, greater cooperation and improved capacity within the region (Department of State, 2013b).

Several initiatives are also underway as Track II diplomacy. For instance, the Centre for Strategic and International Studies (CSIS) and the China Institute of Contemporary International Relations (CICIR) have held a number of meetings on cybersecurity with participants including a broad range of US and Chinese officials and scholars. Known as Track 2 Sino-US Cybersecurity Dialogue, this series of meetings has an objective of reducing misperceptions and to increase transparency on both sides, improve mutual understanding of how each country approaches cybersecurity and to identify areas of potential cooperation, including confidence-building measures (Centre for Strategic and International Studies, 2013).[5]

The origins for these activities are twofold. First, the reports about China's cyber-espionage in the United States – including on military targets – have been causing uneasiness in Washington security circles and provided a significant stimulus to the development of the US cyber-capabilities. At the same time, the developments in United States cyberpolicy gave rise to concerns in China. In March 2013 General Keith B. Alexander, director of National Security Agency and Commander of US Cyber Command, suggested that the United States has the best cyber-offensive in the world. He argues that with potential adversaries demonstrating a rapidly increasing level of sophistication in their offensive cyber-capabilities and tactics, the Department of Defense must 'continue the rapid development and resourcing of out cyber mission forces' (US House of Representatives, 2013). The United States' focus on cyber-offensive capabilities and training programs raised suspicions about US intentions and its wish for cyber dominance and as such posed a serious challenge to cyber stability (Lewis, 2013).

Capacity building: Addressing blurred lines between internal and external security

Due to the global nature of the digital environment, the distinction between internal and external security in cyberspace is almost non-existent. Dealing with uncertainties in cyberspace requires tackling the problem of cybersecurity capacities in different parts of the world. To that end there is a constant need not only to develop cooperation between actors with already advanced cyber policies but in particular to support 'weakest link countries' where the absence of legislation or effective law enforcement mechanisms could offer a fertile ground for cybercrime to thrive, and which could eventually become safe havens for criminals. The report presented by the GGE in 2010 recommends that countries where the skills and expertise are lacking should be supported by briefings, workshops, and joint training (United Nations, 2010).

A number of activities to that end are coordinated, among others, by the International Telecommunications Union (ITU) which developed an extensive network of centres of excellence and created the Cybersecurity Gateway that serves as a platform for sharing information between partners in civil society, private sector and governments. Furthermore, the challenge of capacity building cannot be properly addressed without recognizing the importance of its multi-stakeholder nature, including the role of the private sector as one of the key players. This is the main rationale behind the International Multilateral Partnership Against Cyber Threats (ITU-IMPACT) that supports various actors in the creation of cybersecurity strategies and critical information infrastructure protection (CIIP). The ITU-IMPACT collaboration recognizes that most developing countries do not have sufficient expertise to design and implement such strategies and offers cyber training programmes at both technical and managerial level.

The focus on capacity building is important for building trust at the global level but also for economic and security reasons. A recent report by the Centre for Strategic and International Studies points out that cybercrime (namely, criminal acts that can only be committed through the use of ICT or Internet technology) represents between 0.4 to 1.4 per cent of global GDP – even though the total cost might be higher if the indirect costs (for instance, direct disruption of operations and payment transactions, theft of sensitive data such as trade secrets and credit card information, legal liability, and long-lasting harm to a business's brand) are included. For this reason most of the efforts focus on creating the right conditions for an effective fight against cybercrime. For instance, law enforcement authorities are involved in multinational operations targeting various forms of crime, including online child sexual abuse file sharing networks (Operation Icarus) or child sexual exploitation (Operation Atlantic). One of the most prominent examples of international capacity-building efforts is a joint initiative by the EU and the United States targeting child sexual abuse online. A Global Alliance against Child Sexual Abuse Online launched in December 2012 gathers ministers of the interior and justice from over 50 countries.[6] More specifically, the countries participating in the Alliance have undertaken the commitment to enhance efforts in four specific areas:

1. identification and assistance to victims;
2. investigation of cases of child sexual abuse online and prosecution of the offenders;
3. awareness-raising among children, parents, educators and the community;
4. reducing the availability of child pornography online and the re-victimization of children (European Commission, 2012b).[7]

In order to assess their level of preparedness, as a part of the capacity-building efforts, several national and international bodies engage in cyber-exercises that are an important tool in assessing the preparedness against cyber-attacks.[8] According to ENISA, the number of cyber-exercises in recent years has increased mostly due to the overall policy context and increased threat of incidents and attacks (ENISA, 2012). Their aim is usually to build awareness about cyber threats, examine the capabilities and readiness of participants to deal with them, identify and highlight their specific roles and to build trust among participants (ENISA, 2012). The formats of exercises vary depending on their goal – from a desk check for an early stage validation of a new plan or amendments to an old one to full simulation to stress test the responses with a real time environment (Table 2.3).

One example of a table-top exercise is 'Cyber Atlantic' organized and planned by the EU and the United States in November 2011. This initiative – one of the activities under the umbrella of the EU-US Working Group on Cybersecurity and Cyber Crime established at the EU-US summit of 2010 – was the first joint EU-US cyber exercise and had an exploratory nature. Facilitated by the European Network and Information Security Agency (ENISA) and Department of Homeland Security (DHS), the exercise included 20 countries.[9]

The objective of the exercise was to explore the ways in which the United States and the EU Member States would engage during cyber crisis management activities. Given the differences between European and American procedures, the exercise also meant to identify issues that could potentially play a role during a cyber crisis. Finally, both sides agreed to exchange good practices on their respective approaches to international cooperation (ENISA, 2011). The scenario of the exercises was divided into two parts. First, the participants had to address an Advanced Persistent Threat (APT) scenario whereby a hacker group attempts to exfiltrate sensitive documents from the EU Member States' government agencies in order to publish them on the 'Euroleaks' website. The second scenario focused on vulnerabilities of the Supervisory Control and Data Acquisition (SCADA) systems in power generation equipment. The lessons identified during the exercise included the need for increased participation from all stakeholders involved (i.e. law enforcement, technical and policy) and a desirability of exchanges of Standard Operating Procedures (SOPs), trainings and exercises. Even though the exercise revealed that the mechanisms for cross-border cooperation exist, there was also a clear realization that the

Table 2.3 Types of cyber-exercises

What	Why	How
Desk check	Early stage validation of a new plan or amendments to a plan	One-to-one discussion with the author of the planned procedures against a simple scenario to demonstrate the stages that are in place and how they operate
Comms check	To validate systems or infrastructures	A different form of initial activity used to validate communication methodologies or notification systems
Walk through	The first time the response team convenes to consider the planned procedures and their roles	The response team is convened in one room and a simple scenario is used to demonstrate the progression of the planned responses and what each respondent should do
Workshop	A scenario-based rehearsal of responses and actions in open forum, to allow discussion of activities	A development step in the building of capability, using a scenario to rehearse in an open forum the responses of teams and actions without any time pressure
Table-top	To validate plans and integration of procedures prior to moving on to more complex, team-based activities	Scenario-based, open forum discussions with no external pressures. Responses are stepped through in a measured fashion and each aspect is discussed if needed before moving on
Distributed table-top	To test plans and procedures	Scenario-based, players act according to routine
Command post	To enable the team to rehearse using their own response facilities. Usually only management level involvement	Response centre based but with role play of the external environment and players
Full simulation	To stress test the responses with a real time environment, as close to reality in every aspect as possible	Players respond in real time as information is received, interacting with other teams and role players as the response requires

Source: ENISA 2012.

communications options needed to be further identified and communicated to the stakeholders.[10]

Another example of a cross-regional cooperation effort is the US-ASEAN Cybercrime Capacity-Building initiative with the focus on requirements and models for national high-tech crime investigative units and digital forensics programs. According to the Department of State, the cybercrime initiative would 'address the authorities, tools, and techniques necessary for law enforcement agencies to effectively investigate cybercrime and process electronic evidence for any type of crime; and effectively use formal and informal international cooperation mechanisms for assistance in cybercrime investigations and other investigations involving electronic evidence' (Department of State, 2013a). These efforts are accompanied by intraregional initiatives like the development of the ARF Work Plan on Cyber Security formulated jointly by Malaysia, Australia and Russia as co-lead countries. In light of considerable differences in the level of technological advancement of different countries, their legal systems and institutions, the member countries of the ARF recognized the need to develop the capacities of governments and enhance cooperation in bringing about the culture of cybersecurity (ASEAN, 2013).

Conclusions

With cybersecurity rapidly climbing the policy (and political) agendas, it is necessary to clearly identify the remaining challenges. The ever-evolving nature of the digital environment makes it almost impossible for the governments and private actors alike to adjust in time the regulatory frameworks which provide the basis for their operation. The asymmetry resulting from the diffusion of cyber-authority and cyber-capabilities to non-governmental actors further complicates the debate about the governance of cyberspace. These individual aspects are at the source of legal and political uncertainties that to a large extent determine international relations nowadays.

This chapter provides an overview of two layers through which this challenge can be addressed. First, the European Union and many individual countries around the world deal with cybersecurity by focusing on improving their own resilience and building up their cyber-capabilities. This, however, may create uncertainties as to the peaceful nature of those efforts that in turn need to be accompanied by political initiatives like confidence-building measures. Second, and because there is no physical border at which cyber threats would stop, many actors acknowledge the need to deal with cyber threats through political and capacity-building measures. There is also a widespread recognition among policymakers that capacity building is a global effort and needs to take place in cooperation with the private sector and civil society.

Notes

1 The views expressed in this chapter are those of the author only and are not an official position of the EU Institute for Security Studies.
2 See also Chapter 5.
3 Some of the topics examined in this chapter have also been analysed in Chapter 8.
4 The scholarship distinguishes between CBMs, Confidence and Security Building Measures (CSBMs), Transparency and Confidence Building Measures (TCBMs) where there is a direct link to military and security domain and Civil Confidence Building Measures (CCBMs) designed to build trust and confidence among ethnic groups, etc. See: Neuneck (2013a), Organization for Security Cooperation in Europe (2012), Tulliu and Schmalberger (2003).
5 See the Center for Strategic and International Studies at http://csis.org/program/china-institute-contemporary-international-relations-cicir (accessed 20 August 2013).
6 Among other countries there are Cambodia, Georgia, Ghana, Moldova, Montenegro, Nigeria, Norway, Philippines, Serbia and Ukraine.
7 The next conference to assess the progress towards the goals of the Global Alliance is planned before December 2014.
8 See the ENISA website (On National and International Cybersecurity Exercises: Survey, Analysis, Recommendations) October 2012 at www.enisa.europa.eu/activities/Resilience-and-CIIP/cyber-crisis-cooperation/cyber-exercises/exercise-survey2012 (accessed 20 August 2013).
9 See ENISA at www.enisa.europa.eu/activities/Resilience-and-CIIP/cyber-crisis-cooperation/cyber-atlantic/cyber-atlantic-2011 (accessed 20 August 2013).
10 Interview with a Department of Homeland Security Official, November 2012, Washington, DC.

References

ASEAN (2013), Co-chairs' Summary Report, ASEAN Regional Forum Inter-sessional Support Group on Confidence Building Measures and Preventive Diplomacy,

Beijing, 27–28 April 2012, http://aseanregionalforum.asean.org/files/library/
ARF%20Chairman's%20Statements%20and%20Reports/The%20Twentieth%20
ASEAN%20Regional%20Forum,%202012-2013/08%20-%20Co-Chairs%20
Summary%20Report%20-%20ARF%20ISG%20on%20CBMs%20and%20PD,%20
Beijing.pdf (accessed 20 August 2013).

Baseley-Walker, B. (2011), 'Transparency and confidence-building measures in
cyberspace: towards norms of behaviour', *Disarmament Forum*, 4: 31–40.

Council of the European Union (2013), 'Council Conclusions of the Commission and
the High Representative of the European Union for Foreign Affairs and Security
Policy Joint Communication on the Cybersecurity Strategy of the European Union:
An Open, Safe and Secure Cyberspace', Luxembourg, 25 June 2013.

Demchak, C. C. and P. Dombrowski (2011), 'Rise of a cybered westphalian age',
Strategic Studies Quarterly, 5: 32–61.

Department of State (2013a), 'The ASEAN-US Ministerial Meeting', Fact Sheet,
Washington, 1 July, www.state.gov/r/pa/prs/ps/2013/07/211389.htm (accessed 20
August 2013).

—(2013b), 'US Engagement in the 2013 ASEAN Regional Forum', Fact Sheet,
Washington, 2 July 2013, www.state.gov/r/pa/prs/ps/2013/07/211467.htm (accessed
20 August 2013).

—(2013c), 'Fact Sheet on Outcomes from US-China Strategic Dialogue', Washington,
12 July 2013, http://iipdigital.usembassy.gov/st/english/texttrans/2013/07/20130712
278542.html (accessed 20 August 2013).

ENISA Pan-European Cyber Exercise 2011 and 2012, www.enisa.europa.eu/activities/
Resilience-and-CIIP/cyber-crisis-cooperation/cce/cyber-europe/cyber-europe-2012.

Eric Engleman and Chris Strohm, 'Cybersecurity disaster seen in U.S. Survey citing
spending gaps', Bloomberg, 30 January 2012, www.bloomberg.com/news/2012-
01-31/cybersecurity-disaster-seen-in-u-s-survey-citing-spending-gaps.html
(accessed 5 May 2014).

European Commission (2012a), 'Cyber Security. Report', *Eurobarometer* 390, Special
Issue, July.

—(2012b), 'Declaration on the Launch of the Global Alliance against Child Sexual
Abuse Online, Brussels, 5 December 2012.

—(2013), 'Cybersecurity Strategy of the European Union: An Open, Safe and Secure
Cyberspace, Brussels, 7 February 2013.

Fryer-Biggs, Z. (2013), 'US Sharpens Tone on Cyber Attacks From China',
Defence News, 19 March 2013, www.defensenews.com/article/20130319/
DEFREG02/303190026/U-S-Sharpens-Tone-Cyber-Attacks-From-China (accessed
20 August 2013).

Gellman, B. and E. Nakashima (2013), 'US Spy Agencies Mounted 231
Offensive Cyber-Operations in 2011, Documents Show', *The Washington
Post*, 30 August 2013, http://articles.washingtonpost.com/2013-08-30/

world/41620705_1_computer-worm-former-u-s-officials-obama-administration (accessed 20 August 2013).

Lewis, J. A. (2011), 'Confidence-building and international agreement in cybersecurity', *Disarmament Forum*, 4: 51–60.

—(2013), 'Conflict and Negotiation in Cyberspace', Centre for Strategic and International Studies, February.

Mandiant (2013), 'APT1: Exposing One of China's Cyber Espionage Units', Report, Washington, http://intelreport.mandiant.com/Mandiant_APT1_Report.pdf (accessed 15 September 2013).

Neuneck, G. (2013a), 'Types of Confidence Building Measures', in J. A. Lewis and G. Neuneck (eds), *The Cyber Index: International Security Trends and Realities*, UNIDIR/2013/3, New York and Geneva.

—(2013b), 'Towards CTBMs in the Cybersphere', in J. A. Lewis and G. Neuneck (eds), *The Cyber Index: International Security Trends and Realities*, UNIDIR/2013/3, New York and Geneva.

—(2013c), 'Transparency and Confidence-building Measures: Applicability to the Cyberspace?', in J. A. Lewis and G. Neuneck (eds), *The Cyber Index: International Security Trends and Realities*, UNIDIR/2013/3, New York and Geneva.

Organization for Security Cooperation in Europe (2012), 'OSCE Guide on Non-Military Confidence-Building Measures (CBMs)', Vienna: OSCE.

Security and Defence Agenda (2012), 'Cyber-Security: The Vexed Question of Global Rules: An Independent Report on Cyber-Prepardness around the World', Brussels, www.securitydefenceagenda.org/Contentnavigation/Library/Libraryoverview/tabid/1299/articleType/ArticleView/articleId/3063/SDA-report-Cybersecurity-The-vexed-question-of-global-rules.aspx (accessed 20 August 2013).

Tulliu, S. and T. Schmalberger (2003), 'Coming to Terms with Security: A Lexicon for Arms Control, Disarmament and Confidence-Building', Vienna: UNIDIR.

United Nations (1988), 'Special Report of the Disarmament Commission to the General Assembly at its Third Special Session Devoted to Disarmament, United Nations A/S-15/3', 28 May 1988.

—(2010), 'Group of Governmental Experts on Development in the Field of Information and Telecommunications in the Context of International Security', United Nations A/65/201, 30 July 2010.

US House of Representatives (2013), 'Information Technology and Cyber Operations: Modernization and Policy Issues To Support Future Force', Hearing before the Subcommitee on Intelligence, Emerging Threats and Capabilities of the Committee on Armed Services, Washington, DC: US Government Printing Office.

Xinhua News (2013), 'China's Cyber Security Under Severe Threat: Report', 19 March 2013, http://news.xinhuanet.com/english/china/2013-03/19/c_132246098.htm (accessed 20 August 2013).

3

WikiLeaks and State Control of Information in the Cyber Age

Judith Reppy

Introduction

On 28 November 2010 documents from a cache of over 250,000 confidential – and in some cases, classified – US diplomatic cables were released to the general public by the *New York Times*, the *Guardian* and *Der Spiegel*. The newspapers had received the documents from WikiLeaks, a web-based organization that defines its purpose as bringing important news and information to the public.[1] WikiLeaks, in turn, had received the cables from Pfc. Bradley Manning, US Army, who had access to them in the course of his duties as an intelligence specialist. Manning was arrested in May 2010; his first hearing took place in December 2011, more than 18 months after his arrest; and formal court martial proceedings began on 23 February 2012. His trial finally took place in summer 2013; he was found guilty on 20 counts, including violations of the Espionage Act, and sentenced to 35 years in prison.[2]

WikiLeaks had previously made available large numbers of government documents relevant to US policies and actions – including in 2010 a video, 'Collateral Murder', showing an attack by a US helicopter on civilians in Iraq which killed two Reuters journalists, and two other releases of US documents related to the Iraq and Afghanistan wars – without triggering a strong reaction from the government or the American public. But the exposure of US diplomatic practices in the 'Cablegate' leaks struck a more sensitive nerve. Although only a small fraction (6 per cent) of the leaked cables was classified secret, much of the official reaction focused on the charge that US security had been compromised. Of course, 6 per cent of a large number is a large number: in this case it included approximately 15,652 cables, with over a quarter of those marked NOFORN, meaning no foreigners ('What do the Diplomatic Cables Really Tell Us?' 2010).

The US government reacted to Cablegate with threats of legal action against Julian Assange, the founder and chief spokesperson for WikiLeaks, and an order banning all government employees from visiting WikiLeak websites. It exerted pressure on the organizations hosting WikiLeaks to disable the sites and on financial institutions in the United States and abroad to block donations. And it moved to tighten controls on information sharing within the government, potentially re-introducing the 'information stovepipes' that, in the wake of the 9/11 attacks on the World Trade Center and Pentagon, were criticized as crippling the ability of the government to identify and track terrorist threats. Notably, however, the release of so much confidential information, some of it revealing corruption in friendly governments, secret US operations in Pakistan and Yemen and other damaging stories (Gallagher, 2011), did not result in any significant changes in US foreign policy.

Despite the US government's steps to tighten controls on information and prosecute individuals implicated in leaks, the release of the diplomatic cables was not the last of massive leaks to the press. On 9 June 2013, Edward Snowden, who had worked as a contractor for the National Security Agency (NSA), revealed that he was responsible for leaking documents to the *Guardian* and *Washington Post* detailing the NSA data collection programs. The NSA programs swept up data on telephone conversations and email correspondence, using techniques that can access specific content and also analyse 'metadata' in order to identify patterns of communication and track the location of individuals. Although these programs originated in the perceived need to track communications among terrorists after the 9/11 attacks, they inevitably swept up data of US citizens, and, once exposed, their legality was challenged in the courts. Snowden, meanwhile, sought asylum in Russia.

These events raise a host of interesting questions that go beyond the media interest in the fates of Julian Assange, Bradley Manning and Edward Snowden or the specific revelations of the leaked cables and NSA documents. In this chapter I discuss the challenge that WikiLeaks – and other websites that resemble it – poses to the ability of national states to control information flows and the globalized infrastructure of the Internet, as well as the implications of the response to the leaks for other government policies, such as the protection of whistleblowers. These questions lie at the nexus of relationships in cyberspace among all three levels addressed in this volume – individuals, infrastructure, and national states – and they are a good example of why it is impossible to discuss one dimension of cyberspace in isolation from the others.

WikiLeaks in action

Modus operandi. The emergence of WikiLeaks in early 2007 as a conduit for anonymous sourcing of leaked information was possible because of the dispersed structure of the Internet, the developments in technology and software which provide the capability to handle large data files online, and the concept of crowd sourcing through the wiki model. In fact, however, WikiLeaks operated only briefly in the wiki mode (i.e. allowing edits and comments from users) before converting its practices to something more akin to a secure drop box. Submitted documents are reviewed by an editorial board and then re-routed using standard tools such as tor to protect the identity of the leaker. The documents are published on a website, accompanied by a brief commentary on the topic. The website is based in Sweden – a relatively safe haven because of its strong laws on the protection of information – and maintained by a group of associates and volunteers from around the world organized by Assange. In addition there are numerous mirror sites, designed originally to get around censorship filters in countries such as China and to provide protection against denial-of-services attacks; in 2010–11 these sites proved useful in overcoming the blocks imposed by US and European financial institutions in retaliation to the Cablegate leaks.

The relative independence of the Internet has been essential to protecting WikiLeaks from government controls. Governance of the Internet is the joint product of hundreds of decisions made by actors, both public and private. Governments have played a role, particularly in developing the technologies that made the Internet possible, but the day-to-day operations of the net are governed by the many technical agreements reached by standards committees, private companies, and even individuals working on design features (DeNardis, 2010). This network of actors constitutes a largely invisible economy, one that functions to provide access, connectivity, resilience, and a degree of security to the Internet; notably it has been a global economy, although not all regions are equal. To the extent that the Internet 'has politics.' it has been the politics of open access and transparency.

WikiLeaks relies on the structural features of the Internet to provide anonymity to leakers and connectivity to the broader public. The possibility of remaining anonymous on the Internet is a needed protection for users of the WikiLeaks site who might face government repression if their identities were known. The privacy features that underlie WikiLeaks are related to a general line of technical development in distributed peer-to-peer applications designed to foil surveillance and censorship (The Tor Project, n.d.). Essentially, the systems generate anonymity through a decentralized structure consisting of a large number of redundant nodes to store and search for documents that have been randomly distributed across the network. Communication between the nodes is encrypted and re-encrypted at each step, and the identities of the requester and provider of the information are hidden from all other nodes. Thus, Julian Assange could plausibly claim that he 'never heard of the name of Bradley Manning before it appeared in the media' (Miklaszerski, 2011).

In the eight years that it has been operating, WikiLeaks has acquired and published a number of data caches from a variety of governments and organizations: e.g. documents concerning extrajudicial assassinations in Kenya; the Church of Scientology; the membership list of the British National Party; tax evasion strategies of major banks; and the Australian government's plans in 2009 to censor Internet sites. WikiLeaks claims to provide anonymity for leakers and wide dispersion of the leaked information via its website, and these claims seem to be valid. (The arrest of Bradley Manning in connection with the leaked US data files was the result of his communications with another hacker, not any information acquired from WikiLeaks.) The editorial review process, however, is not the same thing as a guarantee of authenticity and accuracy, something that would be near impossible to provide, given the size of the data files and the relatively few people working for WikiLeaks.[3] Problems of authenticity and accuracy are, of course, not unique to WikiLeaks, but are a feature of all sources that involve large data files. There have, however, been very few challenges to the authenticity of the data published by WikiLeaks.

Prior to the 2010 releases of the video 'Collateral Murder', the US documents on the wars in Iraq and Afghanistan, and the State Department cables, WikiLeaks enjoyed a generally favourable reputation and it received two international awards honouring its role in promoting openness (Lynch, 2010: 310). It did not, however, receive the wide attention to its releases which it felt the material deserved, and this was a source of frustration to Assange and his colleagues. WikiLeaks struggled to get mainstream journalists to write about the materials that it was posting – that is, to provide the broader context and interpretation that would make the information legible to the general public. From the perspective of the journalists, however, WikiLeaks' practice of making the materials available to all on an equal footing eliminated the incentive of an exclusive scoop, and in many cases the journalists were overwhelmed by the sheer volume of information and the difficulty in organizing it into compelling narrative.

After the release of 'Collateral Murder', which was covered in the mainstream media mainly as a story about a security leak rather than evidence of US atrocities in Iraq, WikiLeaks altered its practices for the release of the Iraq and Afghanistan war files to form direct alliances with the mainstream media. It offered three selected newspapers – *The Guardian, The New York Times* and *Der Spiegel* – exclusive access to the files before they were released to the public. For the Cablegate release, the number of partners was increased to include other leading papers, such as *Le Monde* in France and *El País* in Spain; in addition the local press in some smaller countries was given access to the cables pertaining to their own countries (Hrafnsson, 2011).

The rationale for the change in policy was to provide an incentive to the traditional media to promote the leaked material by making them partners in the endeavour and in effect creating the conditions for a journalistic scoop. In addition, WikiLeaks was able to share the job of reviewing, and in some cases redacting, the files with the experienced journalists on the newspaper staffs, and indeed, the newspapers devoted major resources to reviewing the documents before their publication and put the stories on the front page. Finally, the connection to leading newspapers conferred a kind of legitimacy on the operation as well as immunity against government crackdowns, at least until the release of the Cablegate files. Ironically, although WikiLeaks was neither the source of the leaked files nor the only organization to publish them, it has, along with Bradley Manning, borne the brunt of the US government's retaliation, while the newspapers have not been prosecuted.

Relationship with journalism. Julian Assange describes himself as a journalist, and WikiLeaks includes a number of journalists among its active members. Mainstream journalists, however, have had mixed reactions to the emergence of WikiLeaks and similar sites. On the one hand, WikiLeaks has facilitated the publication of large amounts of information that governments and other institutions would like to keep secret, and it has maintained access to the files in cases in which court ordered injunctions have restricted the media from reporting on stories (Bruns, 2009). As such, it has been a valuable resource for journalists. At the same time, however, it competes with the traditional press by providing an alternative source of information, even as traditional journalism struggles to survive in the face of the rise of the Internet as the preferred news source for many people. This tension between WikiLeaks' dual roles as resource and competitor were not resolved by the alliances formed by WikiLeaks and major newspapers to publish the files on Iraq and Afghanistan and the diplomatic cables, and numerous accounts of the negotiations between the major players attest to the difficulties that beset their relationships (e.g. Hrafnsson, 2011; Leigh and Harding, 2011; Keller, 2011; Rosenbach and Stark, 2011). If, however, imitation is the sincerest form of flattery, it is worth noting that the *Wall Street Journal* and *Al Jazeera* set up their own secure drop boxes to bypass WikiLeaks, and even the *New York Times*, which had a special relationship with WikiLeaks, seriously considered doing so (Carr, 2011; McMillan, 2011).

In the sense that it publishes newsworthy material and provides at least some context for the items on its website, WikiLeaks practises a form of journalism. However, it challenges conventional models of journalism and investigative reporting by acquiring the leaked material outside the usual relationship of journalist and trusted informant. Traditional journalists typically build their stories by developing trusted sources, whose identity they have to protect in order to receive privileged access in the future, and they judge the validity of the information, based in part on the presumed motivation of the leaker, before deciding whether to publish the story. Inevitably, the journalists are vulnerable to being co-opted by the interests of the individuals and organizations they are covering, a tendency that was particularly evident in the United States in the aftermath of the 9/11 attacks, when dissent or criticism of government actions in the mainstream media was considerably muted.

By contrast, in the WikiLeaks model the anonymity of the leakers makes assessing their motivation moot in most cases, and the relationship between a source and the organization is not expected to be a continuing one. To the extent a relationship of trust can be imputed, it rests on the technology for guaranteeing anonymity. WikiLeaks's commitment to radical transparency tilts the balance between public good and possible private harm strongly in the direction of the presumed public good; the consequences of publication on the subjects of the story are not seen as a legitimate reason not to publish except in extreme cases of harm – for example, something that might result in the death of a source (Lynch, 2009).[4] WikiLeaks did, however, cooperate in the redaction of sensitive information from the Afghanistan files and the diplomatic cables (Benkler, 2011). It is interesting to note that Edward Snowden went directly to a trusted journalist, Glenn Greenwald, rather than utilizing WikiLeaks. He thus retained some control over the document he had taken. Only after he had revealed his identity as the source did he seek help from WikiLeaks in organizing his appeals for asylum (Shane, 2013).

The US Constitution explicitly protects the freedom of the press.[5] There is, however, no federal law protecting reporters who refuse to disclose their sources – for example, during grand jury proceedings – and although most states have passed 'shield laws', they are a mixed bag, especially as the question of who counts as a journalist has been complicated by the proliferation of online news sources (Policinski, 2011). During the Obama administration there have been attempts by the government to prosecute reporters as accomplices in leak cases (Aftergood, 2013). Thus, WikiLeaks' guarantee of anonymity to its sources falls in contested territory in the United States. Following Cablegate, Julian Assange became the focal point for criticism, with many commentators in the United States calling for his prosecution (and even execution), despite his status as a journalist and the fact that he was not the person who originally leaked the files. The situation in other parts of the world varies from the strong protection provided in Sweden, where journalists are legally bound not to reveal their sources if anonymity has been requested, to countries like Nicaragua, where journalists are required to reveal their sources (Goldstein, 2008).

Secrecy and the US state

The release of the State Department cables, along with WikiLeaks' earlier releases of secret documents on the Iraq and Afghanistan wars, dropped into a long-running debate on government secrecy and democracy.[6] WikiLeaks' extreme position on transparency contrasts with most of the discourse on openness in government, which is best described as a debate over the correct balance between disclosure and secrecy. Nevertheless, for those who consider that the existing situation in most (perhaps all) countries is tilted toward too much secrecy, the WikiLeaks model, which combines cyberspace capabilities with the goal of full transparency, offers the possibility of a vast expansion in public access to information with built-in protection for those leaking the information.

US classification policy. In 1940, Franklin D. Roosevelt signed Executive Order 8381, which established three categories of classification of information for reasons of national security. Ever since there have been cycles in the US government's policies for classification and transparency. Over time the levels of classification and types of protected information have increased, along with the number of government officials deputized to implement classification actions. In FY 2011, the latest year for which data are available, there were over 92 *million* classification actions and 2,362 'original classification authorities' (US Government, 2012: 5). Although most observers agree that overclassification is a serious problem because of the administrative burdens it places on individuals and agencies, there have been few incentives in the system to reduce the tendency to stamp a document classified rather than risk being wrong and exposing a secret to the enemy. Initiatives to reduce the number of classified documents and speed up declassification of earlier materials have not succeeded in making much headway against the entrenched culture of classification.

Governments have many reasons for wanting to keep secrets: to safeguard national security, to enhance their own power by restricting access to politically significant information, or to limit criticism by concealing mistakes and violations of the law. The first category of secrets, which encompasses confidential information – for example, in diplomatic matters – as well as classified military secrets, carries the most legitimacy; unfortunately, national security is regularly invoked as a cover in situations where other motives are the real reason for imposing secrecy. Citizens in a democracy share the government's interest in protecting secrets that are crucial to national security, but they also have a strong interest in transparency so that they can judge the performance of the people they have elected. In countries with a tradition of a free press, journalists play an important role in providing that transparency, and web-based media and crowd sourcing have greatly expanded the possibilities for citizens to be better informed. Whereas traditional journalism has relied on personal contacts with informants and whistleblowers when reporting on classified or confidential matters, online media have facilitated distributed sourcing and anonymous attribution, making prosecution for revealing protected information more difficult.

The WikiLeaks phenomenon impinges on another area of government secrecy policy – the safeguards provided by the law for whistleblowers. Whistleblowing is the act of disclosing wrongdoing by an employer or government agency which results in harm to the public. In principle, reports to higher authorities within the chain of command could serve as a check on illegal or corrupt behaviour, thus providing much the same benefit to society as leaks do. In many cases, however, a 'shoot the messenger' mentality prevails, and the whistleblower suffers from ostracism, direct retaliation, or, at the least, some hefty legal fees.

Although there are laws to protect whistleblowers, in the United States they vary by state, and federal employees face a particularly complex set of rules (Devine and Clark, 2012). The situation in most other countries is even worse (Coliver, 2011).

When an organization fails to respond to an internal complaint, whistle-blowers may go to the media with their allegations and thus become the source of leaks. Edward Snowden claims to have tried to bring his concerns about the constitutionality of the NSA programs to the attention of his superiors before contacting journalists; the NSA says it has no record of such conversations (Gellman, 2013). Perhaps the most famous example of such a leak is that of the Pentagon Papers, a massive history of the US involvement in Vietnam between 1945 and 1967, which Daniel Ellsberg leaked to the *New York Times* and *Washington Post* in 1971. The Nixon administration sought an injunction to prevent publication of further instalments of the leaked documents, and the ensuing court case confirmed the principle that newspapers have a First Amendment right to publish which is not subject to prior restraint. But Ellsberg himself, as the person who had illegally acquired the documents and disseminated them, stood trial under the Espionage Act of 1917, and might well have gone to jail except for the grave misconduct of the government in prosecuting the case, which led the judge to dismiss all charges against him.[7]

Some analysts have argued that a strengthened system of protection for whistleblowers would reduce the incentive for persons with damaging information about government actions to leak it to the media because they could hope to use internal reporting procedures without fear of retaliation. The validity of this argument depends on an analysis of the motives for leaking information, the probability that the law can successfully protect those whistle-blowers, and the claim that the benefits of keeping charges of malfeasance inside the system outweigh the benefits of wider public knowledge of the problems. There is an important difference between revealing cover-ups of illegal behaviour – e.g. bribery or police brutality – and breaking the law by leaking classified information, even when that information could be vital to an informed public understanding of government policy; in the latter case the leaker is subject to prosecution, not just reprisals in the workplace. Of course, many leaks do not pose a danger to national security, or at least not at a level commensurate with the benefits of an informed citizenry. Ironically, overclassification encourages a climate in which leaking seems harmless and is tolerated, thus putting legitimate secrets at greater risk.[8]

In Cablegate, many of the leaked cables appear to fall into the category of information that should not be classified, but which nevertheless is appropriately kept from the public for the period of time during which its release might cause harm to important government goals or allow identification of intelligence sources. Radical transparency, as embodied in some statements from WikiLeaks, has no place for diplomatic confidentiality. In practice, however, the WikiLeaks collective, working with its chosen newspapers, redacted some information that would have served to identify individuals who might be harmed. In the case of the Afghanistan documents, a large number of documents were held back for further review because of their level of classification (Harrell, 2010). The files containing the diplomatic cables were scanned and redacted, but an unredacted master file became publicly available, so the care taken to protect identities was for naught (Tiffen, 2011). WikiLeaks, however, was not solely responsible for the release of the unredacted file of the original cables; instead it was *Guardian* editor David Leigh who published the password in his quickie book on WikiLeaks and made it possible for knowledgeable users to find and open the file (Leigh and Harding, 2011; MargaretMitchellEffect 2013). A number of news stories point to the dangers that foreign informants would face once their identities were revealed, but it is not clear whether any harm can be directly tied to the Cablegate leaks (McManus, 2011; Ball, 2011).

The documents leaked by Edward Snowden were greater in number and carried a higher level of classification: the number of documents Snowden downloaded is estimated to be as many as 1.7 million and many were classified as 'Top Secret' or 'Special Intelligence' (Wall Street Journal, 2014). The contents were even more embarrassing for the US government than the Cablegate leaks because they revealed that the United States was spying on leaders of friendly countries, such as Germany, Brazil and Indonesia, as well as collecting data of American citizens at home and abroad. By the end of 2013, only a fraction of the leaked documents had been published, but revelations in addition to the existence of the data gathering programs include information about NSA cooperation with its British counterpart, Government Communications Headquarters (GCHQ) to tap data of US from abroad; the co-option of companies such as AT&T, Google and Microsoft to gain access to company data records; programs to tamper with computers during shipment (i.e. before they have been delivered to the customers who ordered them) in order to circumvent protective encryption; and finally, the weakness of the court set up under the 1978 Foreign Intelligence and Surveillance Act (FISA), which is supposed to supervise the NSA programs, but has seen its rulings ignored (Gellman, 2013; Hirsh, 2013; Lizza, 2013).

The US government reacts. The Obama administration came into power promising to increase government transparency. In January 2010 the White House issued a new executive order that called for fundamental review of the classification system leading to revised classification guidelines and, in addition, created a National Declassification Center to accelerate the declassification of older documents. Even before Cablegate, however, the administration had stepped up the rate at which it prosecuted security leaks (Gerstein, 2011), and after Cablegate the government moved quickly to tighten controls on classified information. The emphasis shifted to additional layers of security controls rather than more transparency. In a controversial move, the executive branch told its employees and contractors not to visit the WikiLeaks site, and Congress followed suit.[9] The Air Force actually issued a statement that accessing WikiLeaks by persons related to Air Force employees could be considered a violation of the Espionage Act (the Act under which Bradley Manning is being prosecuted), a position so clearly outrageous that it was almost immediately rescinded (Aftergood, 2011b). Members of Congress were also active in condemning WikiLeaks and in proposing new legislation to increase penalties for leaking information.

After WikiLeaks published the Afghanistan files in July 2010, the Department of Defense moved to limit access to the SIPRNet database[10] that had housed the leaked cables by limiting the number of machines from which data could be downloaded and adding a monitoring system to track all downloads (Montalbano, 2011). Immediately after Cablegate, the State Department cut the link between its own computerized system for sharing classified information and SIPRNet (Calabresi, 2010), an action akin to closing the stable door after the horse has bolted. At least three US ambassadors were recalled and other diplomats were reassigned because of the leaked cables, and the entire State Department was involved in damage control from the week of the first cable release and continuing for many months. The direct and indirect effects of the leaked cables on international relations and security are discussed below, but it is clear that in the short run Cablegate was considered a foreign policy crisis.

The Snowden revelations triggered a similar response. Somewhat belatedly, the NSA imposed a 'two-man rule' for work on highly classified systems (Sanger and Schmitt, 2013). NSA and CIA officials made repeated claims of extreme damage to US interests; questions were raised about the number of contractors, as distinct from government employees, with access to classified information; and espionage charges were filed against Snowden, himself. But the government also responded to the outrage of US citizens and friendly governments on learning the global scope of the NSA surveillance. President Obama expressed uneasiness about some of the intelligence-gathering practices and called for a national debate. A Review Group on Intelligence and Communications Technology was established, which released a report in December 2013 with 46 recommendations for changes in US policy (Clayton, 2013). At the time of writing, however, it is not possible to say what impact these changes, if enacted, might have on the intelligence-gathering operations, or, indeed, to judge the repercussions of the Snowden leaks for US national security, beyond the obvious problems they created with alliance relations. Some of the issues will be adjudicated in the courts: two opposing opinions on the legality of the NSA programs were issued in December 2013, guaranteeing that the Supreme Court will be asked to render a decision (Liptak and Schmidt, 2013).

Reprisals against the leakers. After the release of the diplomatic cables the US government went on the attack against WikiLeaks and Julian Assange. In doing so, it went beyond the use of 'soft power' to enrol allies in its campaign against leaks of national security information and condoned extremist statements and explicit threats of coercion. Leading members of the administration and in Congress castigated WikiLeaks and Julian Assange in public statements and exerted pressure on commercial providers of services to WikiLeaks to impose sanctions on WikiLeaks, sanctions that the government itself had no grounds under US law to impose itself (Benkler 2011). Senator Joseph Lieberman was particularly active, with his staff making phone calls to Amazon.com and other service providers and Lieberman himself calling for a general boycott of services to WikiLeaks (Lieberman, 2010). This effort to generate a hostile environment was successful: the financial institutions, which included the Bank of America, Visa, MasterCard, PayPal and Western Union, blocked payments to the WikiLeaks accounts, with the result that contributions to the organization dropped sharply. The Bank of America apparently hired, through its law firm, a group of security firms to prepare a campaign to destroy WikiLeaks, a plan that included planting false documents on the WikiLeak website (Greenwald, 2011). A kind of proxy war broke out between supporters of WikiLeaks, especially the hacker group Anonymous, and the corporations that cooperated in the anti-WikiLeaks campaign, which were targeted by numerous cyber-attacks.

The anti-WikiLeaks campaign was only partially successful. Although WikiLeaks was damaged, it was able to use the redundancy built into the Internet to move its operations to other servers and to create alternative ways to receive donations (Benkler, 2011). But the organization struggled financially, and in late October 2011 it suspended its website for several weeks (by the end of December 2011, however, it was again posting new material). The long-run effect of the actions taken against WikiLeaks may well be counterproductive from the government's point of view: WikiLeaks, the organization, may or may not survive its financial problems, but the model for handling large-scale leaks anonymously is available for others to use. Indeed, several similar organizations were established after the attacks on WikiLeaks to extend its work to new areas (Benkler, 2011: 350).

The US government also put considerable resources into seeking a basis to prosecute Julian Assange for his role in the release of the leaked documents. A grand jury was impanelled in Virginia in January 2011 to hear charges against Assange, with the suggestion that Assange might be indicted under the Espionage Act. In an effort to establish a connection between Assange and Bradley Manning, US prosecutors requisitioned the Google and Twitter accounts of persons connected with Assange, actions that have drawn condemnation from privacy advocates and run counter to European Union privacy laws. At first, it seemed that the government strategy would fail, for no direct link between Assange and Manning was publicly identified, and direct prosecution of Assange would be precedent breaking, given that he is not a US citizen and WikiLeaks is not a US organization. Technically speaking, espionage is a form of treason and treason can only be committed by a person who owes allegiance to the country harmed (Elsea, 2011). Moreover, WikiLeaks' and Assange's role in publishing the leaked documents is exactly the same as that of the cooperating newspapers and should be accorded the same First Amendment protection from prosecution as the newspapers. It is worth noting that no US newspaper has ever been prosecuted for publishing leaked information, even where the potential harm was far greater than the damage that could be imputed to the leaked State Department cables (Benkler, 2011).

Edward Snowden enjoys some protections unavailable to Assange, but they do not include whistleblower protection because he was not a government employee at the time he released the documents, but rather worked for a contractor, Booz Allen Hamilton. As an American citizen he is subject to the Espionage Act, and the government filed charges against him under that law in

June 2013. He cannot be prosecuted, however, until he is taken into custody, and as of January 2014, he is residing in Moscow, with no intention of returning to the United States. It is also possible that he will eventually win official recognition as a whistleblower – a title that the American public has been willing to give him in recognition of the fact that he disclosed instances of the NSA breaking the law and violating the individual privacy of American citizens (Wasserman, 2013). Indeed, on 2 January 2014, *The New York Times* and the *Guardian* both published editorials calling for the United States government to negotiate conditions for his return, including some form of clemency in recognition of the service he rendered by making public the nature and scale of the NSA programs (Condon, 2014).

Impacts on security

If one were to take seriously the closing arguments of the government in the pre-trial hearing for Bradley Manning, one would conclude that US and world security had been irreparably damaged by the leaks, which reportedly were greeted by Al Qaeda with great interest as a guide to vulnerable targets (Thompson, 2011). The more certain effects were much more limited. The State Department was embarrassed and had to devote large resources to apologizing for the breach of security and the content of some of the cables. Hillary Clinton described her January 2011 tour of Middle Eastern states as an 'apology tour', and said 'I think I will be answering concerns about WikiLeaks for the rest of my life, not just the rest of my tenure as Secretary of State' (United Press International, Inc., 2011). The early claims of serious damage to US security now seem overblown; Secretary of Defense Gates probably got it right when he said in late November 2010:

> The fact is, governments deal with the United States because it's in their interest, not because they like us, not because they trust us, and not because they believe we can keep secrets.
>   . . . . some governments deal with us because they fear us, some because they respect us, most because they need us. We are still essentially, as has been said before, the indispensable nation. So other nations will continue to deal with us. They will continue to work with us. We will continue to share sensitive information with one another. Is this embarrassing? Yes. Is it awkward? Yes. Consequences for US foreign policy? I think fairly modest. (Maxwell, 2010)

But it is likely that diplomatic relations will be affected, at least for some time, by self-censorship between and within governments, especially with regard to back channels and inter-departmental negotiations over policy (Dickey, 2010).

Some consequences of Cablegate appear to have been favourable for US policies (Kayyem, 2011). Many commentators observed that the cables showed US diplomats doing their jobs competently, upholding US policy goals and engaging with their host countries. In countries where the news media are controlled, the cables were a welcome source of news (Schwartz, 2011), and in the case of Tunisia, they are credited with providing encouragement to the uprising that began the 'Arab Spring' of 2011. Where the information in the cables and in the earlier releases of the Afghanistan and Iraqi files showed the United States in a bad light, e.g. in the cables reporting on conditions at Guantanamo, civilian deaths in Iraq, or US actions designed to weaken the outcome of the Copenhagen climate change summit, the government was able to avoid damage through a strategy of suggesting that the revelations were 'nothing new'.

The domestic political impact has been less benign. The Cablegate leaks prompted a crackdown in the area of information security and undercut efforts after 9/11 to eliminate the 'stovepipes' that limited intelligence sharing necessary to 'connect the dots' (Kimery, 2011). The furore over WikiLeaks probably was the cause of the failure to pass a federal statute to shield journalists' use of confidential sources, a law that had been expected to pass after many years of patient work by its proponents (Abrams, 2010). It is also possible that the prosecution of Bradley Manning will deter future whistleblowers, although Manning's defence team based their defence in part on his mental state and the Army's failure to supervise him properly, rather than relying solely on a claim that he was motivated to leak the files because he saw in them evidence of violations of international law (Thompson, 2011).

The outpouring of vitriol against Julian Assange, including calls for his execution, debased public discourse by ignoring the limits of US jurisdiction and the tradition of applying First Amendment rights to news publishers. Rodney Tiffen, an Australian observer, comments, 'Perhaps the most troubling aspect of the reactions was the way in which so many (mainly American) political and media figures talked so glibly and casually of Assange being executed or assassinated. It is a further chilling reminder of just how routinely barbaric American right-wing rhetoric has become' (Tiffin, 2011). The power of the state to enrol the private sector to carry out actions that would be illegal if pursued by the state, while not new, is also troubling. The general, if mercifully brief, hysteria in the press and public pronouncements over the Cablegate leaks produced an environment in which fundamental rights and legal protections were ignored.

The Snowden case presents similar issues. Although the NSA leaks on domestic intelligence practices seem likely to generate a national discussion and greater protection for individual privacy, the benefits must be weighed against the impact of the revelations on alliance relations and the possibility that necessary intelligence gathering will be hampered now that its targets have knowledge of NSA methods. In addition, companies in the information technology sector have reduced their cooperation with the government, and some analysts predict a balkanization of the Internet to protect against the kind of surveillance practices that the NSA programs represent (Brown, 2013).

Conclusions

The cases of WikiLeaks – particularly the Cablegate leaks – and the NSA leaks provide a lens through which we can view the contested terrain where the state's interest in maintaining controls on information comes up against the opportunities afforded by new technology that make the release of a large number of documents easy and the detection of the leaker difficult. The radical transparency championed by WikiLeaks and Julian Assange turns out to be an ideal that is not easily attainable – perhaps not even possible – without severe consequences for individual actors. By enrolling the legacy media in the large scale leaks of US government files WikiLeaks obtained greater public exposure and a degree of legitimacy from its association with mainstream journalism, but it also came under attack for not conforming sufficiently to the standard practices of journalism with respect to redacting names and accommodating the government's concerns over the possible impact of the leaks on foreign policy and national security.

The media's focus on the role of WikiLeaks and Julian Assange in the publication of the files detracted from the stories portrayed in the cables themselves. The state showed itself able to inflict damage on WikiLeaks through its influence on ostensibly independent private providers of Internet services. It also demonstrated a different kind of power: although there were many instances of questionable practices and illegal behaviour revealed in the 'Collateral Murder' video and the Afghanistan and Iraqi files, there is no evidence that their exposure had any impact on government policy. The media paid more attention to the act of leaking than to what the leaks revealed, and the government was able to avoid any serious political consequences of having the information made public.

Perhaps because American citizens and their constitutional rights are central to the NSA leaks, the media have focused more on the content of Edward Snowden's leaks than they did in the Cablegate case. That content shows dramatically the secret expansion of government surveillance operations since 9/11 and the power of the government to co-opt major corporations in what is arguably an illegal enterprise of collecting data on US citizens inside the country. Moreover, Snowden is a more sympathetic, if less newsworthy, subject than Bradley Manning and Julian Assange: he has consistently claimed that he acted in the public interest to reveal illegal government actions, and he is widely regarded as a whistleblower, not a traitor. As of January 2014, it appears that his actions may well have a lasting effect on US government policies, at least with respect to limiting surveillance of American citizens.

A striking feature of the debate over the meaning of these leaks for governance and public policy is the extent to which it has been cast in the language of technological determinism. For every commentator who called on the government to shut down WikiLeaks and arrest Assange, there has been another voice saying, in the words of Secretary of Defense Robert Gates, 'Get used to it.' The argument is that changes in information technology have made leaking vastly easier, and that even if WikiLeaks can be suppressed, equivalent organizations will spring up to replace it, as indeed they have. The risk of leaks by insiders may be reduced by new security measures, but no one expects that it can be eliminated. Beneath these arguments lies the view that the technological trajectory of information technology, a trajectory that produced an Internet that favours open exchanges, will continue into the future: the state and individuals alike are not able to stop these developments.

Future developments, however, could change this projection, either because of commercial interests or because states intervene more directly to control access to the Internet and eliminate the possibility of anonymity.[11] China, for example, has been reasonably successful in restricting domestic access to the Internet, even though technically adroit users can circumvent the control. The 2012 decision by Twitter to permit individual countries to censor individual 'tweets' provides yet another example of the possibility that the best allies for repressive state policies may be the private providers of Internet services (Hodal, 2012). In the United States, the government's expanded prosecution of cases involving leaked information, with its reliance on secret court orders to search email and telephone records, has demonstrated that the Internet provides tools for control as well as for dissemination of information (Aftergood, 2013).

On balance, it would seem that while WikiLeaks, the organization, may or may not survive its legal and financial problems, the model it presents for handling large-scale leaks anonymously is available for others to use. Controls, if they are to be effective, will need to focus on blocking the acquisition of information that the government wants to keep secret, because once leaked, publication is much more certain than in the old days when newspaper editors routinely consulted with government lawyers before publishing sensitive news stories. The Obama administration's emphasis on investigating and prosecuting leaks may well discourage whistleblowers as well as other leakers, but as the 2013 NSA leaks by Edward Snowden show, even draconian policies cannot completely eliminate the insider threat.

Notes

1 See the statement on the WikiLeaks website http://wikileaks.ch/About.html
2 Manning was found not guilty of aiding the enemy, a charge that carries a life sentence. Under military law he will be eligible for parole in seven years (Tate, 2013).
3 In 2010 there were between 15 and 20 people on the WikiLeaks payroll, and a much larger number of volunteers. A few spokespersons aside from Assange have emerged, including some disillusioned members who have left the organization, but most of the members of the WikiLeaks cooperative remain anonymous, in part as protection against the threats made against WikiLeaks (Hrafnnsson, 2011).
4 WikiLeaks is not the only web-based source that espouses this position. The Cryptome website, run by John Young, has the following policy: 'Cryptome welcomes documents for publication that are prohibited by governments worldwide, in particular material on freedom of expression, privacy, cryptology, dual-use technologies, national security, intelligence, and secret governance – open, secret and classified documents – but not limited to those. Documents are removed from this site only by order served directly by a US court having jurisdiction. No court order has ever been served; any order served will be

published here – or elsewhere if gagged by order. Bluffs will be published if comical but otherwise ignored'. See http://cryptome.org/

5 The First Amendment states 'Congress shall make no law respecting an establishment of religion, or prohibiting the free exercise thereof; or abridging the freedom of speech, or of the press; or the right of the people peaceably to assemble, and to petition the Government for a redress of grievances.'

6 For a sampling of the literature on government secrecy, see: Foerstal (1993); Maret and Goldman (2009); Bannister and Connolly (2011); and the special issue of *Social Research* on 'Limiting Knowledge in a Democracy' (2010). See also the resources posted by the Project on Government Secrecy at the Federation of American Scientists website, www.fas.org/sgp/index.html

7 See Ellsberg (2002). Ellsberg has supported Bradley Manning and Edward Snowden as fellow whistleblowers, although others have argued that the documents released by WikiLeaks do not reveal an abuse of power that would justify their publication (Abrams, 2010).

8 Steven Aftergood (2010b) has pointed out that one way to reduce the risk of leaks would be a wholesale reduction in the number of classified documents, but there is no sign that his suggestion will be followed.

9 In a concession to reality, the Senate allows its employees to access news reports about the leaked cables, but not the cables themselves. Library of Congress employees, including the staff of the Congressional Research Service, however, are blocked from accessing WikiLeaks (Aftergood, 2011a, 2010a).

10 The acronym stands for the Secure Internet Protocol Router Network. It was created by the Department of Defense in 1995, and linked to the Net-Centric Diplomacy database at the State Department (Calabresi, 2010).

11 The technical community has its own ideas about the future and steps that can be taken to maintain openness. See, e.g. Kurtz (2011).

References

Abrams, F. (2010), 'Why WikiLeaks is Unlike the Pentagon Papers', *Wall Street Journal*, 29 December 2010, http://online.wsj.com/article/SB1000142405297020452780457604402039660 1528.html (accessed 8 September 2013).

Aftergood, S. (2010a), 'Blocking Access to Wikileaks May Harm CRS, Analysts Say', *Secrecy News*, 6 December 2010, http://blogs.fas.org/secrecy/2010/12/crs_block/ (accessed 8 September 2013).

—(2010b), 'Shrink the Classification System', *Secrecy News*, 16 December 2010, http://blogs.fas.org/secrecy/2010/12/shrink/ (accessed 8 September 2013).

—(2011a), 'Senate Offices Told to Avoid WikiLeaks', *Secrecy News*, 21 January 2011, http://blogs.fas.org/secrecy/2011/01/senate_wikileaks/ (accessed 8 September 2013).

—(2011b), 'Air Force Rescinds New Guidance on WikiLeaks', *Secrecy News*, 9 February 2011, http://blogs.fas.org/secrecy/2011/02/af_rescinds_guidance/ (accessed 8 September 2013).

—(2013), 'Reporter Deemed "Co-Conspirator" in Leak Case', *Secrecy News*, 20 May 2013, http://blogs.fas.org/secrecy/2013/05/kim-rosen-warrant/ (accessed 8 September 2013).

Ball, J. (2011), 'WikiLeaks Publishes Full Cache of Unredacted Cables', *Guardian*, 2 September 2011, www.theguardian.com/media/2011/sep/02/wikileaks-publishes-cache-unredacted-cables (accessed 8 September 2013).

Bannister, F. and R. Connolly (2011), 'The Trouble with Transparency: A Critical Review of Openness in e-Government', *Policy & Internet* 3: 1–30, http://onlinelibrary.wiley.com/doi/10.2202/1944-2866.1076/abstract (accessed 9 September 2013).

Benkler, Y. (2011), 'A Free Irresponsible Press: Wikileaks and the Battle over the Soul of the Networked Fourth Estate', *Harvard Civil Rights-Civil Liberties Law Review*, 46: 311–96.

Brown, I. (2013), 'Will NSA Revelations Lead to the Balkanisation of the Internet?', *Guardian*, 1 November 2013.

Bruns, A. [Snurb] (2009), 'Wikileaks and its Relationship to Journalism', *Snurblog*, 9 October 2009, www.snurb.info/node/1171 (accessed 1 September 2013).

Calabresi, M. (2010), 'State Pulls the Plug on SIPRNet', *Time Swampland*, 29 November 2010, http://swampland.time.com/2010/11/29/state-pulls-the-plug-on-siprnet/ (accessed 8 September 2013).

Carr, D. (2011), 'Is This the WikiEnd?', *New York Times*, 5 November 2011, www.nytimes.com/2011/11/06/sunday-review/is-the-wikileaks-movement-fading.html?pagewanted=all (accessed 1 September 2013).

Clayton, M. (2013), 'Obama Task Force's NSA Proposals Go "Much Further" Than Anyone Expected', *Christian Science Monitor*, 18 December, 2013, www.csmonitor.com/World/Security-Watch/2013/1218/Obama-task-force-s-NSA-proposals-go-much-further-than-anyone-expected-video

'Clinton on a WikiLeaks "Apology Tour"' (2011), UPI, 10 January 2011.

Coliver, S. (2011), 'National Security Whistleblowers: The Radical Dissenters of the 21st Century', *World Politics Review*, 22 November 2011. www.worldpoliticsreview.com/features/74/human-rights-a-closer-look (accessed 6 September 2013).

Condon, S. (2014), 'Newspapers Urge Obama to Treat Edward Snowden as a Whistleblower', CBS, 2 January 2014.

DeNardis, L. (2010), 'The Emerging Field of Internet Governance', *Yale Information Society Project Working Paper Series*, 17 September 2010, http://ssrn.com/

abstract=1678343 or http://dx.doi.org/10.2139/ssrn.1678343 (accessed 8 September 2013).

Devine, T. and L. Clark (2012), 'Now More Than Ever, Stronger Whistle-blower Protection Essential', *Federal Times*, 19 May 2012, www.whistleblower.org/press/gap-op-eds/2225-federal-times-now-more-than-ever-stronger-whistle-blower-protection-essential (accessed 8 September 2013).

Dickey, C. (2010), 'Transparency Will be the First Casualty of the WikiLeaks State Department Revelations', *Daily Beast*, 28 November 2010, www.thedailybeast.com/newsweek/2010/11/28/transparency-is-first-casualty-of-wikileaks-state-department-revelations.html (accessed 8 September 2013).

Ellsberg, D. (2002), *Secrets: A Memoir of Vietnam and the Pentagon Papers*, New York: Viking Press.

Elsea, J. K. (2011), 'Criminal Prohibitions on the Publication of Classified Defense Information', *Congressional Research Service R41404*, September 2011, www.fas.org/sgp/crs/secrecy/R41404.pdf (accessed 8 September 2013).

Foerstal, H. N. (1993), *Secret Science: Federal Control of American Science and Technology*, Westport, CT: Praeger.

Gallagher, R. (2011), 'What Has Wikileaks Ever Taught Us?', *OpenDemocracy*, 17 February 2011, www.opendemocracy.net/ryan-gallagher/what-has-wikileaks-ever-taught-us-read-on (accessed 8 September 2013).

Gellman, B. (2013), 'Edward Snowden, After Months of NSA Revelations, Says his Mission's Accomplished', *The Washington Post*, 23 December 2013.

Gerstein, J. (2011), 'Obama's Hard Line on Leaks', *Politico*, 7 March 2011.

Goldstein, N. (2008), 'An International Assessment of Journalist Privileges and Source Confidentiality', *New England Journal of International and Comparative Law*, 14: 103–34.

Greenwald, G. (2011), 'The Leaked Campaign to Attack WikiLeaks and its Supporters', *Salon.com*, 11 February 2011, www.salon.com/2011/02/11/campaigns_4/ (accessed 8 September 2013).

Harrell, E. (2010), 'Defending the Leaks: Q&A with Wikileaks' Julian Assange', *Time* 27 July 2010, http://content.time.com/time/world/article/0,8599,2006789,00.html (accessed 8 September 2013).

Hirsh, M. (2013), 'How America's Top Tech Companies Created the Surveillance State', *National Journal*, 25 July 2013, www.nationaljournal.com/magazine/how-america-s-top-tech-companies-created-the-surveillance-state-20130725

Hodal, K. (2012), 'Thailand Backs Twitter Censorship Policy', *Guardian*, 30 January 2012, www.theguardian.com/world/2012/jan/30/thailand-backs-twitter-censorship-policy (accessed 9 September 2013).

Hrafnsson, K. (2011), 'How WikiLeaks Will Transform Mainstream Media', Presentation at the Sydney Ideas and Department of Media and Communications, Sydney, Australia, 17 June 2011, http://sydney.edu.au/sydney_ideas/lectures/2011/kristinn_hrafnsson.shtml (accessed 9 September 2013).

Kayyem, J. (2011), 'WikiLeaks' Favor to Diplomacy', *Boston Globe,* 8 December 2011, www.bostonglobe.com/opinion/editorials/2011/12/08/wikileaks-favor-diplomacy/kZDiwPbutSFapenqZfgbkL/story.html (accessed 9 September 2013).

Keller, B. (2011), 'Dealing with Assange and the WikiLeaks Secrets', *New York Times,* 26 January 2011, www.nytimes.com/2011/01/30/magazine/30Wikileaks-t.html?_r=1&ref=global-home&pagewanted=all (accessed 9 September 2013).

Kimery, A. (2011), 'Information Technology: An End to Infosharing?', *Homeland Security Today,* 1 February 2011, www.hstoday.us/focused-topics/information-technology/single-article-page/an-end-to-infosharing/55915db66128bc355cd71ca0eeb13a6a.html (accessed 8 September 2013).

Kurtz, D. (2011), 'More on Egypt and the Internet', *TPM Blog,* 28 January 2011. www.talkingpointsmemo.com/archives/2011/01/more_on_egypt_and_the_internet.php#more (accessed 8 September 2013).

Leigh, D. and L. Harding (2011), *Wikileaks: Inside Julian Assange's War on Secrecy,* New York: Public Affairs.

Lieberman, J. (2010), 'Internet Company had Hosted WikiLeaks Website', Senate of The United States, 1 December 2010, http://lieberman.senate.gov/index.cfm/news-events/news/2010/12/amazon-severs-ties-with-wikileaks (accessed 8 September 2013).

Liptak, A. and M. Schmidt (2013), 'Judge Upholds NSA's Bulk Collection of Data on Calls', *The New York Times,* 27 December 2013.

Lizza, R. (2013), 'State of Deception', *The New* Yorker, 16 December 2013, www.newyorker.com/reporting/2013/12/16/131216fa_fact_lizza

Lynch, L. (2009), 'A Toxic Archive of Digital Sunshine: WikiLeaks and the Archiving of Secrets', Paper presented at conference on Media in Transition, MIT, 24–26 April 2009, http://web.mit.edu/comm-forum/mit6/papers/Lynch.pdf (accessed 8 September 2013).

—(2010), 'We're going to crack the world open', *Journalism Practice,* 4: 309–18.

Mack, A. (ed.) (2010), 'Limiting knowledge in a democracy', *Social Research* (special issue) 77.

Maret, S. L. and J. Goldman (2009), *Government Secrecy: Classic and Contemporary Readings,* Westport, CT: Libraries Unlimited.

MargaretMitchellEffect (2013), 'David Leigh's 'Encryption Key Fiasco', 19 January 2013, www.marthamitchelleffect.org/redactions-and-propaganda-2/4575255397

Maxwell, D. (2010), 'Quotable: Secretary Gates on WikiLeaks', SWJ Blog Post, 30 November 2010, http://smallwarsjournal.com/blog/quotable-secretary-gates-on-wikileaks

McManus, D. (2011), 'Damage "fairly modest"', *Miami Herald,* 3 February 2011.

McMillan, G. (2011), 'Will the New York Times Set Up its own WikiLeaks Portal?' *Techland Time,* 25 January 2011, http://techland.time.com/2011/01/25/will-the-new-york-times-set-up-its-own-wikileaks-portal/ (accessed 8 September 2013).

Miklaszerski, J. (2011), 'US Can't Link Accused Army Private to Assange', *MSNBC*, 24 January 2011, www.sott.net/article/222045-US-Cant-Link-Accused-Army-Private-to-Assange (accessed 9 September 2013).

Montalbano, E. (2011), 'DOD Taking Steps to Prevent Another Cablegate', *InformationWeek*, 15 March 2011, www.informationweek.com/government/security/dod-taking-steps-to-prevent-another-cabl/229300963 (accessed 8 September 2013).

Policinski, G. (2011), 'These Days It's Harder to Identify Who is a Journalist', *First Amendment Center* www.firstamendmentcenter.org/these-days-it%E2%80%99s-harder-to-identify-who-is-a-journalist (accessed 10 September 2013).

Rosenbach, M. and H. Stark (2011), 'Lifting the Lid on WikiLeaks: An Inside Look at Difficult Negotiations with Julian Assange', *Speigel Online*, 28 January 2011, www.spiegel.de/international/world/lifting-the-lid-on-wikileaks-an-inside-look-at-difficult-negotiations-with-julian-assange-a-742163.html (accessed 10 September 2013).

Sanger, D. and E. Schmitt (2013), 'N.S.A. Imposes Rules to Protect Secret Data Stored on Its Networks', *The New York Times*, 18 July 2013.

Schwartz, C. (2011), '"If They're Collecting all of this Information, They're Surely Using it, Right?"', WikiLeaks' Impact on Post-Soviet Central Asia', *Global Media Journal*, 5(1) www.commarts.uws.edu.au/gmjau/v5_2011_1/schwartz_essay.html (accessed 8 September 2013).

Shane, S. (2013), 'Offering Snowden Aid, WikiLeaks Gets Back in the Game', *The New York Times*, 23 June 2013.

Spiegel Online (2010), 'What do the Diplomatic Cables Really Tell Us?', *Spiegel Online*, 28 November 2010, www.spiegel.de/international/world/wikileaks-faq-what-do-the-diplomatic-cables-really-tell-us-a-731441.html (accessed 10 September 2013).

Tate, J. (2013), 'Judge Sentences Bradley Manning to 35 Years', *Washington Post*, 21 August 2013, http://articles.washingtonpost.com/2013-08-21/world/41431547_1_bradley-manning-david-coombs-pretrial-confinement (accessed 8 September 2013).

Thompson, G. (2011), 'Hearing in Soldier's WikiLeaks Case Ends', *The New York Times*, 23 December 2011, www.nytimes.com/2011/12/23/us/hearing-in-private-mannings-wikileaks-case-ends.html (accessed 8 September 2013).

Tiffen, R. (2011), 'WikiLeaks and mega-plumbing issues – – unresolved dilemmas revisited', *Global Media Journal* 5(1), www.commarts.uws.edu.au/gmjau/v5_2011_1/tiffen_ra.html (accessed 8 September 2013).

United Press International, Inc. (2011), 'Clinton on a WikiLeaks "Apology Tour"', United Press International, Inc., 10 January 2011, www.upi.com/Top_News/World-News/2011/01/10/Clinton-on-a-WikiLeaks-apology-tour/UPI-30541294675421/ (accessed 8 September 2013).

US Government, National Archives and Records Administration, Information Security Oversight Office (2012), 'Report to the President for Fiscal Year 2011', US

Government, National Archives and Records Administration, Washington DC. www.fas.org/sgp/isoo/2011rpt.pdf (accessed 8 September 2013).

Wall Street Journal (2014), Snowden's Damage', 10 January 2014, http://online.wsj.com/news/articles/SB10001424052702304347904579310813434692676 (accessed 5 May 2014).

WikiLeaks.org (2011), 'Financial Blockade: Chronology', WikiLeaks.org, 24 October 2011, http://wikileaks.org/IMG/pdf/WikiLeaks-Banking-Blockade-Information-Pack.pdf (accessed 11 September 2013).

Zetter, K. (2011), 'Jolt in WikiLeaks Case: Feds Found Manning-Assange Chat Logs on Laptop', *Wired*, 19 December 2011, www.wired.com/threatlevel/2011/12/manning-assange-laptop/ (accessed 11 September 2013).

4

Leaks: Secure Communications and Achieving Nuclear Zero

Bruce D. Larkin

Precis

Today's nuclear weapons and delivery systems largely predate the impact of Net and Web. Nonetheless military capabilities and operational plans – and policy-making and decision – now rely throughout on computing and telecommunications. Society as a whole is tying itself to transportation and energy grids, financial movements, technically 'advanced' design and production, data networks and daily more intensive collaborations – all dependent on exchange of voice and data.

At the same time, there is a growing consensus that nuclear weapons have no practical purpose but carry enormous risk, risk so great that it mandates their elimination. Deterrence? An interim improvisation ... that contributes to risk.

Ongoing management of nuclear weapons depends on rule-adherent performances organized among tens of thousands of men and women, who must talk among themselves and share common understandings, but not with 'the enemy' or 'the proliferator'. As management requires private communication, so will the political process of agreeing to global zero, and then maintaining it.

This chapter explores the cyber requirements of nuclear disarmament, to infer conditions and capabilities that will be required. Because the future is inconveniently unavailable, we look at diverse suggestive prior secrecy breaches. Some concern diplomacy, military preparedness, encryption and communication, while others deal directly with nuclear secrets.

Among concluding observations are that future breaches are certain, that prudent planning for a breach should be built into the new 'zero nuclear weapons' regime, and that operating in daylight is the best preventive of harm through breach. Occasions that seem to require secrecy and secure communications can be avoided by relying on positive assurance, shared assessment, and ready access to disputed sites. This orientation favours ongoing mutual reassurance, public access to evidence and its assessment, and full disclosure, while acknowledging that secrecy may be a useful and ethical choice in some circumstances. For example, negotiations may prove more fruitful when preliminary discussion can take place in private. Assessing a suspected violation of a zero nuclear regime in place may require obtaining evidence acquired only by promising not to reveal its source. Even in such circumstances, however, there should be no presumption favouring classification: no easy path to secrecy. Instead, the burden of justifying secrecy should be on the party proposing it.

Once it is decided to employ secure communications and document classification, this orientation favours ongoing refinement and focused use of standard practices, including encryption, access controls, prudent hardware choices, and appropriate physical security.

Secure communication

Dismantling and prohibiting nuclear weapons, and then maintaining a stable peace in a non-nuclear world, will require ongoing political negotiations and collaborative actions. There will be some people – perhaps some governments – that seek to undermine, distort, preclude, or simply shape that exercise in hope of outcomes judged more in their interest. This is the nature of politics and life in a social world. Negotiation is the distinguishing activity of politics. It is carried on among 'friends', among those in search of the like-minded, but also between 'enemies'. It is carried on within governments, and among 'parties' and their publics.

'Secure communication' implies: (a) a message (document, image, electronic file, sensor stream), from the time it is composed until it is irretrievably destroyed (in every form including drafts and copies, every medium including digital and hardcopy, and however transformed by selection or encryption); (b) grounds to believe – practices in place – that only those authorized by the issuer will have access to the message; and (c) successful handling of the message such that the intent of 'access only by those authorized' is not defeated.

'Secure communication' serves not only the actual negotiation – exchanges between negotiators – but other functions as well: intelligence (gathering 'facts' about the world), coordination (for example, among officials of a government, and between governments), and operations (covert and military).

It is widely believed that governments are advantaged if others do not know the sources, content and quality of intelligence available to them, their internal arguments, and their action plans, both strategic and tactical. (Sometimes, of course, there is advantage in disclosure.) The point of 'secure communication' is to keep messages whole and secret. Many means are employed: selective recruitment, training, document control, penalties for unauthorized disclosure, restriction of access, and physical control of communications. Governments define 'secrets' or 'military secrets' or 'state secrets' and endeavour to prevent their unauthorized 'leakage'.

What political damage can follow a breakdown of security?

General propositions about 'secure communication' are made vivid by examples of actual breakdowns. Of many illustrations we could choose, two not only underscore vulnerability to insider disclosures, but also concern the issue of nuclear disarmament: the Koza email, and one of the more than a quarter-million US Department of State cables disclosed by WikiLeaks in 2010–11.

Frank Koza's memorandum leaked by Katharine Gun (2003)

In the jostling prior to President Bush's attack on Iraq on 19 March 2003, the United States sought to win UN Security Council approval of an attack. What was sought was a 'second resolution'. It was thought that the United Kingdom would not join in war against Iraq unless a 'second resolution' was obtained, but it was not obtained, and the Blair Government still joined the war.

The US version of 'necessity' turned on imminent threat from Iraqi 'weapons of mass destruction', and especially nuclear weapons. At stake was whether the IAEA and UNMOVIC inspections in Iraq should run their course, exhausting the question whether there was evidence that Iraq was moving to acquire 'weapons of mass destruction', or whether the inspections should be shoved aside unless they produced the evidence sought. In this sense the pre-war political manoeuvring of 2002 and early 2003 were homologous with what could be expected of suspicions or charges of 'breakout' from a ZNW world.

While the United States still thought that it might obtain approval by the P5 and sufficient members of the Security Council, Frank Koza, a National Security Agency operative, sent an email requesting acquisition of intelligence about the intentions of states that were members of the Security Council.[1] A copy of this message was (routinely, we presume) sent to the NSA's counterpart in the UK, GCHQ. Katharine Gun, a translator employed at GCHQ, made the text public. She was subsequently placed on trial, but the process was abandoned in midcourse, and she was released.[2]

Comment at the time anticipated issues raised by the Snowden NSA revelations in 2013: how could intimate relations among the 'Five Eyes' states survive disclosure of their widespread surveillance? The text of Koza's message, as reported by the *Observer*:[3]

To: [Recipients withheld]
From: FRANK KOZA, Def Chief of Staff (Regional Targets) CIV/NSA
Sent on Jan 31 2003 0:16
Subject: Reflections of Iraq Debate/Votes at UN-RT Actions + Potential for Related Contributions
Importance: HIGH
Top Secret//COMINT//X1

All,

As you've likely heard by now, the Agency is mounting a surge particularly directed at the UN Security Council (UNSC) members (minus US and GBR of course) for insights as to how to [*sic*] membership is reacting to the ongoing debate RE: Iraq, plans to vote on any related resolutions, what related policies/ negotiating positions they may be considering, alliances/dependencies, etc. – the whole gamut of information that could give US policymakers an edge in obtaining results favourable to US goals or to head off surprises. In RT, that means a QRC surge effort to revive/create efforts against UNSC members Angola, Cameroon, Chile, Bulgaria and Guinea, as well as extra focus on Pakistan UN matters.

We've also asked ALL RT topi's to emphasize and make sure they pay attention to existing non-UNSC member UN-related and domestic comms for anything useful related to the UNSC deliberations/debates/votes. We have a lot of special UN-related diplomatic coverage (various UN delegations) from countries not sitting on the UNSC right now that could contribute related perspectives/insights/whatever. We recognize that we can't afford to ignore this possible source.

We'd appreciate your support in getting the word to your analysts who might have similar, more in-direct access to valuable information from accesses in your product lines. I suspect that you'll be hearing more along these lines in formal channels – especially as this effort will probably peak (at least for this specific focus) in the middle of next week, following the SecState's presentation to the UNSC.

Thanks for your help.

The undisputed reading of the Koza instruction is that the US intercepted communications of UN delegations – after all, NSA deals in communications, not recruiting spies, and that is a reasonable reading of 'accesses in your product lines' and 'domestic comms'. US intrusion may also have included electronic devices – bugs – in UN offices and those of UN delegations. On the day after the prosecution of Katharine Gun was abandoned, former British cabinet minister Clare Short, the BBC reported, said that 'British spies were involved in bugging Mr Annan's office in the run up to war with Iraq. … Asked if Britain was involved in this, she replied; "Well I know – I've seen transcripts of Kofi Annan's conversations"' (BBC World, 2004).

The Bradley Manning deliveries to WikiLeaks (2010–11)

Consider a cable regarding a complex issue expected to come before the 2010 NPT Review Conference. One cable (labeled 10PARIS193) concerns calls for creating a nuclear-free zone in the Middle East, with implications for Israeli nuclear weapons. The United States reveals a design to outflank the Egyptian Foreign Minister by going directly to President Mubarak. Consider this excerpt from the cable 10PARIS193, sent 20 February 2010:

[S E C R E T SECTION 01 OF 03 PARIS 000193

NOFORN
SIPDIS

E.O. 12958: DECL: 02/19/2020
TAGS: PREL PARM MNUC KACT KNNP MARR MCAP NATO CH
IR, PK, FR
SUBJECT: U/S TAUSCHER'S MEETINGS WITH FRENCH OFFICIALS

Classified By: DCM Mark Pekala, Reasons 1.4 (b), (d).

¶1. (C/NF) SUMMARY: Under Secretary of State for Arms Control and

International Security Ellen Tauscher's February 2 meetings with French counterparts from the Elysee (presidency) and MFA included discussions of U.S. disarmament priorities, the NPT Review Conference (NPT RevCon), the Nuclear Security Summit, and missile defense. Meeting separately with NSA-equivalent Jean-David Levitte, Presidency Strategic Affairs Advisor Francois Richier, and MFA Strategic Affairs Director Patrick Maisonnave, U/S Tauscher reassured the French that while "a world without nuclear weapons" is a sincere USG ambition, the United States will not move precipitously and will take allies' interests into account. U/S Tauscher discussed next steps on NPT RevCon preparations, including thinking creatively about outcomes and minimizing the threat of disruptive Egyptian behavior. U/S Tauscher also clarified USG missile defense priorities, especially political support for territorial defense at the 2010 Lisbon NATO summit. END SUMMARY.

¶6. (S/NF) Richier and Maisonnave agreed with U/S Tauscher's analysis that Egyptian FM Aboul-Gheit will, if unchecked, work to undermine the RevCon with an aggressive posture on the Middle East Nuclear Weapons Free Zone (NWFZ) resolution. U/S Tauscher outlined ongoing U.S. efforts to gain consensus language on the NWFZ, but underlined the need to contemplate a more forward-leaning strategy. She suggested considering possible phone calls from Presidents Obama and Sarkozy directly to Egyptian President Mubarak in the mid-March timeframe to sensitize the Egyptian president to the importance of the RevCon in strengthening the NPT and the unhelpful role the Egyptian MFA is playing.[4]

This message illustrates several issues. While the French participants in conversations with Ellen Tauscher knew the content of their talks, other governments – including the Egyptian government – probably did not. US officials had concluded that the likelihood of influencing Egypt's position would be enhanced if both Obama and Sarkozy approached Mubarak by telephone: hence the effort to concert US and French action. Mubarak might suspect that Washington and Paris had exchanged preliminaries about the telephone approach, but would not have had evidence to that effect.

From this cable alone it is not possible to discern what other steps the United States may have been taking to achieve a Middle East resolution to its liking. We do know that at the NPT Review Conference language was reached that no participant rejected, after difficult negotiations.[5]

The WikiLeaks cables put all diplomats on warning that their conversations with counterparts may become public, a problem explored more fully below.

Types of breaches: Leaks, intrusions, thefts and unanticipated inference

An office enters information on a sheet of paper or in an electronic file. The information may be akin to texts in everyday books and newspapers, or specify procedures to be invoked and executed on a computer, sensor, or mechanical device. For whatever reason, the office is determined to control access. Only those whom it authorizes should be privy to the information or able to invoke the procedures. So it intends. In practice, however, unauthorized persons obtain the 'secrets'. How can they do so?

There are many ways. The can be categorized by answering just three questions: was the loss of secrecy due to an insider? An external 'attacker'? Or to someone – not necessarily either insider or attacker – exploiting an insight or happenstance which the office had not anticipated? Then we have:

1 *A leak*. An insider, a person with authorized access to the information, reveals it to an unauthorized recipient. (Example: the WikiLeaks cables (Leigh, 2010; Nakashima, 2011).[6])

2 and 3 *A theft*. An external 'attacker' or 'enemy' succeeds in an attempt to obtain the secret information.

2 *Theft without insider assistance*. The attacker designs and executes a scheme to obtain the information despite whatever precautions the originating office has taken. (Example: US interception of internal Soviet military transmissions by placing a device on a coastal undersea cable.)

3 *Theft with insider assistance*. An attacker colludes with an insider, whom he may have inserted into the pool of authorized recipients, who participates in the execution of a plan to transfer 'secrets' to the attacker. (Example: Israeli collusion with Jonathan Pollard; Soviet collusion with the 'Johnnie Walker' spy ring.)

4 *Unanticipated inference*, either as part of a (2) *theft*, or by any unintended party that exploits weakness of happenstance to obtain the 'secrets'. (Example: journalists' use of aircraft flight plans to infer US movement of captives among 'black sites' during the 'War on Terrorism'.)

Note, however, that leaks, thefts, and inferences often combine. (Example: according to reports, the chance connection of an infected Iranian laptop to the Net enabled Stuxnet to spread and, therefore, forensic laboratories to explore its code and draw conclusions about its probable source.)

5 *Intrusion,* which may be accompanied by *theft*. The intruder enters premises or a computer network or a Smartphone and *alters something* to

her benefit, perhaps by placing on a computer software that will report to the intruder or perform operations on command. (Example: the Stuxnet exploit against Iranian uranium centrifuge enrichment.)

At what points in the chain of custody is a document vulnerable to breach?

We may associate with every document (file, image, stream, etc.) an intended chain of custody and, in contrast, custody as practised. Their elements will be an author, registrar (marking its entry to the chain), issuance custodian, distributor, distribution clerk, and issuance archivist; transmission medium; then reception clerk, reception custodian, addressees and recipient archivists. Transmission may be by courier, post, display, or any digital means. Some elements may not be required; the author, for example, may also act as code clerk and distributor, or the message transmitted in clear ('The cock will crow at dawn.') Additionally, addressees may order further distribution, for example among members of an authorized working group that is to use the information.

Each link of the chain of custody carries the possibility that it will be the site of a breach. We can imagine a *comprehensive security plan* and even strive to follow it … but only if we keep in mind that our expectation of secrecy may fall to an imaginative exploit or to unlikely chance. Consider these vulnerabilities:

- At time of composition. Once-upon-a-time every typewriter used to compose messages left an imprint of strokes keyed on something called a 'ribbon'. Grab the ribbon, read the message. Today the analogue is any device that collects a message while a computer keyboard is used, sensing either electrical emission or movement or characteristic sound of each key, or reading keyboard input.
- While the message is in transit. For the most part, a message must be carried, broadcast, or sent by wire/fibre. Technically ingenious means exist to harvest radio signals or cable traffic and extract the stream of voice messages or data, encrypted or not. The United States placed recording devices on Soviet underwater cables carrying military traffic between two Soviet land centres. Although there was a time when fibre optic cables were thought immune to being tapped without interference with the cable being detected, over time consensus grew that fibre was being tapped.
- Despite encryption. Encryption renders a message 'harder' to read. At best,

it would be too hard for the thief to read with the means available, and 'soon enough' for the information to be useful. The strongest methods now employed on a large scale are implementations of 'public key encryption' (PKE), which exploit one-way mathematical relationships between related keys (Diffie, 1988; Diffie and Landau, 1998, 2007).[7] These can even be used to encrypt a message between two nodes as it makes its way across a net, protecting the message from a tap. World War II Russian Venona communications relied on the only perfect, unbreakable method of encryption, the one-time pad, but its users cheated because the volume of messages exceeded the one-time pads they could supply. Plus, it was far from being adequately effective and adequately practical.[8]

To be practical encryption must be easy to use, by both sender (encrypting) and recipient (decrypting), but resistant to being read by unwanted eyes. Difficulty is usually introduced by adopting some method of rendering the message so changed that a thief cannot read it 'in time' to make use of the information contained. This is what PKE accomplishes. That is: with a powerful enough computer and enough time the encryption might yield, but the thief is otherwise thwarted.

- While the message is stored. The problem is that to be useful, information must not only be stored but must be accessible. It is a standard maxim that if a digital file is so sensitive that it must not fall into the wrong hands, then the storage server and user terminals must be unconnected to the Net and distribution of the file, or its contents, managed user-by-user.
- After decryption and rendering in hard copy. Obviously, files can be rifled.
- Malfeasance or carelessness of authorized personnel. Charges against Bradley Manning assert forbidden conduct. There is no public evidence that he entered the military, or sought the duty he was assigned, in order to reveal secrets. This is an individual act.
- By placing a confederate, or an enabling technology, somewhere in the chain of custody. Some entity – a state, or a group of conspirators – sets out to gain access to secrets, or to communications which the parties assume to be private. Among the charges rumoured to be being made against high Chinese official Bo Xilai is that he tapped into telephone conversations between other high officials. Governments inserting a 'mole' into the apparatus of another state typically do so to gain access to information otherwise inaccessible to them (as well as to act in their sponsors' interests).

- Decision to release, or draw upon, and publish. When is a 'leak' a matter of deliberate policy? A government may want to claim credit for 'successes' previously held as 'secrets', or decide that revealing an issue trumps keeping the 'secret'. And governments have been known deliberately to mislead: can the 'revelation' be trusted?

- Subject and Content. Each text (file, etc.) judged to require classification ('secret', 'top secret', 'SCI', etc.) and the registry of a document for 'secure' handling has its unique content and a place in some practical initiative. In turn, its timeliness and importance to the issuer, vulnerabilities, the breaches to which it could become subject, steps that an 'attacker' might design, and the political and strategic consequences of the document being 'lost' are specific to the message's content and context. The issuer must be rigorous and imaginative in conceiving just how the security of a text (file, etc.) matters. Because my studies focus on weapons denuclearization ('global zero') and the requirements to sustain zero, once it is achieved, it is in that context that I think about security of documents (files, sensor streams, etc.) and how they are shared. My nuclear interest is reflected in this text.

Nuclear-weapon 'management'

In a 2006 paper I posed this question: 'If Washington could get so much wrong in invading Iraq, can we be confident of its management of nuclear weapons?' I concluded that,

> we cannot be confident of the current management of US nuclear weapons. The better posture is one of scepticism toward claims that any system of command and control can meet the standards of coherence, robustness, reliability and performance that ongoing 'nuclear weapons management' requires. (Larkin 2006: 113–14)

That was written before six nuclear-armed cruise missiles were flown from Minot AFB, North Dakota to Barksdale AFB, Louisiana, slung under the wing of a B-52 bomber, on 29–30 August 2007. We are told that no one knew that the six weapons were loose, neither those who had been responsible for their custody nor the crew that flew them across the United States (Warrick and Pincus, 2007). Senior officers and the civilian Secretary of the Air Force lost their jobs. Apropos our topic, accounts attribute the public's learning about this episode to details having been 'leaked by unknown DoD officials'.

Another measure of management is its ability to keep its most salient secrets: management requires keeping secrets, and the secrets themselves must be managed. About sources of possible breakdown I cited 'assumptions about the loyalties and performance of their personnel' and comment by a naval information systems manager that another 'Johnny Walker' cannot be ruled out.[9]

In early 2012 another alleged 'Johnny Walker', Jeffrey Paul Delisle, was arrested and charged by Canadian authorities with delivering secrets to a foreign country. Both the WikiLeaks 'Cablegate' episode and the Delisle case claim acts by a member of the military whose duties gave access.

This chapter centres not on military operations, but on the interplay of politics and communications in achieving and then sustaining global nuclear zero. As some of the examples below illustrate, however, force and statecraft both require secure communications. In both realms 'secrets' are prized. Reliable communication – free from mischief – requires that a mischief-maker be unable to block transmissions, pretend to an identity ('spoof'), alter or insert messages, gain access to elements of a network (computers, servers), or be enabled to command devices – such as military robots, industrial controls, or satellites – via a network.

A brief list of requirements for negotiating nuclear zero would emphasize needs to: (1) negotiate, within each state, whether to commit to zero; (2) negotiate zero in common with other states; (3) conduct ongoing assurance during physical denuclearization; (4) monitor for defection or breakout; (5) establish agreed 'facts' about any perceived threat to the zero regime; and (6) negotiate and conduct whatever response to defection or breakout is to be made, which may include threat or use of force.

Classification in practice

The 'Cablegate' messages contribute nothing to an understanding of how a government or private entity could 'hack' a government's secure communications. Instead, 'Cablegate' confirms the well-understood fact that terming communications 'secure' accepts a risk that some person authorized to access the system will divert or alter its contents. That is what reporters' accounts of the episode have claimed: that a US Army private, with authorized access and a 'Top Secret/SCI' clearance, devised a subterfuge to copy and remove the texts of the cables from a 'secure' facility in Baghdad (Booth, Brooke and Morris, 2010).

As of 2 January 2011 about 2,000 cables had been widely distributed on the Net, and some of them summarized and even reproduced in full (or with selective redactions) by *Der Spiegel, El País, Le Monde, The Guardian* and *The New York Times*. On 1 September 2011 the entire suite of 251,287 cables was made public, when the key to widely distributed encrypted versions – circulated by Julian Assange as an insurance policy to ensure that distribution could not be suppressed – became known.

The US Government confronts the anomaly that texts marked 'Secret' and 'NOFORN' are nonetheless loose in the wild and cannot be recalled. *The New York Times* reported that:

The [US] Air Force is barring its personnel from using work computers to view the Web sites of The New York Times and more than 25 other news organizations and blogs that have posted secret cables obtained by WikiLeaks, Air Force officials said … (Schmitt, 2010)

The American Civil Liberties Union filed suit to force the US Government to confront the contradiction in its insistence that freely-available texts remain 'classified'. The federal court judge was unpersuaded, adopting the argument that classification still mattered as the United States had not admitted that the texts were true. *The New York Times* presented this drama:

'Documents in Plain Sight, but Still Classified'

WASHINGTON – Can a government document be both publicly available and properly classified at the same time?

That is not a Zen riddle. It is a serious question posed in a provocative lawsuit filed last year by the American Civil Liberties Union, and on Monday a federal judge said the answer was yes.

Judge Colleen Kollar-Kotelly of Federal District Court in Washington ruled that the State Department had acted correctly in withholding more than half of 23 classified diplomatic cables sought by the A.C.L.U. – all of which had been posted on the Web months earlier by WikiLeaks. (Shane, 2012)[10]

If Judge Kollar-Kotelly's ruling implies that the White House prizes imaginary doubt over direct admission – and believes that foreign governments are unable to assess whether a cable is authentic or not – it does not resolve the question whether those holding US security clearances jeopardize themselves if they read, or share, texts that are accessible to a billion other people. This must not be a silly question, since Jeffrey Lewis has addressed it on his armscontrolwonk. com blog, in the following way:

> I know that a lot of my readers have .gov and .mil addresses, which means that I need to take special care about how I treat classified material on this website.
>
> I've spent a few days talking to people, and there are no easy answers. Each element of the government seems to have its own policies, which are evolving over time.
>
> Until further notice, I am adopting the following policy when it comes to treating classified material, particularly that released by WikiLeaks (I have updated previous posts to conform with this policy).
>
> 1. Under no circumstance will I post quotations that include security markings. I may quote from documents, but I won't put anyone in the position of having a scarlet S or the dreaded NOFORN appear on their screen and, as a result, in their cache.
>
> 2. Under no circumstance will I post either the full-text of a cable or even consecutive paragraphs. In fact, I doubt that I will ever post the entirety of a paragraph. Any material taken from the cables will appear as it might in the New York Times or Washington Post.
>
> 3. I will do my best to enforce this policy on reader comments.
>
> I hope that this satisfies the majority of readers with day jobs. In any event, I invite readers to comment on the new policy and am prepared to modify it if and when circumstances dictate. (Lewis, 2010)

A commenter, in response to critics of Lewis' decision, wrote that 'You do not understand the problem that Jeffrey is trying to solve' and went on to explain the awkwardness that follows for US Government employees, especially those who hold clearances.[11]

Another reading is possible: that the command norms by which the United States government controls 'classified' material reflect once-upon-a-time and require – if Washington chooses to maintain 'classification' – redesign of the ways in which authority to view and possess files is allocated and enabled in hardware.

Another issue is whether Americans who read WikiLeaks cables may be punished for doing so. Two months after the cables began to appear on the Web, the US Air Force threatened family members of personnel holding security clearances, if the family member read a classified cable. That threat was shortly withdrawn.[12] How is the currency of the 'Cablegate' disclosures relevant to secure communication on the road to nuclear zero?

Secrecy in nuclear weapons: Dispelling fears and verification

'Secure communications' do not matter if the content of those communications is sharable from the start. It is one thing if classification is the default option, declassification requiring that some burden of proof be met, and quite a different matter if non-classification is the default option, against which whoever proposes that the communication be classified must meet some serious demonstration of need and appropriateness.

By clearly distinguishing transactions and texts that require being private from those that do not, and following a policy of full disclosure wherever the requirement of secrecy cannot be persuasively made out, an institution confines its 'secrets' to the smallest number. A firm that designs, manufactures, and sells precision equipment probably has many 'proprietary secrets' that are the basis of its business. But if it finds there is some fault that could harm users or produce anomalous results, it must share that fact with the buyers. Organizations also identify 'personnel' files as private, sometimes for the improper purpose of avoiding litigation, and sometimes with the understanding that papers may be released only with the consent of the employee. The case for secrecy can only be made around particulars.

In the transition to nuclear zero, nuclear-weapon states may claim that as the number of weapons falls their vulnerability increases, with the result that some facts become even more closely held than before. The N5 can tell the world how many nuclear weapons they have, but they will more jealously guard the locations of at least some of those weapons, an argument for the joint 'jump to zero' from several hundred.

Similarly, if the issue is whether nuclear-weapon states have declared all nuclear weapons and fissile material in their possession, there need be nothing 'secret' about the evidence they advance in showing that this is so. A state or authority that suspects error, or misrepresentation, in another state's declarations may appropriately keep its reasons to itself, for example treat an informant's identity as a 'secret', but it must collaborate in the design of tests that will confirm or disconfirm its suspicions in circumstances free of secrecy. The same measure applies mutatis mutandis to other issues of doubt and verification.

Secrecy as a 'wasting asset' ˙

There is another reason why 'secrets' typically matter less than their aura suggests. It is a commonplace among those discussing secrecy to point out that it is a 'wasting asset'. With rare exceptions, secrets are temporary, on their way to becoming non-secrets. Except for something known only to a single individual, there is cost and inconvenience to translating a 'known' into a 'secret'. If the translation includes procedures to 'protect' the secret, such as encrypting it, the cost and inconvenience will grow as more vexing protections are put in place.

British Telecom's posting passwords in plain sight responded to the inconvenience of introducing newcomers to the passwords they needed to do their work. That ministries of external affairs are ready to reveal their communications after 30 or 50 years demonstrates that diplomatic cables' classification can expire. Looking at the header to 10PARIS193 we see that it is already equipped with a 'tell-by' date (DECL: 02/19/2020). The relevant US State Department manual now instructs (emphasis in original) that:

> When possible, the classifier should choose a specific date or event within 10 years for declassification. When this is not feasible, information should be classified for 10 years unless that clearly does not provide adequate protection, in which case the information may be classified for up to 25 years from date of origin. With the two important exceptions outlined in 5 FAH-3 716.2 and 5 FAH-3 716.3 below, *information may not be classified for longer than 25 years at the time of its original classification.*[13]

An earlier version of this section explained that the 'exception' is for 'information that would reveal the identity of confidential human sources or human intelligence sources'.[14] But in the case of 10PARIS193 the sources are neither 'confidential' nor 'intelligence' sources. Today's 716.2 and 716.3 are not included in the version publicly accessible, but 5 FAH-3 H-717.2 explains exemptions from the 25-year rule:

> '5 FAH-3 H-717.2 Exempting Human Source and Certain Information about Weapons of Mass Destruction from Automatic Declassification at 25 Years' (CT:TAGS-44, 01-31-2012).
>
> Given the extreme sensitivity of information that would reveal the identity of confidential human sources or human intelligence sources, and the usual need to protect such information for lifetimes or other long durations, original classifiers may mark this type of information only, at the time of classification,

as exempt from automatic declassification at 25 years by marking 50X1-HUM (formerly X1 or 25X1-human).

Similarly, design and construction concepts for weapons of mass destruction can remain useful and sensitive for longer than 25 years, thus requiring classification beyond 25 years, and restriction from transmission on SMART messaging systems when RD information is present. Information concerning weapons of mass destruction should be marked elsewhere, such as on paper documents, as 50X2-WMD. However, because such Atomic Energy Act information, like Top Secret information, cannot be transmitted via SMART, 50X2-WMD is not a duration marking option in SMART. Therefore, apart from human source information, no other SMART messages may be marked with duration greater than 25 years nor have an exemption category at the time of original classification.

The issue of information provided by foreign government sources is addressed in 5 FAH-3 H-716. One reason that can be entered to explain classification is that it is,

foreign government information (FGI) provided with the expectation of confidentiality (see note below); ...

NOTE: Department of State messages that clearly contain FGI do not require portion markings for FGI per a waiver granted to the Department by the Information Security Oversight Office. However, normally, you must mark messages containing foreign government information (FGI) to show the source government and classification level, for example (UK- Secret). If the identity of the source government must be protected, mark the pertinent portions of the document "FGI" together with the classification. You also must enter this information in the text of the telegram itself.

b. If the fact that information is foreign government information must be concealed, do not use the markings described above; mark the document as if it were wholly of U.S. origin.

Examples (classified for exhibit purposes only):

(S-FGI): (NZ-C, AUS-C, CAN-S)

(S-FGI) Used, for example, if a paragraph of the telegram contains foreign government information (FGI) given with both the expectations of confidentiality and non-attribution to which foreign government it came from.

(S) Used if foreign government source does not want it disclosed that the information came from another government at all.

Note, however, that the language does not preclude a later decision to change the original declassification date. Some WikiLeaks cables (e.g. 01PARIS11204) also illustrate tagging names of people whose views are summarized with the set phrases 'protect' or 'please protect' or 'strictly protect'. The object is to caution against exposing those – usually non-US officials – who share their opinions with an Embassy officer. An officer's ability to interpret a country's politics to Washington depends on having candid and helpful conversations with informed locals. Exposure would not only identify the informant, who might find that embarrassing locally, but also expose the content of his remarks. Would the informant, who may still be deeply engaged in politics in ten years' time, take well to having the declassified contents of the cable spread on local broadsheets? Is the lesson that it is imprudent to say anything to an Embassy officer that one would not say to a crowd in the public square?

This excursion into the Department of State's handbook illustrates that the governing Executive Order anticipates that much 'secret' information will become stale and in just a few years no longer require secrecy.[15]

The secret of the atomic bomb

The very notion of a 'world without nuclear weapons' implies a world in which no one – government, corporation, criminal conspiracy, even the merely curious – can construct a nuclear weapon from scratch. Specialists converge in emphasizing that a nuclear device cannot be made without a sufficient quantity of suitable uranium or plutonium, at a first approximation for practical purposes, hard to get. In addition, the notion circulates that special knowledge is required to make a nuclear weapon, even if you have solved the problem of getting uranium or plutonium. Is it true that there is such special knowledge and, if so, has it leaked, or could it leak, from existing nuclear-weapon programs.

The short answer is that a crude uranium device could be made by a small group of well-selected and competent engineers, using their general knowledge and what is already widely reported in books and journals. It would be a clumsy affair, a terror device, but could prove a highly destructive one. For example, a uranium device assembled in a basement, or assembled vertically, bringing two pieces of uranium together by explosion ('gun type') or gravity. This is not a so-called 'dirty bomb', which does not involve a nuclear detonation but only the scattering of material that includes highly radioactive isotopes.

To build a true weapon, a practical weapon, light enough to deliver by missile, reliable and predictable, a plutonium weapon, and especially a full thermonuclear weapon, would be within the means of a government willing to devote great resources and personnel, but on paths that would not be made much easier by learning any particular 'secret' that might be pilfered from an existing weapons program. That does not mean that the nuclear-weapon states that have invested in finely-calculated and closely-engineered weapons, proven by explosive tests, do not hope to retain as well as they can their monopoly on the knowledge of refined design. But there is no 'secret of the atomic bomb'.

In fact, in 1939 nuclear scientists talked openly about the possibility of building a uranium bomb that could destroy a city. Their speculations were reported by the Associated Press in an article titled 'Vision Earth Rocked by Isotope Blast' published in *The New York Times* the 29 April 1939 (Larkin, 2008: 18). On 6 August 1945 the whole world learnt it was truly possible. The key bottleneck is that plutonium and highly-enriched uranium (uranium rich in ^{235}U) are scarce and are held in significant quantities only by governments or under government regulation – as best we know.

What secrets are 'necessary', or 'useful', in seeking and then sustaining nuclear zero?

Distinguish, at the outset, national requirements from requirements of the nuclear zero regime. Governments committed to nuclear abolition – having decided to work for and achieve a global abolition regime or having inherited as state policy the decisions of earlier governments – are not in a static situation, but must repeatedly reassure themselves, and answer any doubts among their people, that the regime remains real and sustainable. From this follow these state desiderata:

1. means to monitor the regime, relying heavily on national means and cooperation with others, and including measures to detect any conspiracy or clandestine program that aims to breach the regime;
2. persuasive evidence of compliance, whether technical (for instance, sensor data, satellite photographs) or collaborative (for instance contributions from other governments);
3. successive internal assessments of the regime, given the facts as they are understood, and given that there may be significant disagreement about the quality and meaning of 'facts' available;
4. contingency plans (which would include how regime institutions are to

be alerted to suspicions and their capabilities invoked) to be drawn upon should the regime be broken in some respect that could endanger the safety or security of its population.

Each of these requirements depends, to some extent, on some details being 'secret'. The hypothetical challenge posits a state, or some non-state entity, that has resolved to seek advantage by breaching the regime, or creating prerequisites for a prompt breaching of the regime. It may target regime 'secrets'. The seeming paradox is that each state's assuring itself that the regime is sound will necessitate its undertaking planning and collaborations that it will be unwilling to share with all ... with the resulting possibility that others may suspect it of harbouring designs to breach the regime ... and that such suspicions cannot be completely resolved by the available measures of reassurance.

Who would have stakes and dealings in a move to nuclear zero? A schematic of institutions and the fabric of connections within and among them for which a case for 'communications security' can be made would begin with a typical government, its branches by which decisions are made and actions taken, its agencies with custody of nuclear weapons and special nuclear materials, its regulatory framework, and its diplomatic and intelligence contacts with the world beyond its borders. Include germane corporations and research centres. Of 'international organizations' we would posit regional and near-universal bodies analogous to EURATOM and the IAEA; imagine what we will call the Authority that comes to be mandated by treaty to set zero in place and manage its maintenance. There could also be a Common Force, a collective military entity, on which the Authority could call. The UN Security Council, or a group with some of its powers, would backstop the transition to global zero, seen as a key component of global security and stability. Participant states would, of course, remain the actual source of consent and any response to a breach, whose role would be defined by treaty among the universal or near-universal membership of the regime. Still, divided loyalties – is my duty to the international organization in which I serve, or to my native state that now approaches me and asks me to do as it asks? – remain and are an ongoing consideration when one speaks of 'secrecy' or 'communications security' in this context.

Regime institutions and their roles, then, would look something like those with which we are already familiar – IAEA, UNSCOM/UNMOVIC and IAEA in Iraq, the OPCW, and UNSC – and could demonstrate frailties like those seen before. If the Authority were called upon to assess whether a State Party had created unpermitted technical capabilities, capabilities that would enable it to accomplish a prompt breach of the regime, the Authority would need to assess whether it was being given the access required to make that assessment, or was instead in the 'cat and mouse' situation to which Hans Blix frequently referred. There would have to be communications between inspectors and the Authority. If technical monitors were installed, their data would need to be communicated with integrity to the Authority. Politics among states – what shall we do? – will be conducted in large part by electronic means.

Secure communication is not an incidental feature of a zero regime, nor something introduced capriciously, but lies at the very heart of the regime's *raison d'être*. The entire process of negotiating and committing to an abolition regime arises out of peril and distrust. If the weapons were not so destructive 'abolition' might be desirable but not necessary, and if all governments (and groups) could be trusted then formal commitments and regime institutions would be completely unnecessary.

What about 'secure communication' among anti-zero plotters?

Envision a world en route to nuclear zero, or already there. It is possible that a government (or renegades within government) or a group outside government would conspire to defeat the move to zero, or the zero regime itself. This would seem to put global zero regime institutions – alongside governments committed to the regime – into practising something akin to 'cyberwar'.

Several implications follow. Both advocates of zero and 'conspirators' will design and use encryption and decryption techniques. Conspirators may exploit, and the regime seeks to detect, messages hidden in otherwise open transactions (hence fictional messages to the Resistance of the form: 'The crow will fly at dawn.'). Altogether novel means of communication will be sought (recall Herodotus' story of the courier with a message tattooed on his scalp, then hidden by growing hair). Conspirators' obtaining intelligence of the regime's capabilities to detect will be among their highest priorities.

Just how global regime institutions should modulate their transactions with and reliance on States' intelligence capabilities, and the offerings of opposi-tionists and defectors, were well-developed themes in the work of UNSCOM/UNMOVIC and the IAEA in Iraq. Hans Blix refers obliquely to the claim that the United States distorted UN-accepted offers of communications assistance within Iraq to install sensors working for its own anti-Saddam agenda. No general a priori guidance can be given, since the disposition to avoid becoming entangled in member state intrigues and purposes may be outweighed, given circumstances and the threat, by the specifics of any actual endangerment to the regime.

The skills to protect against hostile plotters will reside in governments and private labs (for example, in computer security firms and universities). Will the Authority be comfortable contracting with 'outside' firms or labs for security services? With governments?

If nuclear zero requires 'secure communications', can they be had?

The answer is simple enough: although there is always a risk that important secrets will be lost, or data 'spoofed', or systems entered, there is a well-practised repertoire of means to achieve greater assurance and hedge against risk: hardware configuration, personnel caution, data management, strong encryption, monitoring traffic and, above all, not abandoning prudence in the face of user demands. Was the US Department of Defense exercising reasonable caution when it placed years of Department of State cables on SIPRNET?

How to manage the tension between secrecy and efficacy? Best practice is to conduct study, design, and discussion with others in the open. There, third parties can see the reasons advanced, judge them, and contribute. The object is broad consensus around steps that are informed by differences of interest and approach but, when those are taken into account, are seen as workable and effective.

State planning groups, engaged in intense internal negotiations as well as contacts with their counterparts in other States, may need to keep 'secrets', at least for a time. After all, they must explore the grounds for agreement and bring agreement to completion. Future breaches are certain. Prudent planning for breach should be practised in attaining zero, and built into the subsequent 'zero nuclear weapons' regime.

Operating in daylight is the best preventive of harm through breach: there is no opportunity for a salient breach. Looking at the problem in this way favours ongoing mutual reassurance, public access to evidence and its assessment, and full disclosure, while the drive for durable agreement acknowledges that negotiations are often more fruitful when they can take place in private.

The burden of justifying secrecy lies on whomever proposes it. Technically, this orientation favours ongoing refinement and prudent use of standard practices, including encryption, redundant assurance, shared assessment, and ready access to disputed sites. But those claiming need for 'secrets' bear the burden of proof.

Taking account of the NSA and GCHQ files and other examples

At the time of writing, we have not the slightest idea what else there may be in the files that Edward Snowden has not yet revealed. The NSA Director, General Keith B. Alexander, estimates the number of files in Snowden's hands to be between 50,000 and 200,000; and unnamed British authorities are cited as saying that 'at least 58,000' classified GCHQ documents are in Snowden's possession (Hosenball, 2013). Despite what we do not know, three indicators confirm a surveillance apparatus of unlimited ambition and extraordinary capabilities: files revealed to date are consistent with earlier suspicions and evidences, have not been denied by the United States or Britain, and are complemented by newly-released US Government documents concerning the 'legality' of domestic and foreign collections. Of course it must concern the US and British Governments, and many others, to establish exactly how Snowden accomplished his acquisitions. We have only fragmentary press reports purporting to shed light on that question, none attributed to named sources.[16]

A canvass of cases in which 'secure communications' have been compromised would show that network designers and administrators must anticipate diverse challenges to the integrity of their systems, but that trusted personnel – among them spies, whistleblowers, opportunists, the careless, and even those whose dedication and ambition carry them into unsustainable exploits – often pose the greatest threats.

The themes of ambition and disclosure are illustrated by any number of cases. Technology supplies powerful means of collaboration, but also novel methods of signals intelligence and document access. Readers are likely aware of the Zimmermann Telegram and Pentagon Papers, Stuxnet and kin, Jonathan Jay Pollard, 'Johnny Walker', and the Venona decrypts. There are many other cases from which caution can be learnt.[17]

Further implications

What is said here about a 'global zero' nuclear regime also applies, mutatis mutandis, to other insidious weapons. How can states negotiate measures to prevent harm from genetically engineered biological weapons, or chemical weapons of great toxicity, without communicating among themselves the means to create and disseminate such weapons? What is the tension between providing polities sound information about novel weapons, so that citizens may estimate their risks and judge what to do, and so enabling evildoers with that same information?

More generally, if 'global zero' or its analogues with respect to other threats are judged to require some secrets of great salience, and to place a premium on identifying people with intent or simple capacity to undermine that regime, will the effect be to reinforce the incentives for states – and even private entities – to monitor all communications and harvest from them what they can?

Notes

1   See Bamford (2008: 142). Bamford states that the request was sent to the NSA's signals intelligence partners in Britain, Canada, Australia and New Zealand. In the *Observer*'s published version identity of the recipients is withheld.

2   On the Katharine Gun case, see BBC World (2004), Bright and Beaumont (2004) and Radden Keefe (2004).

3   'US plan to bug Security Council: the text', *Observer*, 2 March 2003: 'Online document: The text of the memorandum detailing the US plan to bug the phones and emails of key Security Council members, revealed in today's Observer'. RT appears to mean the NSA section designated 'Regional Targets', and 'topi' is probably shorthand for 'tactical/operational intelligence'. QRC means 'quick reaction capability'. For use in a US Air Force context, see www.af.mil/shared/media/epubs/AFI14-120.pdf

4   Cable 10PARIS193. NOFORN or NF means 'no foreign dissemination'. [Arkin translates it as 'Not Releasable to Foreign Nationals'.] SIPDIS indicates the message is suitable for dissemination on SIPRNET, the ['Secret Internet Protocol Router Network'].

5   Those negotiations were facilitated by the Irish diplomat Alison Kelly, whose government is among the abolitionist New Agenda Coalition. At a guess her work was largely accomplished in direct conversations, not orchestrated by wire or wireless.

6   David Leigh (2010) recounts Manning's method:

> It was childishly easy, according to the published chatlog of a conversation
> Manning had with a fellow-hacker. 'I would come in with music on a CD-RW
> labeled with something like '"Lady Gaga"' ... erase the music ... then write a
> compressed split file. No one suspected a thing ... [I] listened and lip-synched
> to Lady Gaga's Telephone while exfiltrating possibly the largest data spillage
> in American history'. He said that he 'had unprecedented access to classified
> networks 14 hours a day 7 days a week for 8+ months'.

However, *The Washington Post* cybersecurity reporter Ellen Nakashima (2011) has
been told that Manning did *not* have authorized access:

> He had a top secret security clearance, but that alone does not enable access to
> the full range of material on the SIPRNet – the military's secret-level classified
> network. There are certain portions of the network that are accessible only
> to those with a "need to know" based on their job duties. For instance, my
> understanding is that Pfc. Manning did not have authorized access to the State
> Department's diplomatic cable database, which was accessible through SIPRNet
> to individuals with need to know.

It is clear that Manning had authorized access to the physical location in which,
according to his account, he downloaded the cables. Was there a flaw – a departure
from written requirements – in the installation? *The New York Times* writes that
'Private Manning apparently exploited a security loophole' without identifying
what that 'loophole' might have been. See http://topics.nytimes.com/top/reference/
timestopics/people/m/bradley_e_manning/index.html (accessed 31 January 2013).
For this chapter, the point is that every feature of a 'secure' communications system
is open to being 'flawed': that there are (what are in retrospect) 'normal flaws', by
analogy to the 'normal accidents' of normal accident theory.

7   Briefly, recipient generates a pair of keys: a 'public key' that will be known to all
and a 'private key' known only to its owner. Sender encrypts using recipient's
public key; and recipient uses her corresponding private key to decrypt the
message. PKE's development includes a major breakthrough by three research
scholars, Whitfield Diffie, Martin Hellman and Ralph Merkle. (See Diffie, 1998.)
Diffie and Hellman are also known for their deep interest in nuclear weapons and
risk. On Diffie's studies in communication security see Diffie and Landau (2007),
where the authors mention the role of encrypted commands in the 'permissive
action links' by which control of nuclear weapons is exercised at the warhead level.

8   Imagine that the system uses 256 symbols. Each character in plaintext is
represented by a number from 0 to 255. In place of the n bytes of the original

message, the sender now has a sequence of n numbers. Generate a sequence of 'random' numbers between 0 and 255 ('keys') as long as the message to be encrypted. Place the message sequence 'underneath' ('alongside') the sequence of keys, and add the two numbers. If the sum exceeds 255 subtract 256 from the sum. When all plaintext characters have been replaced, send the message.

The recipient has a copy of the one time pad. She subtracts each 'key' from the corresponding number transmitted. If the result is negative she instead adds 256 to the number transmitted and from the sum subtracts the 'key'. Each character is *individually encrypted* by a key that is not applied to any other character. Note the weakness: the file of modifiers ('keys') must be generated in advance, stored (securely), and a copy conveyed (securely) to the recipient, who must keep the copy (secure) until needed.

9   'Through history people have intentionally or unintentionally passed classified information. There are people like Johnny Walker around. We've had them in the past; we've had them recently. We'll have them again. But, the vast majority of our military people have the personal integrity and the training that keeps them from violating security rules' (Smith, 1998). Issues prior to 1999 are no longer at the original site, but the page is archived at http://web.archive.org/web/20060504113303/chips.navy.mil/archives/98_jul/c_ews3.htm (accessed 31 December 2012).

10 Shane continues:

> The A.C.L.U. filed what it acknowledged was a 'mischievous' Freedom of Information Act request in an effort to force the government to acknowledge counterterrorism operations that it had refused to discuss on secrecy grounds and that were mentioned in the cables. The State Department, acting as if the cables were still secret, withheld 12 of the 23 cables completely and released 11 with some redactions.
>
> The judge ruled, in effect, that a document remains classified until it is officially declassified by the government, even if it has become public through unofficial channels. 'No matter how extensive, the WikiLeaks disclosure is no substitute for an official acknowledgment' that the documents are authentic, Judge Kollar-Kotelly wrote. She said the A.C.L.U. had failed to show that State Department officials had confirmed that the cables posted on the Web by WikiLeaks were real.

Ben Wizner, director of the A.C.L.U.'s speech, privacy and technology project, said the court's decision would 'leave many Americans scratching their heads, and rightly so.' He noted that the 23 cables had been 'published throughout the world' and that the military was prosecuting Pfc. Bradley Manning, an Army intelligence analyst accused of providing them to WikiLeaks. By endorsing the government's 'legal fiction' that the documents remain classified, Mr Wizner said, the court 'does further damage to the government's credibility and undermines the legitimacy of any future government claim of secrecy.'

11 The comment:

> You do not understand the problem that Jeffrey is trying to solve. First, someone who works for the government, in general, and holds security clearances, in particular, are required, by law, to protect classified information. Even if that information has leaked into the unclassified world, it remains classified, by law, until the original classifier (in this case, the State Dept) declares it unclassified. We, with clearances, can read it, but we can't discuss it or confirm it or use it in other writings. That's why Jeffrey has said he won't quote full cables or paragraphs, but will excerpt and paraphrase.
>
> Second, you cannot store or print classified information on an unclassified gov't computer, that pollutes the computer, and requires that all its drives and files be scrubbed, a costly, time-consuming, and fundamentally annoying process.
>
> Hence, Jeffrey's avoidance of paragraphs with paragraph markings. That's to protect us from this procedural annoyance. He's not hiding the information. He's just adjusting its form to make it easier for us to participate in his discussions without breaking the law.

12 See MacAskill (2013). The report states:

> The US air force has backtracked after issuing guidance last week banning the families of staff from reading classified material released by WikiLeaks. The guidance also warned that the families faced prosecution as spies if they read the leaked diplomatic cables. But the air force, seeking to calm a growing row, said on Monday night that the advice had not been sanctioned by headquarters and it had been removed from its website.

13 On this point, see US Department of State (2011).

14 '5 FAH-3 H-700 E.O. 12958, as amended, Telegram Classification Marking (CT:TAGS-40; 07-14-2009)' accessed by archive.org on 22 February 2010. Versions of this document can be found by going to archive.org and entering the URL www.state.gov/documents/organization/89254.pdf in the 'wayback machine' and then selecting a year calendar showing for which dates the document is archived.

15 On the content of Executive Order 12958, see www.archives.gov/isoo/policy-documents/eo-12958-amendment.html (accessed 1 February 2013).

16 Details, Nakashima (2013):

Snowden lifted the documents from a top-secret network run by the Defense Intelligence Agency and used by intelligence arms of the Army, Air Force, Navy and Marines, according to sources, who spoke on the condition of anonymity to discuss sensitive matters.

Snowden took 30,000 documents that involve the intelligence work of one of the services, the official said. He gained access to the documents through the Joint Worldwide Intelligence Communications System, or JWICS, for top-secret/sensitive compartmented information, the sources said.

The material in question does not deal with NSA surveillance but primarily with standard intelligence about other countries' military capabilities … ;

Additional details, in Hosenball and Strobel (2013):

A handful of agency employees who gave their login details to Snowden were identified, questioned and removed from their assignments, said a source close to several U.S. government investigations into the damage caused by the leaks.

"Snowden may have persuaded between 20 and 25 fellow workers at the NSA regional operations center in Hawaii to give him their logins and passwords by telling them they were needed for him to do his job as a computer systems administrator, a second source said.

17 Thumbnails and further sources for additional cases can be read at www.learnworld.com/JOURNAL/DD.136E.Leaks.pdf. Among those briefed are the Conficker worm; Google's charges that hacking originating in China sought its proprietary source code libraries (and Gmail accounts); the attack on Greek mobile phone calls of government and other figures; the case of US FBI agent Robert Hanssen's supplying secrets to the Soviet Union; and even the World War II-era activities of Donald Maclean, First Secretary of the UK Embassy in Washington, supplying information to the Soviet Union.

References

Arkin, W. M. (2005), *Code Names*, Hanover, NH: Steerforth Press.

Bamford, J. (2008), *The Shadow Factory: The Ultra-Secret NSA from 9/11 to the Eavesdropping on America*, New York: Doubleday.

BBC World (2004), 'UK "spied on UN's Kofi Annan"', 26 February 2004, http://news.bbc.co.uk/2/hi/uk_news/politics/3488548.stm (accessed 1 February 2013).

Booth, R., H. Brooke and S. Morris (2010), 'WikiLeaks cables: Bradley Manning Faces 52 years in Jail', *The Guardian,* 30 November 2010.

Bright, M. and Peter Beaumont (2004), 'Britain spied on UN allies over war vote', *The Observer*, 8 February 2004.

Diffie, W. (1988), 'The First Ten Years of Public Key Cryptography', Proceedings of the IEEE, v 76 n 5, May 1988, pp. 560–577, http://cr.yp.to/bib/1988/diffie.pdf (accessed 31 January 2013).

Diffie, W. and S. Landau (1998 [2007]), *Privacy on the Line: The Politics of Wiretapping and Encryption*, Cambridge, MA: MIT Press.

Hosenball, M. (2013), 'NSA Chief Says Snowden Leaked Up to 200,000 Secret Documents', Reuters, 14 November 2013, www.reuters.com/article/2013/11/14/us-usa-security-nsa-idUSBRE9AD19B20131114 (accessed 27 November 2013).

Hosenball, M. and W. Strobel (2013), 'Snowden Is Said to Have Tricked NSA Co-workers into Giving Him Their Passwords, Reuters, 7 November 2013, www.washingtonpost.com/world/national-security/exclusive-snowden-persuaded-other-nsa-workers-to-give-up-passwords--sources/2013/11/07/6bfa9a54-4828-11e3-bf0c-cebf37c6f484_story.html (accessed 27 November 2013).

Keefe, P. R. (2004), 'The Leak Was Me' http://www.patrickraddenkeefe.com/articles/media/NYRB_20040610.pdf (accessed 28 April 2014).

Larkin, B. D. (2006), 'Nuclear Weapons and the Vision of Command and Control', in E. Halpin, P. Trevorrow, D. Webb and S. Wright (eds), *Cyberwar, Netwar, and the Revolution in Military Affairs*, Basingstoke: Palgrave Macmillan, 113–38.

—(2008), *Designing Denuclearization*, New Brunswick, NJ: Transaction.

Leigh, D. (2010), 'How 250,000 US Embassy Cables Were Leaked', *The Guardian*, 28 November 2010.

Lewis, J. (2010), 'A Note to Readers', 9 December 2010, http://lewis.armscontrolwonk.com/archive/3356/a-note-to-readers (accessed 31 January 2013).

MacAskill, E., N. Davies, N. Hopkins, J. Borger and J. Ball (2013), 'GCHQ Intercepted Foreign Politicians' Communications at G20 Summits', *The Guardian,* 16 June 2013 (accessed 16 June 2013).

Nakashima, E. (2011), 'Live Q&A's', *The Washington Post*, 9 May 2011, http://live.washingtonpost.com/wikileaks-who-is-bradley-manning.html (accessed 4 February 2011).

—(2013), 'Officials Alert Foreign Services that Snowden has Documents on their Cooperation with US', *The Washington Post*, 24 October 2013, www.washingtonpost.com/world/national-security/officials-alert-foreign-services-that-snowden-has-documents-on-their-cooperation-with-us/2013/10/24/930ea85c-3b3e-11e3-a94f-b58017bfee6c_story.html (accessed 27 November 2013).

Schmitt, E. (2010), 'Force Says Leaked Cables Are Off Limits On Its Network', *The New York Times,* 15 December 2010, A1.

Shane, S. (2012), 'Documents in Plain Sight ... But Still Classified', *The New York Times,* 23 July 2012, www.nytimes.com/2012/07/24/us/government-documents-in-plain-sight-but-still-classified.html (accessed 31 January 2013).

Short, C. (2004), 'Clare Short: What Happened when I Told the Truth about the Bugging of Kofi Annan', *The Independent* (London), 25 October 2004, www.independent.co.uk/news/uk/politics/clare-short-what-happened-when-i-told-the-truth-about-the-bugging-of-kofi-annan-6159202.html (accessed 2 February 2013).

Smith, E. (1998), 'Email and Internet Services to the Fleet, A Report on the US Navy's Unified Atlantic Region Network Operations Center (UARNOC)' (July 1998), United States Navy, http://www.chips.navy.mil/archives/98 jul/c_ews3.htm (accessed 26 April 2003).

Warrick, J. and W. Pincus (2007), 'Missteps in the Bunker', *Washington Post*, 23 September 2007 and 'How Warheads Made an Unplanned Flight', *The Los Angeles Times*, 23 September 2007, http://articles.latimes.com/2007/sep/23/nation/na-bomber23 (accessed 31 January 2013).

5

Establishing Norms of Behaviour in Cyberspace: The Chinese Viewpoint

Chunmei Kang[1]

Change in cyberspace

In general, cyberspace implies the vast and growing logical domain composed of public and private networks and virtually every networked device in the world. There are more than 4 billion digital wireless devices in the world today (White House, 2011). Individuals and communities worldwide connect, socialize and organize themselves in and through cyberspace. From 2000 to 2010, global Internet users increased from 360 million to over 2 billion people (US DoD, 2011). Almost a third of the world's population uses the Internet and countless more are affected by it in their daily lives.

Clearly, the growth of these networks supports prosperous economies and society. Moreover, the continuing growth of networked systems, devices, and platforms means that cyberspace is embedded into an increasing number of capabilities upon which states and people rely to complete their mission. People trade goods and services in cyberspace, moving assets across the globe in seconds. In addition to facilitating trade in other sectors, cyberspace is in itself a key sector of the global economy. Cyberspace has become an incubator for new forms of entrepreneurship, advances in technology, and new social networks that drive our economy and reflect our principles. Today, societies are increasingly relying on networked information systems to control critical infrastructures (CI) and communications systems essential to modern life. Critical life-sustaining infrastructures that deliver energy (electric power, oil and gas) and water, food, transportation (rail, air, merchant marine), finance and banking, information and telecommunications, public health, emergency services and so on, all depend on networked information systems.

Although it brings opportunities to our society, cyberspace also brings significant challenges. Today, resources for conducting harmful cyberspace attacks are widely available and inexpensive, creating a low cost of entry for any adversary. The tools and techniques developed by cyber criminals are increasing in sophistication at an incredible rate, and many of these capabilities can be purchased cheaply on the Internet. As the main theme of this volume shows, the targets can range from states to individuals. Well-planned attacks on key nodes of the cyberspace infrastructure have the potential to produce network collapse and cascading effects that can severely affect critical infrastructures locally, nationally, or possibly globally. Many states' networks and information infrastructure that these states depend on for their operations suffer from exploitation, penetration, disruption, degradation and sabotage from states and non-state actors. Potential cyber-attacks may include:

- Theft or exploitation of data. Successful penetration would lead to the loss of thousands of files from networks.
- Disruption or denial of access or service that affects the availability of networks, information, or network-enabled resources. Given the integrated nature of cyberspace, computer-induced failures of power grids, transportation networks, or financial systems could cause massive physical damage and economic disruption.
- Destructive action including corruption, manipulation, or direct activity that threatens to destroy or degrade networks or connected systems.
- Anti-government activities. Some anti-government group may make political statements, or express personal disappointment in their government that could be devastating to national security.

Challenge in cyberspace governance

The necessity of establishing behavioural norms in cyberspace

Because of the global nature of cyberspace, the vulnerabilities that exist are open to the world and available to everyone, anywhere, with sufficient capability to exploit them. China as a developing country is far less capable of maintaining Internet security than developed countries, facing a much bigger threat of online attacks. According to information released by China Internet Network Information Centre (CNNIC) (Qian, 2011) in the past years, China Internet continues to maintain fast development momentum.[2] To the end of November 2011, Chinese Internet users had over 500 million online attacks with a penetration rate of 37.7 per cent. Although China possesses maximum Internet users, its development level is relatively low compared to developed countries (Figure 5.1).

As the network becomes more and more popular in China, it has also turned into a major concern for China's national security authorities (Xinhua News Agency, 2013). In recent years, China's vulnerable network has repeatedly been a victim of major overseas hacker attacks. Qian Xiaoqian, the Deputy Director of China Internet Information Office, pointed out that more than 4.5 million Chinese PCs had been attacked by Trojan viruses from IPs abroad in 2010, an increase of more than 16 times since 2009 (Qian, 2011).

According to data released by Chinese National Internet Emergency Centre at the annual meeting of Chinese Internet Security, nearly 4,635 Chinese government websites were tampered in 2010, nearly half of these following attacks from abroad (Chinese National Internet Emergency Centre, 2010).

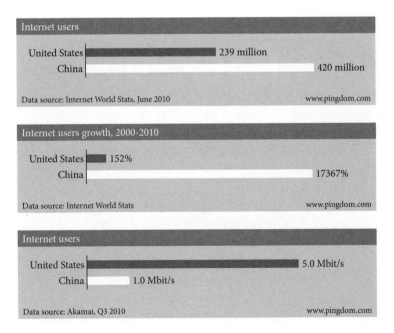

Figure 5.1 Comparative Internet users and development levels in China and the United States

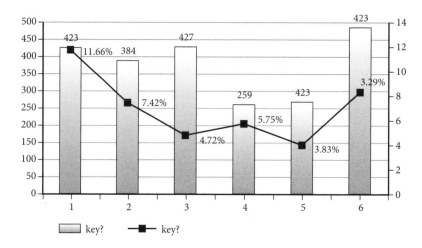

Figure 5.2 Amount of tampered Chinese government websites compared with total number of tampered websites (mainland China)

Figure 5.2 shows the amount of tampered Chinese governmental websites and its proportion to the whole of tampered websites of mainland China. Figure 5.3 shows the main page of a government website that was tampered.

Figure 5.3 Example of the main page of a tampered government website

In 2010, monitoring data from the Emergency Centre shows that nearly 480,000 Trojans controlled terminal IP, of which 221,000 are located outside. Among them, America (14.7 per cent) and India (8 per cent) are the two biggest states where the virus originated (Chinese National Internet Emergency Centre, 2010). In addition, a total of 13,782 zomby networks controlled terminal IP, 6,531 of them located outside. The top three are the United States (21.7 per cent), India (7.2 per cent) and Turkey (5.7 per cent) (Chinese National Internet Emergency Centre, 2010). According to the data submitted by Internet network security information units of the Ministry of Industry and Information, more than half of the hostile domains that linked China pages to phishing and other malicious wrongdoing websites are registered abroad (Xinhua News Agency, 2011; see also 2013).

The following are some examples of cyber-attack and crime executed through the Internet. In December 2011, a famous Chinese network community, the Tianya community, suffered repeated hacker attacks. About 40 million users' information leaked out which made those game players suffer a lot (People Henan Channel News, 2011). Sometimes even more serious criminal behaviour may happen through the Internet. For example, in June 2011, Chinese police in Hangzhou, China, seized a criminal group that had first stolen users' bank account numbers and then transferred them to their accomplices abroad (Zhejiang News, 2011). Through Internet operations, they finally took out users' money stored on the bank cards, which caused substantial problems for those bank clients.

Hacker attacks cause enormous losses to Internet users. For promoting the use of information and cyber-technology in advancing economic and social development and people's welfare, standards of behaviour and related law should be established. Considering that different countries have different historical and cultural traditions, economic and social development levels, standards of cyber behaviour could first be established nationally. International cooperation can first be conducted in the fields with common views and common laws, such as anti-terrorism and inhibiting criminal behaviour.

Technical difficulties in Internet governance

It is generally believed that cybercrime should be inhibited and international norms and measures on cybercrime should be developed bilaterally and multilaterally. Cyberspace governance is a complex issue and should be considered and discussed carefully (Brenner, 2010; Brown and Poellet, 2012). For example, it was thought that DNS blocking and filtering would be an effective measure when we take charge of illegal sites, yet, there are technical issues that need to be considered thoroughly. If ISPs redirect a website to other sites, it should alter records in the Net's system for looking up DNS, so that users could not navigate to the site. Opponents of this measure consider that this would harm the usefulness of the Domain Name System Security Extensions (DNSSEC), a set of protocols developed by the Internet Engineering Task Force (IETF) for ensuring Internet security. A white paper by the Brookings Institution (Friedman, 2011) aptly noted that 'The DNS system is based on trust', adding that DNSSEC was developed to prevent malicious redirection of DNS traffic, and other forms of redirection would break the assurances from this security tool, which means core Internet infrastructure may be changed.

In a lawsuit argued in November 2011, both of DNS blocking methods mentioned above were applied. Luxury goods maker Chanel won lawsuits against hundreds of websites trafficking in counterfeit luxury goods (Anderson, 2011). A federal judge in Nevada has agreed that Chanel can seize the domain names in question and transfer them all to the US-based registrar GoDaddy, where they would all be redirected to a page serving notice of the seizure. In addition, a total ban on search engine indexing was ordered. The judge ordered 'all Internet search engines' and 'all social media websites' – explicitly naming Facebook, Twitter, Google+, Bing, Yahoo, and Google – to 'de-index' the domain names and to remove them from any search results. It was not entirely certain that those domains might not even be registered in the United States and the judge's ban on search engines and social media indexing apparently extended to the entire world. This case shows that international cooperation is necessary in catching Internet criminals.

Cybercrime detection has also proved to be a challenge. Unlike cybercrimes such as child pornography that could be blocked voluntarily by media websites using methods that begin by detecting skin tones, other cybercrimes, such as copyright infringement, are much harder to detect. Media websites must rely on copyright holders to bring offending material to their attention. In the copyright lawsuit mentioned above, the luxury goods maker Chanel hired a Nevada investigator to order from three of the 228 sites in question (Anderson, 2011). When the orders arrived, they were reviewed by a Chanel official and declared counterfeit. The other 225 sites were seized based on a Chanel anti-counterfeiting specialist browsing the Web. These techniques greatly increase the difficulties of cybercrime detection.

Just as personal behaviour should be bounded by cyber behaviour norms, nations' actions should also be guided by responsible behaviour norms to prevent the misunderstandings that could lead to conflict. In these years, cyberspace has been regarded by some countries as an effectively 'independent military operation domain', like the air, land, sea and space (*The Economist*, 2010). The United States National Military Strategy for Cyberspace operations (NMS-CO) (Chairman of the Joint Chiefs of Staff, 2006) which was issued by the Chairman of the Joint Chiefs of Staff was a product of significant reflection and debate within US military and government. NMS-CO is the US Armed Forces' comprehensive strategic approach for using cyberspace operations to assure US military strategic superiority in the domain. In the document (US Chairman of the Joint Chiefs of Staff, 2006), cyberspace is not only treated by the US military as a cyberspace-specific operations domain, but it is also pivotal to ensure success in the other domains included. NMS-CO reported that 'the integration of offensive and defensive cyberspace operations, coupled with the skill and knowledge of our people, is fundamental to this approach'. In fact, as early as 2004, the US National Military Strategy pointed out that 'The Armed Forces must have the ability to operate across the air, land, maritime, space and cyberspace domains of the battle space' (US Chiefs of Staff, 2004). Here, cyberspace was for the first time mentioned as an independent operation domain in US official documents (see also the US Army War College Library, 2013: 6–10).

Actually, US departments and services have published several documents related to cyberspace in recent years (for instance, the US Chairman of the Joint Chiefs of Staff, 2006; the US Air Force Cyber Command, 2008; the US Army, 2010; Department of Defense, 2011; The White House, 2011). From these documents, it can be seen that the US Cyberspace strategy has gradually changed from strategic defensive to strategic offensive.[3] The 'International Strategy for Cyberspace' that was released by the US government in 2011 stated the US was 'to build and enhance existing military alliances to confront potential threats in cyberspace' (The White House, 2011).

The concept of cyberspace operations domain makes Internet governance an even more complex issue. At least three questions need to be answered for countering against cyber-attacks from hostile countries or groups of individuals. First, how can the origin of the attack be confirmed? Be as it may, cyber-attacks require only commodity technology and to enable attackers to obfuscate their identities, locations, and paths of entry. When hackers from a distance attack states' infrastructures, how can the state identify precisely the sources and/ or geographical location of the attack? Second, the decision-making process is too short for cyberspace operation. The lack of geopolitical boundaries and natural boundaries of the electromagnetic spectrum allow cyberspace operations to occur rapidly nearly anywhere. Commanders in the cyberspace war need to make decisions in a very short time that inceases the possibility of misjudgement. The probabilities of making wrong decisions would increase. Third, the concept of cyberspace operation would block development and popularization of Internet.

All countries have the right and responsibility to protect their information technology and cyberspace and critical information infrastructure from threats, disturbance, attack and sabotage. At the same time, information technology and cyberspace should not become a new battlefield.

Conclusions

At present, the information technology and cyberspace security represents a major non-traditional security challenge confronting the international community. Inter-connectivity of information and cyber networks have contributed to 'make countries of the world 'a community of common destiny' in which states' security is inseparably linked together' (Wang, 2011). Therefore, the international community should work together towards a peaceful, secure and equitable information technology and cyberspace. The issue of cyberspace is now more than a technical issue. It is also an issue related to social, political, economic and cultural traditions of a country, which means that it has to be be considered carefully. In our opinion, the following norms should be established in the field of cyberspace.

The principle of peace

The international community should engage in active preventive diplomacy and promote the use of information and cyber-technology in advancing economic and social development and people's welfare and in maintaining international peace, stability and security. At the same time, countries should work to keep information and cyberspace from being a new battlefield, to prevent an arms race in information technology and cyberspace, and to settle disputes on this front peacefully through dialogue.

The principle of sovereignty

While ensuring the healthy development and effective utilization of information technology and cyberspace, it is also necessary to keep information and cyber-technology from being turned into another tool to interfere in internal affairs of other countries. In this area, respect for sovereignty and territorial integrity enshrined in the UN Charter and other universal basic norms of international relations should also be respected.

The sovereign countries should establish mutual respect and enhance understanding. Different countries have different historical and cultural traditions, different levels of economic and social development. As far as the existence of different opinions towards the Internet are concerned, we should not focus on the differences, but in a mature, responsible manner, respect and take care of each other's concerns, seek common ground for mutual cooperation and development through frank dialogue and exchange. Such common topics and issues may include: forensics and attack attribution; protection of networks and systems critical to national security, indications and warnings; protection against organized attacks capable of inflicting debilitating damage to the economy; fostering the establishment of national and international supervision and warning networks to detect and prevent cyber-attacks as they emerge and so on.

Rule of law

We should build and sustain an environment in which norms of responsible behaviour guide states' actions. Adherence to such norms brings predictability to state conduct, helping to prevent misunderstandings that could lead to conflict. Cooperation in this area should be conducted in the framework of the UN Charter and other universal basic norms of international relations. This cooperation is most effective and meaningful when countries have common cybercrime laws, which facilitate evidence sharing, extradition, and other types of coordination. International society could first try to establish rule of law in this common field, such as criminal law to prevent terrorism and criminal behaviour.

Technical standards in Internet governance

Unique attributes of networked technology require additional work to clarify how these norms apply and what additional understandings might be necessary to supplement them. Considering its complexity and importance in people's lives and national security, technical standards and governance structures should be established gradually among international societies after careful discussion. Norms of behaviour should be negotiated after considering national security and various interests, but not only in those counties with strong advantages in the field of cyberspace and information technology.

Cyberspace is now embedded in an increasing number of capabilities upon which states and people rely to complete their mission. Because of the global nature of cyberspace, the vulnerabilities that exist are open to the world. China as a developing country is far less capable of maintaining Internet security than the developed counties, and faces a much bigger threat of online attacks. For promoting the use of information and cyber-technology in advancing economic and social development and people's welfare, behaviour norms and related law should be established.

Most importantly, cyberspace is now beyond mere technology. It is also an issue related to social, political, economic and cultural traditions of a country, which makes it a topic that needs to be considered carefully. Considering that different countries have different historical and cultural traditions, economic and social development level, cyber behaviour norms could first be established nationally. International cooperation could, for example, be first implemented in fields of common interests and where common legislation exists, such as anti-terrorism and the prevention criminal behaviour.

Notes

1 This chapter was completed with the help, as co-authors, of Qiang Zhao, Hao Shen and Jianbin Shi. All authors are from the China Academy of Engineering Physics.
2 See for example www.cert.org.cn/publish/main/index.html (accessed 29 June 2013).
3 Editor's note: for a different perspective on this issue see the Mandiant report 'APT1: Exposing One of China's Cyber Espionage Units' (2013) at http://intelreport.mandiant.com/Mandiant_APT1_Report.pdf (accessed 15 September 2013).

References

Anderson, N. (2011), 'US judge orders hundreds of sites "de-indexed" from Google, Facebook', Ars Techinca, 29 November 2011, http://arstechnica.com/tech-policy/2011/11/us-judge-orders-hundreds-of-sites-de-indexed-from-google-twitter-bing-facebook/ (accessed 14 September 2013).

Brenner, S. W. (2010), *Cybercrime: Criminal Threats from Cyberspace*, Santa Barbara, CA: Praeger.

Brown, G. and K. Poellet (2012), 'The Customary International Law of Cyberspace', *Strategic Studies Quarterly* 6: 126–145, www.au.af.mil/au/ssq/2012/fall/brown-poellet.pdf (accessed 14 September 2013).

Chinese National Internet Emergency Center (2010), 'Chinese Internet Security Report 2010' (original in Chinese), www.cert.org.cn/publish/main/46/2012/20120330183838603351566/20120330183838603351566_.html (accessed 20 December 2010).

Economist (The) (2008), 'War in the Fifth Domain; Cyberwar', 3 July 2010: 25–8.

Friedman, A. A. (2011), 'Cybersecurity in the Balance: Weighing the Risks of the PROTECT IP Act and the Stop Online Piracy Act', Brookings, 15 November 2011,www.brookings.edu/research/papers/2011/11/15-cybersecurity-friedman (accessed 14 September 2013).

People Henan Channel News (2011), 'Tianya Community Admitted To Be Hacked and 40 Million Users' Information Leaked', 26 December 2011 (original in Chinese), http://henan.people.com.cn/news/2011/12/26/587148.html (accessed 27 December 2011).

Qian, X. (2011), 'Keynote Speech', The Fifth China-US Internet Forum, (original in Chinese), www.chinadaily.com.cn/hqzx/zmhlwlt_5/2011-12/09/content_14238668.htm (accessed 20 November 2011).

US Air Force Cyber Command (2008), 'Air Force Cyber Command Strategic Vision', February, www.dtic.mil/cgi-bin/GetTRDoc?AD=ADA479060 (accessed 14 September 2013).

US Army (2010), 'The United States Army's Cyberspace Operations Concept Capability Plan 2016-2028', February TRADOC Pamphlet 525-7-822 February, www2.gwu.edu/~nsarchiv/NSAEBB/NSAEBB424/docs/Cyber-033.pdf (accessed 14 September 2013).

US Army War College Library (2013), 'Cyberspace: A Selected Bibliography', US Army War College, Carlisle, PA, www.carlisle.army.mil/library/bibs/Cyberspace2013.pdf (accessed 14 September 2013).

US Chairman of the Joint Chiefs of Staff (2006), 'The National Military Strategy for Cyberspace Operations', December, http://itlaw.wikia.com/wiki/National_Military_Strategy_for_Cyberspace_Operations (accessed 14 September 2013).

US Chiefs of Staff (2004), 'The National Military Strategy of the United States of America: A Strategy for Today, A Vision for Tomorrow' (2004), www.bits.de/NRANEU/others/strategy/NMS04.pdf (accessed 14 September 2013).

US DoD (2011), 'Department of Defense Strategy for Operating in Cyberspace', July. www.defense.gov/news/d20110714cyber.pdf (accessed 14 September 2013).

Wang, Q. (2011), 'Speech by H.E. Ambassador Wang Qun at the First Committee of the 66th Session of the GA on Information and Cyberspace Security', October (original in Chinese).

White House (The) (2011), 'International Strategy for cyberspace – Prosperity, Security, and Openness in a Networked World, Washington, DC, May, www.whitehouse.gov/sites/default/files/rss_viewer/international_strategy_for_cyberspace.pdf (accessed 14 September 2013).

Xinhua News Agency (2011), 'A Large Number of User Data Leakage Afflicts Chinese Network Security', 27 December 2011 (original in Chinese), http://news.xinhuanet.com/society/2011-12/27/c_111318683_2.htm (accessed 14 September 2013).

—(2013), 'China's Cyber Security Under Severe Threat: Report', 19 March 2013, http://news.xinhuanet.com/english/china/2013-03/19/c_132246098.htm (accessed 20 August 2013).

Zhejiang News (2011), 'Hangzhou Police Broke the First Transnational Network Fraud and Arrested 36 Suspects, 30 June 2011 (original in Chinese), http://news.zj.com/detail/1346241.shtml (accessed 30 June 2011).

Part Two

The Infrastructure
and the Individual

Einstein on the Breach: Surveillance Technology, Cybersecurity and Organizational Change

Andreas Kuehn and Milton Mueller*

Introduction

In May 2009, US President Obama announced 'a new comprehensive approach to securing America's digital infrastructure'. In the course of describing this new initiative, he stated that 'Our pursuit of cybersecurity will not – I repeat, will not – include monitoring private sector networks or Internet traffic. We will preserve and protect the personal privacy and civil liberties that we cherish as Americans.' In the same speech, he also stated 'Let me be very clear: My administration will not dictate security standards for private companies' (The White House, 2009a).

Promoting security while avoiding surveillance or regulation of the private sector is proving to be more complicated and difficult than Obama's speech let on. In fact, as the structure of this volume suggests, policy efforts to secure the Internet affect the intertwined concepts of nations, infrastructure and individuals, and have implications for Internet governance (for example, Kuehn, 2013). While the boundaries of these three levels merge in cybersecurity discussions, this chapter focuses particularly on the effects on the infrastructure level. The Internet creates major interdependencies between the networks of government agencies and the networks supplied and used by the private sector. Additionally, the implementation of security technologies has an inherent tendency to alter lines of responsibility, management and control. Security technologies can, for example, create hierarchies where before there were market transactions or looser, networked forms of cooperation (for example, Kuerbis and Mueller, 2011).

This chapter addresses how cybersecurity technology implementation has altered, or threatened to alter, organizational relationships among civilian and military government agencies, Internet service providers, private businesses and users. As part of a larger project on the impact of deep packet inspection (DPI) technology on Internet governance,[1] it examines the implementation of IDS/IPS by US government agencies. Two federal cybersecurity initiatives involved DPI: (1) the 'Einstein' program, administered by the US Department of Homeland Security (DHS); and (2) the Defense Industrial Base (DIB) and Enhanced Cybersecurity Services (DIB/ECS) program initially administered by the US Department of Defense (DoD).

IDS/IPS is intended to shield federal agencies against cyber-espionage, data exfiltration, malware, DDoS attacks and other network-based security threats. IDS/IPS employs deep packet inspection (DPI) capabilities to scan and analyse data flowing over networks in real time. Based on automated recognition of threats, it issues alerts (IDS) or makes decisions about how to handle incoming and outgoing network traffic (IPS).

Broadly, we are interested in the extent to which attempts to improve cyber-security are leading to more state-based hierarchy and centralized control over the production of Internet access. The liberalization and privatization of telecommunications in the 1980s and 1990s moved the supply of information and communication services, standards and equipment away from the state or state-delegated monopolies into a private sector-led, competitive market economy. The Internet accelerated this revolution by facilitating the creation and interoperability of an unprecedentedly large number of private data networks. The social, economic and cultural gains of this massive proliferation of devices and networks have been enormous. But those very same features make nation-states, infrastructure and individuals in cyberspace potential targets and security initiatives vastly more complex. Hence, this case study focuses on the infrastructure and its stakeholders to investigate the way the US federal government's implementation of cybersecurity policies and technologies altered organizational arrangements. These changes affected the federal government itself as well as the relationships between the government and the private sector actors who supply the government with Internet access and military products and services.

Drawing on theories of economic organization, specifically the theory of the firm, our research asks: How did the US federal government's cybersecurity initiatives alter the organizational arrangements among the federal agencies and the private sector parties with which they cooperated? To what extent did the uncertainties associated with cyber risks lead to more hierarchical control and the internalization of functions and operations formerly provided by the private sector?

We show that the implementation of cybersecurity policies and technologies led to reassessing and revising the roles and responsibilities of various actors. With respect to the first aspect of our research question, we find that the federal government did consolidate Internet access and strengthen hierarchical control over federal agencies' Internet access. We also see efforts to extend surveillance and regulation to private, civilian networks, but document how political resistance and mistrust of government intelligence agencies prevented this in some cases and limited its scope in others.

Theory and method

The theory of the firm provides a useful lens with which to analyse the organizational impact of federal cybersecurity initiatives, as it brings into relief many of the factors that created pressure for, and resistance to, organizational changes. The *firm* is the economist's term for the basic decision making unit for production (Williamson and Winter, 1993). A variant of public choice theory considers the state to be a firm that supplies so-called 'public' goods (Auster and Silver, 1979; Forte, 2010).[2] Like a firm, the state draws on information, technology and its own managerial capabilities to combine factors of production into the types and quantities of services society signals that it wants the state to produce. Demand for the state's services however is conveyed not through the market price system but through political mechanisms such as voting, lobbying, political campaigns, rent-seeking and so on.

Transaction costs

A major preoccupation of firm theory has been to explain what is produced within an organization (in-sourced) and what goods and services are acquired across firms through markets or contractual agreements (out-sourced). Transaction costs (TC) are the costs of engaging in the search, negotiation, monitoring and enforcement needed to support a market exchange, whereas management costs (MC) are the equivalent costs associated with supervising the execution of the task internally. All things being equal, the lower TC relative to MC, the more organizations will tend to acquire goods and services from other firms as opposed to making them within the organization; conversely, the higher TC relative to MC, the more likely they will be internalized in a hierarchical organization. Hierarchy can be used to resolve differences among actors via managerial fiat, as well as to gain access to information that would otherwise not be available. Production costs, and especially the presence or absence of scale economies, is another significant factor affecting the boundaries of the firm.[3]

Governments, like private firms, are constantly faced with the question of which functions and services to in-source and which to out-source. Research and policy work in public administration emphasizes the way out-sourcing to more specialized, efficient private firms can reduce governments' costs while retaining and even enhancing their role in public policy implementation; there is also some literature on the reversal of privatizations (for instance, Warner and Hefetz, 2012).

Cybersecurity presents a complex picture with respect to in-sourcing and out-sourcing. One potentially relevant strand of TC theory emphasizes the way in-sourcing can eliminate uncertainty about the supply of or access to a required input. By taking direct control of security management, the government can be more certain that it is actually achieving security objectives that have become politically salient. Deep, operational knowledge of the specific configuration and architecture of a network might also be considered a form of asset specificity, which would militate against out-sourcing. On the other hand, computer and network security operations clearly involve forms of expertise that might be best concentrated in specialized firms and acquired through out-sourcing. Research in this area emphasizes how performance-based contracts can reconcile a managed security services provider's incentive to shirk and their need to maintain a good reputation to remain competitive (Ding and Yurcik, 2005).

Public vs. private security

One of the benefits of a firm-theoretic approach is that it highlights and clarifies an important distinction between two aspects of the federal government's pursuit of cybersecurity. On the one hand, the government can act to improve the security of its *own* networks. In this respect, security is pursued as a private good, not much differently from a private firm. On the other hand, the government can try to provide Internet security as a public good for the country as a whole.[4] The two objectives, though interrelated, must be kept distinct. The organizational arrangements that might optimize security for the federal government's own systems are not necessarily the same as those required for optimizing security across the Internet as a whole. Indeed, in this case study we can see tensions between those two agendas in play.[5]

The internally-oriented federal cybersecurity initiatives described below consisted largely of getting a diverse set of agencies and departments to participate in new, centrally-directed, common security arrangements. On the whole, security management responsibility for the government's own networks seems to have been drawn inward and made more hierarchical and coordinated. Governmental efforts to promote cybersecurity as a public good, on the other hand, had important implications for private sector suppliers of Internet access and the general public. Efforts by the military and the NSA to apply IDS/IPS to the public 'critical infrastructure' would have created new forms of surveillance or supervision of the private sector by the US government. There was, as we shall see, significant resistance to that.

The shifting of these boundaries is an accelerated repetition and temporal extension of what Dunn Cavelty described as a *threat frame*, that broadens the threat landscape from US government networks to critical infrastructure and finally to the entire society. Consequently, the distinction between internal and external threats and private and public spheres of action becomes contentious (Dunn Cavelty, 2008). While those boundaries are shifted and threats and enemies remain ambiguous, cybersecurity and national security tend to meld due to calls to use the military/intelligence expertise and capabilities to secure both US government networks and public infrastructure.

Method

This research follows a case study approach (Eisenhardt, 1989; Yin, 2008). To understand the organizational impact of the IDS/IPS initiatives, we first systematically reviewed the documentary evidence of the federal government's cybersecurity policy initiatives after 9/11. This included the high-level executive orders and Presidential directives as well as the legally-required privacy impact assessments filed regarding the Einstein program. We also conducted interviews with technology vendors, government officials, academics and activists involved in these initiatives during the summer of 2012. We categorized the Einstein program into three phases. Phase 1 corresponds to the implementation of

Einstein 1; phase 2 to the implementation of Einstein 2. Phase 3, which involved the third iteration of the Einstein program, we classify as a period of *blurred boundaries* between the government and the private sector. It includes the DIB/ECS program as well as Einstein 3 and focuses on the expansion of IDS/IPS into the private sector.

To track the first aspect of the research question, we have broken down the basic elements of government agency Internet access into a simplified list of component parts. For each of the phases noted above, we schematized the extent to which they were in-sourced and out-sourced. Tables with these schemata are found at the end of each section. Additionally, in the next section we explain more specifically the key economic components of an IDS/IPS system, and discuss the various modes of economic organization that might be associated with its implementation.

Deep packet inspection and the firm

Deep packet inspection (DPI) is a technology for scanning and analysing Internet traffic and making decisions about how to handle it in real time. It is an enabling technology that can be used for many different applications. For instance, in addition to detecting and blocking network security threats through IDS/IPS applications, it can be used to prevent exfiltration of private or classified information, for censorship and surveillance, for bandwidth management, for copyright policing, and for online behavioural advertising (Kuehn and Mueller, 2012; Mueller and Asghari, 2012; Mueller, Kuehn, and Santoso, 2012).

DPI capabilities were first developed for intrusion detection and prevention systems. IDS's allowed network operators to passively detect incoming or outgoing traffic associated with recognized forms of malware (viruses, Trojans, worms, and other dangerous codes). IPS's utilize IDS but supplement its recognition capabilities with programmed actions that stop or block the intrusion (Sourdis, 2007). Both IDS and IPS are based on signatures, a predefined set of values that describes a particular pattern in the network traffic. If the signature matches a particular pattern associated with malware or attacks, predefined actions are triggered. An IDS merely recognizes and reports suspect network activities, whereas an IPS takes automated actions to stop them. Thus, signature-based IDS/IPS can only prevent attacks previously known to the signature provider. Appendix B contains a sample signature. In organizing the implementation of a DPI capability, one must make decisions about two key aspects of the system. First, what is the source of the signatures that will be used to detect threats? Second, where will the DPI box itself be situated and who will be responsible for operating it?

With respect to the signatures, a number of options regarding the production and sharing of threat recognition information are possible. The government can produce its own signatures. Conversely, the government could stay out of signature production altogether and rely on private sector actors to produce signatures. Or there could be a mixed regime, with a variety of sources producing signatures. Aside from who produces them, there is the issue of how signatures are distributed or shared. The various parties can pool the signatures and share them freely, restrict their distribution, or share some and restrict others. We try to encapsulate these as nine options in the simplified matrix in Table 6.1; the darkened cell shows where we are in the real world.

Table 6.1 Possible methods of organizing IDS/IPS signature production

Signature producer	Shared	Not shared	Mixed
Government			
Private sector			
Both			

Source: Authors' elaboration.

As the empirical evidence will show, the production and sharing of threat information was a key point of negotiation and concern in the organization of cybersecurity implementations. Open sharing of signatures makes the most efficient use of a non-rival informational resource and may have good security results; however, the NSA insisted on keeping some of its signatures classified in order to prevent adversaries from knowing that it recognizes its exploits. Reliance on military or intelligence agency signatures and threat information would benefit from the specialized expertise of the agencies, but could also restrict sharing and use of the signatures, which can create their own set of security pathologies. There might also be a less than perfect match between the signatures produced by military and intelligence agencies and the actual threats and vulnerabilities routinely faced by the private sector and the public. In an environment of secrecy there is also the possibility of abuse of the signature production function for unlawful surveillance purposes.

Decisions about the operation of the DPI box also have significant implications for both efficiency and security. Is it located in the public ISP, where it can inspect traffic from any user, or is it confined to the organizational gateway of the government agency? Is the box administered by the ISP, or by the individual government agency at its link to the Internet, or by a centralized government agency working across multiple gateways and agencies? How are the signatures fed into the machine and how are they updated? If some signatures are classified special procedures must be in place to shield the information and restrict distribution. What are the policies that specific threat recognition alarms will trigger? How widespread are the notifications? Who must take action based on the notification? The empirical evidence below will show that these issues, too, loomed large in the implementation of the Einstein and DIB/ECS programs.

Due to privacy law considerations, the creation of signatures for the Einstein program follows a review process that addresses personally identifiable information (PII). PII can only be used upon approval and to detect targeted threats. The procedures in place are supposed to avoid the collection of irrelevant network traffic (DHS, 2012a). Bellovin et al. (2011) discussed the architecture and limitations of IDS/IPS systems, using the US example of the Einstein 3 program.

Cybersecurity policy and technology

In response to the developing threat landscape, intense policy making efforts took place over the last two Presidential administrations to improve the security cyberspace. What follows is a brief account of the major policy decisions and related technology deployments. Appendix C contains a timeline that depicts the major elements of the policy development.

Policy development

Our narrative begins with the 9/11 terrorist attacks in the US, which greatly affected both cyber- and physical security policy. In 2002, a secret executive order signed by then President Bush authorized the National Security Agency (NSA) to deploy DPI to intercept and inspect telecommunication and Internet networks without a court warrant. Domestic as well as foreign traffic was included in its scope. Deep packet inspection equipment was secretly installed at major network nodes with the cooperation of private US telecom firms AT&T, Verizon and BellSouth.

Monitoring domestic communication contravened NSA's governing law, the Foreign Intelligence Surveillance Act of 1978, (FISA). Once the program was exposed by a whistleblower, it fuelled fears that the NSA's spying capabilities were also directed towards American citizens and domestic communication (Klein, 2009; Landau, 2010: 2; Wu, 2010: 238). Fears and concerns about NSA involvement in cybersecurity efforts stemming from the warrantless wiretapping program played an important role in future negotiations over the Einstein program.

With the creation of the Department of Homeland Security (DHS) in late 2002, a 'National Strategy to Secure Cyberspace' was issued (DHS, 2003a). The Bush administration put forward a bottom-up approach by coordinated efforts with state and local governments and the private sector to address cybersecurity policy issues and challenges (Harknett and Stever, 2011). In the same year, the Federal Information Security Management Act (FISMA, 44 USC § 3541, et seq.) was enacted. FISMA required all federal agencies to implement effective information security controls to protect information and information systems. In late 2003, the DHS became responsible for coordinating plans to protect critical infrastructure (DHS, 2003b). In September 2003, the United States Computer Emergency Readiness Team (US-CERT) was formed as a partnership between the DHS and the private sector to coordinate response to Internet security threats. The Federal Computer Incident Response Center (FedCIRC) located at the General Service Administration (GSA) was the US-CERT's predecessor with similar duties: response coordination, incident reporting and sharing of vulnerability information across the federal agencies (Dacey, 2002).

Einstein 1: Early monitoring capabilities

The organized deployment of federal government-wide cybersecurity monitoring capabilities began in 2003 when US-CERT, the operational arm of the Department of Homeland Security's National Cyber Security Division (NCSD), developed and initiated the Einstein program (DHS, 2010a). The objectives of Einstein 1 were to improve cyberthreat monitoring and response capabilities at civilian federal government agencies by generating and sharing better information about network activity. For the agencies that installed a sensor, Einstein 1 automatically collected network flow information at Internet gateways, allowing US-CERT to correlate and analyse it to detect anomalies that might indicate security threats. Network flow information includes sending and receiving of IP addresses, sending and receiving of port numbers, a number indicating the protocol used, the number of packets and bytes sent, the start and end time of the connection, the name of the sensor that collected the information, and a few other items. Appendix A contains a more detailed explanation and example of a flow record.

In *firm-theoretic* terms, Einstein 1 established a specialized functional capability (US-CERT) within the civilian federal agencies. Flow records indicating malicious activities were sent to US-CERT for further investigation, which could then (in theory) coordinate threat mitigation with associated government networks and share network security information with the public and private sectors. But this was a passive data collection capability; it created records that could be shared and analysed by experts but did not fully leverage the state-firm's hierarchical organizing capabilities. Agency participation in the program was voluntary. Adoption by federal agencies remained at a low level, which was predictable given the budget and time constraints affecting agency managers.

As of 2005, only three agencies had deployed Einstein 1; as of December 2006, the circle of participating agencies had expanded to only eight out of several hundred (DHS, 2007). Furthermore, even though information was being collected, the procedures for sharing it in real time and for developing coordinated responses were not well developed. Neither the technology nor the organizational arrangements behind Einstein 1 automated response mechanisms. Finally, the initiative was confined to the civilian agencies and was not integrated or well-coordinated with the capabilities of military and intelligence agencies.

Einstein 2 and the trusted Internet connection initiative

Phase 2 of the state-firm's response involved greater consolidation of Internet access and greater automation and centralization of monitoring and control. In late November 2007, under the auspices of the Office of Management and Budget (OMB) and the DHS, a federal government-wide initiative known as the Trusted Internet Connections (TIC) program was instituted. TIC was aimed at consolidating external network access points and improving their security.[6] Up to this point, federal agencies could autonomously transact for their own

Internet connections. The number of such connections was approaching 5,000. The original target was 50 external access points. This is a reduction by a factor of 100 (from 5,000).[7]

The initial deadline for the TIC implementation across the federal government was June 2008, but was later postponed to December 2009 (GAO, 2010a). From a network security perspective, there are two reasons to consolidate external network connections: (1) a smaller number of external access points can be centrally monitored more easily and offers adversaries fewer targets for security exploits; and (2) the TIC locations can be used to deploy an IDS/IPS capability more economically. Aside from a few exceptions, the TIC program required external connections to be routed through approved TIC access points (GAO, 2010a).

The major formal policy milestone in the US debate on cybersecurity came in January 2008 with the still-classified Comprehensive National Cybersecurity Initiative (CNCI).[8] CNCI was based on National Security Presidential Directive 54 *Cyber Security and Monitoring* (NSPD 54) which was also referred to as Homeland Security Presidential Directive 23 'Cyber Security and Monitoring' (HSPD 23). The CNCI set in motion a dozen initiatives, centralized earlier efforts and integrated the Einstein program's progression towards IDS and IPS and the TIC Program's progression towards a lower number of external network gateways. Under CNCI, federal agencies can only obtain Internet access in four ways: (1) by becoming a TIC access provider (TICAP) after successful certification and providing their own access service; (2) by seeking access from another TICAP; (3) by obtaining access through an approved commercial provider through a Managed Trusted IP Service (MTIPS); or (4) some hybrid of the above (GAO, 2010a). Figure 6.1 shows the four options. The vast majority of agencies get access through a TICAP.[9] Commercial service providers ('Networx vendors') provide flexibility in obtaining access services; most agencies indicated that they will obtain managed security capabilities as part of their TIC implementation (GAO, 2010a). Small agencies may share TICs, while larger agencies may need several secured external Internet gateways.

The CNCI's vision was to manage the federal government's civilian agency networks as a single network. Concerns about privacy and civil liberties arose because CNCI remained classified. Briefly after CNCI was issued, public and closed Congressional hearings took place (US House of Representatives, 2008; US Senate, 2008). Newly-elected President Obama's Cyberspace Policy Review provided key recommendations with regards to CNCI and assured that attention was given to privacy rights and civil liberties (The White House, 2009b). The incoming Obama administration also addressed complaints about the previous administration/DHS's approach to taking too long. Consequently, the new administration shifted its policy efforts to what Harknett and Stever (2011) described as a top-down, rational, comprehensive approach by putting the White House in charge of cybersecurity. An early 2008 TIC evaluation report articulated the need for coordination regarding implementation of technical requirements, including 'deep packet inspection of encrypted sessions, storage volume requirements, uniform time services, the sharing and use of custom IDS signatures, and Sensitive Compartmentalized Information Facility (SCIF) requirements'. It also addressed the Einstein deployment and international TIC locations (DHS, 2008).

Based on IP address ranges, traffic is monitored to identify malicious traffic by deploying signature-based and anomaly-based IDS at the agency's TIC gateways. The scanning is not directly in-line; a temporary copy of the traffic is created and scanned for suspect patterns (Bradbury, 2009). As Bellovin et al. (2011) observed, cutting the number of external access points was a crucial

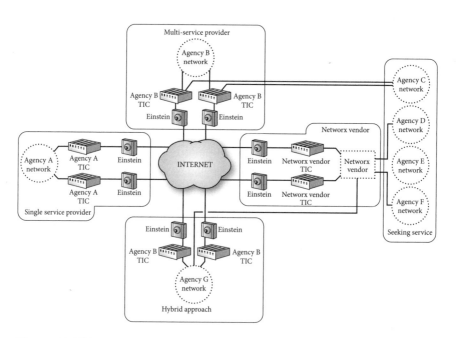

Figure 6.1 TIC access service options – interaction of TIC and Einstein

prerequisite for the Einstein 2 capability. It cut down the number of monitoring points, allowing more expensive and sophisticated detection technology to be deployed at those points. But it also posed challenges; the new gateways had to be secure and scalable enough to handle higher levels of network traffic; the routing architecture also had to be modified (Juniper Networks, 2008).

Einstein 2 strengthened US-CERT's ability to surveil security incidents across federal civilian networks. Its facilities combined commercial, off-the-shelf and government-developed technology. It deployed an intrusion-detection system that used DPI capabilities to scan for malicious activities in incoming and outgoing network traffic. Most of the network data scanned by Einstein 1 was contained in the packet header, but Einstein 2 looked inside the payload of the packet for signatures of threats. The ability to detect network security threats is based on a predefined set of custom signatures that formally describe malicious network traffic (DHS, 2012a). If a signature matches a specific network traffic pattern, US-CERT is alerted (for instance, a specific email attachment that contains a computer virus might trigger such a notice).

As of September 2009, none of the 23 reviewed agencies had met all TIC requirements. Sixteen agencies that opted to provide access themselves cut down the number of external access points from 3,286 to approximately 1,753 (GAO, 2010a). Similarly, agency participation in the Einstein effort lagged at the outset. Subsequently, Einstein 2 was made mandatory for all federal agencies, as part of a push to gain situational network security awareness (OMB, 2007). Notably, the Department of Defense and intelligence agencies were exempted from the Einstein program, as they already had their own IDS capabilities. As of September 2009, Einstein 2 was deployed at six agencies (GAO, 2010a). In 2011, 15 agencies providing Internet access and four private telecommunications service providers (Managed Trusted Internet Protocol Services) had fully deployed and activated Einstein 2 (GAO, 2011).

Blurring boundaries

In Phase 3, attention shifts from government agencies to the relationship with the private sector. The overlap and tensions between the federal government's narrower requirement to secure its own networks and its broader mandate to provide cybersecurity as a general public good create a period of confusion and negotiation. There were criticisms aired that the information sharing between the public and private sector were not working. There were 'research' initiatives that toyed with the idea of placing government-operated sensors to detect malicious network activities in private sector infrastructure. The NSA's role as a provider of threat signatures became more openly asserted and generated political concern. The federal government's cybersecurity efforts were extended to private firms in the so-called Defense Industrial Base (DIB). In this phase, the control of cybersecurity information and monitoring capabilities are re-negotiated among the public and private sector and, within the federal government, between the military and civilian branches. In this section we try to describe and explain the equilibrium that was reached.

Role of the NSA

The NSA, a military agency, took the lead in pushing a more expansive approach toward the achievement of public security, involving a stronger role for government in producing technology for the private sector and in monitoring private infrastructure. In September 2007 the *Baltimore Sun* newspaper revealed that Director of National Intelligence Mike McConnell, a former NSA chief, was coordinating a highly classified 'Cyber Initiative' with NSA, DHS and unspecified 'other federal agencies' to monitor civilian networks for unauthorized intrusions (Gorman, 2007). This foray into securing domestic private communications would be a significant change in NSA's role, which was supposed to be confined to foreign targets.

Coming not long after public exposure of the warrantless wiretapping program in late 2005, fears of privacy violations and government surveillance were aired. As Landau (2010: 119) pointed out, when asked 'how do you protect civilian networks without observing the traffic on them?' the administration was not forthcoming with an answer. The *Baltimore Sun* story was the first indication that efforts to secure cyberspace were not limited to US government networks (see also the next chapter in this book).

The NSA's role in domestic wiretapping was also demonstrated in the summer of 2007, when the controversial Protect America Act (PAA) (Pub. L. 110-055) was passed, thus making significant changes to FISA. A retroactive attempt to legalize what the Bush administration had done years before, PAA allowed warrantless wiretapping if it was 'reasonably believed' that one end was outside the US (Bellovin et al., 2008). In the meantime, an AT&T switching office in San Francisco was exposed as being involved in redirecting domestic traffic to NSA (Wolfson, 2007–8; Mossavar-Rahmani, 2008; Landau, 2010: 2).

Continuing in this vein, the summer of 2010 saw the NSA award a classified contract worth up to US$91 million and lasting at least through September 2014 to defence contractor Raytheon regarding protection of critical infrastructure (Gorman, 2010; NSA, 2012). The project, named 'Perfect Citizen', was to study sensors in critical infrastructure to detect malicious network activities, particularly utilities and the electrical power grid. Where the Einstein program focused on shielding federal communications networks, Perfect Citizen targeted sensitive control systems (SCS) or industrial control systems (ICS), including communications for supervisory control and data acquisition (SCADA) used for automated control and data collection of distributed utilities (NSA, 2010, 2012).[10] Of particular concern were control systems that were originally designed as independent, stand-alone units but were later connected to the Internet, sometimes without adopting necessary security requirements. Just as the prospect of extending Einstein 3 to the public Internet drew critical reaction, negative public reaction to Perfect Citizen forced NSA to respond that these were purely research efforts; real sensors would not be placed nor networks monitored in the private sector (Singel, 2010).

'The exercise'

In 2010 an attempt was launched to add intrusion prevention (IPS) capabilities to the existing IDS capabilities of the Einstein program. Like IDS, IPS makes use of deep packet inspection technology, but not only identifies but also acts upon predefined threat signatures. IPS was considered the third phase of the Einstein program.

A small-scale trial of IPS, referred to as 'The Exercise' in government memos, was conducted. A commercial Internet service provider (ISP) provided with Einstein capabilities redirected traffic to and from an undisclosed, single medium-sized federal civilian agency (DHS, 2010b). In the beginning of Einstein 3, in particular during 'The Exercise', commercial and government technologies were combined at the agency TICAPs; the trial used NSA-developed IPS technology. The network traffic in question was routed from the agency's TICAPs to a secured room within the access provider where the DHS itself operated the government-owned IPS boxes. After the network traffic passed through the intrusion prevention devices, it was directed back to the participating agency (DHS, 2010b).

As the federal government stood poised to implement Einstein 3 in full, fears were expressed by some prominent technical experts that government-controlled Einstein IDS/IPS capabilities would be extended into the private sector infrastructure (Bellovin et al., 2011). The legacy of mistrust generated by the NSA contributed to these fears. These kinds of concerns tended to push the administration to bring the civilian agency (DHS) into the lead over NSA as the intermediary between the private sector and the government in federal cyberse-curity efforts. While early instances of Einstein 3 relied heavily on government furnished equipment, in later instances technology use shifted significantly to ISP owned and operated equipment for active monitoring. Direct NSA partici-pation was reduced and only the DHS deployed signatures.

Government-private sector sharing of information

The issue of how information generated by IDS/IPS would be shared posed another area of blurred boundaries between the public and private sectors. As the Einstein program progressed, one report recommended DHS to evaluate 'the feasibility of sharing federally developed technology capabilities' with critical infrastructure providers (DHS, 2010a). An independent GAO report in 2010 unveiled crucial issues in the sharing of security incident information. It concluded that public-private partnerships intended to exchange timely and actionable cyber-threat information were not working (GAO, 2010b). While federal agencies were not meeting private sector expectations, some private companies were not willing to share sensitive, proprietary information with the government. A related 2008 GAO report had identified these challenges two years earlier, but was met with little interest (GAO, 2008). However, a report from the DHS' Inspector General revealed that even the sharing of cyber-threat information coming out of Einstein was marginal. Einstein was called an 'effective tool' while US-CERT was said to be 'unable to share near real time data and classified and detailed information to address security incidents' (Skinner, 2010; DHS, 2010c).

Einstein information is shared only within DHS; otherwise a Memorandum of Agreement is required. In early 2012, it was reported that international information-sharing agreements with Israel and India existed. US-CERT shared information with these two governments through the use of Einstein 2 technology (DHS, 2012a). Other DHS partnerships on cybersecurity with foreign governments, including Australia, Canada, Egypt, the Netherlands and Sweden, have existed since 2009 (Napolitano, 2013).

Extending network protection to defence contractors

Network protection efforts were also extended into the private sector through the Department of Defense, based in part on the evolving Einstein model. The networks and information systems of military contractors, known in Washington as the Defense Industrial Base (DIB) companies, contain sensitive US military information and intellectual property, and have been repeatedly targeted in cyber-attacks. In 2011, the Department of Defense conducted a pilot, referred to as DoD Defense Industrial Base Opt-in Pilot Exploratory Cybersecurity Initiative, under its DIB Cyber Security/Information Assurance (CS/IA) Program. During the 90-day voluntary pilot, Tier 1 Internet service providers deployed signatures provided by the NSA to monitor the participating DIB companies' networks (DoD, 2011).

The pilot contained network prevention capabilities, analogous to Einstein 3 but not in its full extent; as a senior DoD official stated '[...] by way of analog, it [DIB Opt-in Pilot] is looking for part of the dot-com to bring what Einstein 3 is supposed to bring to dot-gov' (Miller, 2011). According to a *Washington Post* article, AT&T, Verizon, and CenturyLink took part in this pilot to protect the networks of 15 defence contractors, among them Lockheed Martin, SAIC and Northrop Grumman (Nakashima, 2011). While the DIB companies obtained a higher degree of network security, network traffic monitoring was conducted by the ISPs, not DoD. The contractors were not required to report cybersecurity incidents detected during the DIB Opt-in Pilot to DoD.

In January 2012, it was announced that the Pentagon handed over the DIB Opt-in Pilot to the DHS to jointly undertake another proof of concept. Consequently, the pilot was renamed the 'Joint Cybersecurity Services Pilot (JCSP)' but participation in it remained voluntary. The operational relationships with the Internet service providers were shifted to DHS. Henceforth, DHS furnished unclassified and classified indicators to the Internet service providers which converted those into machine-readable signatures for their intrusion detection and prevention systems. DHS continued the two cyber-threat countermeasures in the JCSP that were already in operation at the Pentagon pilot, deployed at the Internet service provider site: first, the DNS sinkholing (if a signature matches outbound DNS requests to a known, malicious domain (for example, botnets, spyware), this traffic is redirected to a 'sinkhole server', effectively blocking DNS communications); and second, email filtering (if a signature matches an infected attachment of an incoming email, the messages is quarantined) (DHS, 2012b).

After the six-month joint proof of concept was completed, it was turned into a voluntary program. The 'Joint Cybersecurity Services Program (JCSP)' was opened up to all of the more than 200 eligible DIB companies in May 2012 (Fryer-Biggs, 2012). JCSP became the optional component known as the DIB Enhanced Cybersecurity Services (DECS) in the Defense Department's voluntary cyber-threat information and best practices sharing efforts (CS/IA) program. DHS acted as a point of contact for the participating Internet service providers – AT&T and CenturyLink – offering Einstein 3-like capabilities, while DoD managed the relations to the DIB companies (DoD, 2012a). DoD lacked the authority to require DIB companies to participate in DECS, but encouraged them to do so (DoD, 2012b). At the beginning of the new JCSP, emphasis was put on the DIB companies already participating in the CS/IA program, but the purpose of program was to broaden the protection to critical infrastructure (DHS, 2012c).

In February 2013, the White House issued executive order 13636 'Improving Critical Infrastructure Cybersecurity' and Presidential Policy Directive 21 'Critical Infrastructure Security and Resilience', effectively extending the program to all operators and owners of critical infrastructure and, once again, renaming the program. The program was now called 'Enhanced Cybersecurity Services (ECS)' (DHS, 2013; The White House, 2013). DHS will provide the same threat indicators with approved private Internet service providers that are used to protect civilian federal government networks; these Internet service providers then may enter contractual relations with providers of critical infra-structure (Napolitano, 2013). Defense contractors Lockheed Martin (2013), Raytheon (2013), Northrop Grumman (2013), and SAIC (2013) joined ranks with AT&T and CenturyLink as approved commercial service providers (CSPs) offering ECS to critical infrastructure operators. DHS uncovered plans that threat indicators will include classified software vulnerabilities, so-called zero day exploits (Menn, 2013).

For ECS participants this would increase their protection in an area that would have been extremely difficult to protect otherwise. The executive order is also seen as a reply to the failure of the controversial Cyber Intelligence Sharing and Protection Act (CISPA, H.R. 3523 and H.R. 624), a bill intended to foster sharing of cyber-threat information between the government and private companies. The executive order comes after a decade of legislative efforts; while legislative proposals were plenty, since FISMA in 2002 no major legislation has been passed that addresses cybersecurity specifically. The executive order neither grants expansive powers nor legal immunity to private companies. However, the Department of Justice has quietly issued so-called 2,511 letters to telecommunication companies, providing them legal immunity from violations under the US Wiretap Act (EPIC, 2013).

This policy and its technological consequences constitute a fundamental shift that institutionalizes how the US government and private companies share cyber-threat information and consequently how these networks are protected.[11] Adoption of the ECS program could become mandatory for companies that are regulated by federal agencies with responsibilities towards securing critical infrastructure; this might include companies in specific sectors, such as the defence, health, transportation, chemical and food industries (Perera, 2013).

Discussion

This discussion section will briefly review the development of the Einstein and the ECS program with regards to organizational changes and further the discussion on related transaction costs. Table 6.2 provides a summary of the two different programs and their iterations.

The provisioning of secure Internet access, first for USG networks and later for DIB companies and private operators for critical infrastructure (CI), can be conceptualized as four components of a bundle of products and services. It includes: (1) transport (i.e. connectivity to the rest of the Internet); (2) devices and applications; (3) gateway management and configuration (firewalls, security, identity); and (4) information about threats and anomalies. The sourcing of the components of this bundle reflects organizational changes and the expansion of cybersecurity. Table 6.3 tabulates these components and categorizes for each phase whether or not they are in-sourced (IN), out-sourced (OUT), mixed (MIX) or projected (PROJ); also the changes are briefly described. By 'projected' we mean that the federal government extended supply, standards or requirements *to* the private sector.

Transaction costs considerations

While the federal government never attempted to extend its control or management to Internet connectivity (transport) or to devices and applications, it established firmer hierarchical control over the gateways between federal

Table 6.2 Overview Einstein and ECS programs

Networks	Program phase	Development Started	Deployment Launched	Description
USG Federal Civilian Networks	Einstein 1	2003	2005	(Block 1.0) Network Flow Information ('NetFlow'), including centralized data storage.
	Einstein 2	2008	2008	(Block 2.0)Intrusion Detection System, to assess network traffic for malicious activities; (Block 2.1) Security Incident and Event Management (SIEM), to enable data aggregation, correlation, and visualization; (Block 2.2) to augment threat information visualization and to provide mechanism for information sharing and collaboration.
	Einstein 3	2010	2012	(Block 3.0) Intrusion Prevention System.
Private Sector Networks	Enhanced Cybersecurity Services (ECS)	2011	2013	ECS was originally introduced by the DoD as the DIB Opt-in Pilot that was handed over in 2012 to DHS as Joint Cybersecurity Services Pilot (JCSP) and evolved into the Joint Cybersecurity Services Program (JCSP), the DIB Enhanced Cybersecurity Services (DECS), and most recently the Enhanced Cybersecurity Services (ECS). ECS has Einstein 3-like capabilities.

Source: Authors' elaboration.

Table 6.3 Changes in pattern of secure Internet access production for government agencies

	Pre-Einstein	Einstein 1	Einstein 2	Einstein 3	ECS	Changes
Networks		USG networks			Private networks	
Boundaries	within USG			blurred, extended		
			Source			
Components						**Changes**
Transport	OUT	OUT	OUT	OUT	–	From agency level autonomy to TICAP requirements for USG networks and accreditation for CSPs.
Devices and applications	OUT	OUT	OUT	OUT	–	Agency level decisions within FISMA standards; OMB audits for USG networks. Separate norms for CI.
Gateway management and configuration	MIX	MIX	IN	PROJ	PROJ	From variation across agencies, to agency level decisions within FISMA standards; OMB audits, to TIC program. Separate norms for CI.
Information about threats and anomalies	MIX	IN	IN	PROJ	PROJ	From ad hoc sharing across agencies to US-CERT as coordinator for information sharing to mandatory use of Einstein 2 for USG networks. Voluntary for DIB and CI.

Source: Authors' elaboration.

networks and the public Internet, which made it easier and more efficient to implement IDS/IPS throughout the federal government. After the high initial set-up costs of these programs, transaction costs to interface with private sector Internet services probably declined, as IDS/IPS came integrated in standardized access services from various commercial Internet service providers. Thus, switching costs or lock-in effects stemming from those managed, out-sourced cybersecurity services may be lower than earlier literature on this topic would suggest.

After establishing this capability for federal networks, and sometimes in parallel with the Einstein program, the military and defence agencies moved to project its gateway management and signature production and scanning capabilities into private sector networks. Some of the more ambitious thrusts in this direction (for instance, Perfect Citizen) were blunted by public pressure but ISPs serving government agencies and defence industry firms gain access to classified and unclassified cyber-threat information provided by US-CERT and compiled by the US intelligence community.

Conclusion

Following this book's theme on security in cyberspace, this chapter focused on the infrastructure level, exploring the way cybersecurity technology alters organizational relationships. It examined how deep packet inspection capabilities in the form of intrusion detection and prevention systems were deployed in US government networks. Co-evolving with this technology development and deployment were various cybersecurity and national security policies. As part of the Comprehensive National Cybersecurity Initiative (CNCI), the US government decided to monitor its federal civilian networks with IDS/IPS capabilities. These capabilities were advanced and extended into private networks via commercial Internet service providers. The NSA and DHS as points of contact provided approved Internet service providers with unclassified and classified cyber-threat indicators and signatures to protect federal government networks, DoD defence contractors and operators of critical infrastructure.

Over several phases from 2003 to 2013, responsibilities and organizational boundaries were reassigned and negotiated among different actors. Negotiations focused on the following points: where would the DPI equipment be located? Who would be responsible for operating it? How would it interact with prior security measures? How would compliance with privacy laws be taken into account; how are cybersecurity risks distributed; and how is the control over the new cybersecurity capabilities assigned; what would be classified and what would be open?

The initial steps of the IDS/IPS implementation involved consolidating the federal government's Internet access points and asserting stronger and more centralized control over each agency's arrangements. As the Einstein program went through three different phases, the DPI technology required greater coordination and some degree of organizational centralization. Responsibilities for monitoring and responding to threats are reassigned from individual government and private entities to an intermediary entity, the US-CERT. This equates to a shift from cybersecurity self-production to a more coordinated and consolidated responsibility for US-CERT, which takes a central role in the exchange of information from all levels of government, industry, academia and international partners. It releases alerts about cyber threats and attacks, but also became the central point of contact for the deployment of Einstein. The relationships between DHS, the military agencies and the intelligence community were progressively restructured in ways that changed the relationship between ISPs and government agencies. As the program progressed, the capabilities were continuously extended to include private Internet service providers, state government networks, defence contractors and finally private sector operators of critical infrastructure.

This proved to be politically sensitive and generated pushback from civil society and the private sector. In particular, due to privacy and surveillance concerns the civilian agency DHS had to serve as the 'trusted intermediary' between the private sector actors and the other government agencies, especially the military and intelligence-oriented ones. The ISPs retained control of the DPI equipment but were given signatures by the military and civilian agencies.[12]

The key site of tension and negotiation was the supply of the threat signatures and the situation of the signature monitoring capabilities. In the last phase we saw those capabilities go from being internalized by the federal government and detached from the private sector, to being placed in the private sector network operators' infrastructure but controlled by the government, to being delegated to the private sector actors while making use of some government-supplied signatures, both classified and unclassified.

In this chapter, we argued that these policy changes are fundamental, leading to greater interdependence among federal agencies and between federal government and privately-supplied infrastructure. The effects of this extension are observable on several independent levels: the scope of monitored networks; the scope of technological capabilities that determines what can and cannot be monitored; a shift from direct monitoring of networks to an indirect, delegated monitoring through commercial Internet service providers; and a switch from voluntary participation to mandatory requirements of such programs. Establishing norms in the form of technology deployments, formal organizational agreements, Presidential directives and executive orders and pending cybersecurity legislation are manifestations of the institutionalization of cybersecurity practices.

Depending on one's view, when government agencies seize control over cybersecurity in privately owned Internet and other critical infrastructure, the shifting of boundaries comes with certain benefits or costs. Risk and control are redistributed; some would argue that this reallocation is unilateral. Given the different risk profiles from the military/intelligence, civilian government and private sector but just one infrastructure, securitization of one area affects other interdependent areas accordingly. While the US military/intelligence saw the early Einstein 3 pilots as a model of something bigger, extendable to critical infrastructure, opponents pointed out a narrow path between protecting networks and gathering intelligence information while monitoring them.

Notes

*   The authors would like to thank the four anonymous reviewers from the Twelfth Workshop on the Economics of Information Security 2013, where an earlier version of this chapter was first presented. This work has received financial support from the US National Science Foundation (Award SES-1026916). The opinions expressed here are those of the authors and do not necessarily represent those of the National Science Foundation.

1   In other research, we have argued that DPI is a potentially disruptive technology due to its clash with three pre-established principles of Internet governance: the end-to-end argument, users' expectations regarding the confidentiality of their communication, and the legal immunities offered ISPs for the actions of their users. As a potentially disruptive technology, DPI may dramatically change the architecture, governance and use of the Internet. At the same time, it is also possible that DPI will be domesticated and regulated in ways that will make its use consistent with the principles and norms of the existing Internet. The research attempts to determine whether the use of DPI catalyses changes in law, regulation

and governance of Internet service providers, or whether those pre-established principles act to curb or limit the use of DPI. See http://deeppacket.info

2 We use the term 'public goods' reluctantly because of the huge disjunction between the formal economic definition of a public good and the goods that states actually provide. Many if not most of the services the state provides do not qualify as public goods, in that they are neither non-rival in consumption nor non-exclusive. Colloquially, however, it has become common to deem anything the state provides as a public good precisely because the state provides it.

3 As Demsetz (1988) has noted, even if transaction costs are zero, goods or service might still be produced by a firm if there are increasing returns to scale, as demand for additional units of the good can more efficiently be met by expanding a firm's output as opposed to purchasing the service from diverse smaller suppliers in a market.

4 The idea of 'cybersecurity in one country' is probably an oxymoron; any attempt to provide cybersecurity as a public good would probably have to entail transnational efforts.

5 Public and private security can be complements. While security is generally considered a public good and one of the primary functions of the state, it is also true that both public and private goods are usually employed to fulfil the public's demand for security. Protection against crime, for example, is provided by bodyguards, watchdogs, alarms and locks as well as by the police. Abstract arguments that security is a public good tell us very little about which mix of public and private security measures is optimal.

6 All federal agencies, except for the Department of Defense, were required to implement the TIC initiative (GAO, 2010a).

7 As of January 2008, over 4,300 connections existed; this number was reduced by May 2008 to 2,758; the revised target number of connections is smaller or equal to 100 (DHS, 2008).

8 A summary of the CNCI was declassified and made available to the public by the Obama Administration in 2010 (The White House, 2010).

9 As of 2008, 144 federal agencies (35 per cent of solicited agencies) reported that 82 per cent will seek service, where as 15 per cent will provide single service and 3 per cent will provide multi service (DHS, 2008).

10 The US-CERT has a specialized program, the Control Systems Security Program (CSSP), which addresses control systems within the US critical infrastructure, the Industrial Control Systems CERT (ICS-CERT). See http://ics-cert.us-cert.gov

11 The executive order includes critical infrastructure providers and all private and public companies that 'transport information electronically'.

12 The 2013 NSA surveillance scandal (Gellman and Poitras, 2013; Greenwald and

MacAskill, 2013) heightened public attention on the dilemma between security and surveillance. Leaked NSA information showed that the NSA and the FBI were accessing stored, comprehensive Internet communications on servers of nine leading US Internet companies. While there seems to be no link between the NSA surveillance scandal and the programs considered in this chapter, it is likely that the new public awareness regarding the extent of the surveillance and the technical capabilities may shape the public perception on DPI-enabled cybersecurity and potential risks to civil liberties.

References

Auster, R. D. and M. Silver (1979), *The State as a Firm: Economic Forces in Political Development* (Vol. 3), The Hague: Martinus Nijhoff.

Bellovin, S. M., M. A. Blaze, W. Diffie, S. Landau, P. Neumann and J. Rexford (2008), 'Risking communications security: potential hazards of the protect America act', *IEEE Security and Privacy*, 6: 24–33.

Bellovin, S. M., S. O. Bradner, W. Diffie, S. Landau and J. Rexford (2011), 'Can it really work? problems with extending Einstein 3 to critical infrastructure', *Harvard National Security Journal*, 3: 1–38.

Bradbury, S. G. (2009), 'Legal Issues Relating to the Testing, Use, and Deployment of an Intrusion-Detection System (Einstein 2.0) to Protect Unclassified Computer Networks in the Executive Branch', Department of Justice, Opinions of the Office of Legal Counsel, in Vol. 33, 9 January 2009, www.justice.gov/olc/2009/e2-issues.pdf (accessed 30 August 2013).

Dacey, R. F. (2002), 'Critical Infrastructure Protection, Significant Homeland Security Challenges Need to Be Addressed', Testimony July 9, before the Subcommittee on Oversight and Investigations, Committee on Energy and Commerce, House of Representatives, www.gao.gov/assets/110/109467.pdf (accessed 1 September 2013).

Demsetz, H. (1988), 'The theory of the firm revisited', *Journal of Law, Economics and Organization*, 4: 141–61.

DHS (2003a), 'National Strategy to Secure Cyberspace', Department of Homeland Security, 14 February 2003, www.dhs.gov/files/publications/editorial_0329.shtm (accessed 30 August 2013).

—(2003b), 'Homeland Security Presidential Directive-7 (HSPD 7)', Critical Infrastructure Identification, Prioritization, and Protection, 17 December 2003, www.dhs.gov/homeland-security-presidential-directive-7 (accessed 1 September 2013).

—(2007), 'Challenges Remain in Securing the Nation's Cyber Infrastructure', Department of Homeland Security, Office of the Inspector General (OIG-07-48),

June, http://web.archive.org/web/20090326172325/http://www.dhs.gov/xoig/assets/mgmtrpts/OIG_07-48_Jun07.pdf (accessed 1 September 2013).

—(2008), 'Trusted Internet Connections (TIC) Initiative, Statement of Capability Evaluation Report', Department of Homeland Security, 4 June 2008, www.whitehouse.gov/sites/default/files/omb/assets/egov_docs/2008_TIC_SOC_EvaluationReport.pd (accessed 1 September 2013).

—(2010a), 'Privacy Impact Assessment Update for the EINSTEIN 1: Michigan Proof of Concept', Department of Homeland Security, 19 February 2010, www.dhs.gov/xlibrary/assets/privacy/privacy_pia_nppd_einstein1michigan.pdf (accessed 1 September 2013).

—(2010b), 'Privacy Impact Assessment for the Initiative Three Exercise', Department of Homeland Security, 18 March 2010, www.dhs.gov/xlibrary/assets/privacy/privacy_pia_nppd_initiative3exercise.pdf (accessed 1 September 2013).

—(2010c), 'US Computer Emergency Readiness Team Makes Progress in Securing Cyberspace, but Challenges Remain (OIG-10-94)', Department of Homeland Security, Office of Inspector General, June, http://web.archive.org/web/20100705034034/http://www.dhs.gov/xoig/assets/mgmtrpts/OIG_10-94_Jun10.pdf (accessed 1 September 2013).

—(2012a), 'Privacy Compliance Review of the EINSTEIN Program', Department of Homeland Security, 3 January 2012, www.dhs.gov/xlibrary/assets/privacy/privacy_privcomrev_nppd_ein.pdf (accessed 8 September 2013).

—(2012b), 'Privacy Impact Assessment for the National Cyber Security Division Joint Cybersecurity Services Pilot (JCSP)', Department of Homeland Security, 13 January 2012, www.dhs.gov/xlibrary/assets/privacy/privacy_nppd_jcsp_pia.pdf (accessed 8 September 2013).

—(2012c), 'Privacy Impact Assessment Update for the Joint Cybersecurity Services Program (JCSP), Defense Industrial Base (DIB) –Enhanced Cybersecurity Services (DECS)', Department of Homeland Security, 18 July 2012, www.dhs.gov/xlibrary/assets/privacy/privacy-pia-update-nppd-jcps.pdf (accessed 8 September 2013).

—(2013), 'Privacy Impact Assessment for the Enhanced Cybersecurity Services (ECS)', Department of Homeland Security, 16 January 2013, www.dhs.gov/sites/default/files/publications/privacy/privacy_pia_nppd_ecs_jan2013.pdf (accessed 8 September 2013).

Ding, W. and W. Yurcik (2005), 'Outsourcing Internet Security: The Effect of Transaction Costs on Managed Service Providers', Paper presented at the International Conference on Telecommunication Systems – Modeling and Analysis, Dallas, TX, 17–20 November.

DoD (2011), 'Privacy Impact Assessment for the Defense Industrial Base (DIB) Cyber Security/Information Assurance Activities', Department of Defense, http://dodcio.defense.gov/Portals/0/Documents/DIB%20CS-IA%20PIA_FINAL_signed_30jun2011_VMSS_GGMR_RC.pdf (accessed 8 September 2013).

—(2012a), 'DIB Enhanced Cybersecurity Services (DECS) Procedures', Department of Defense, www.dc3.mil/dcise/DIB%20Enhanced%20Cybersecurity%20Services%20 Procedures.pdf (accessed 8 September 2013).

—(2012b), 'Defense Industrial Base Cyber Security, Memorandum', Department of Defense, 31 October, http://www.acq.osd.mil/dpap/policy/policyvault/OSD012537-12-RES.pdf (accessed 8 September 2013).

Dunn Cavelty, M. (2008), *Cybersecurity and Threat Politics: US Efforts to Secure the Information Age*, London: Routledge.

Eisenhardt, K. M. (1989), 'Building Theories from Case Study Research', *The Academy of Management Review*, 14, 532–550.

EPIC (2013), 'EPIC FOIA Request Reveals Details About Government Cybersecurity Program', Electronic Privacy Information Center, 24 April 2013, http://epic. org/2013/04/epic-foia-request-reveals-deta.html (accessed 9 September 2013).

Forte, F. (2010), *Principles of Public Economics: A Public Choice Approach*, Cheltenham and Northampton, NH: Edward Elgar.

Fryer-Biggs, Z. (2012), 'Cyber Sharing Program Formally Expanded', *DefenseNews*, 11 May 2012, www.defensenews.com/article/20120511/DEFREG02/305110001/Cyber-Sharing-Program-Formally-Expanded (accessed 9 September 2013).

GAO (2008), 'Cyber Analysis and Warning: DHS Faces Challenges in Establishing a Comprehensive National Capability (GAO-08-588)', Government Accountability Office, 31 July 2008, www.gao.gov/products/GAO-08-588 (accessed 9 September 2013).

—(2010a), 'Information Security – Concerted Effort Needed to Consolidate and Secure Internet Connections at Federal Agencies (GAO 10-237)', Government Accountability Office, 12 March 2010, www.gao.gov/new.items/d10237.pdf (accessed 9 September 2013).

—(2010b), 'Critical Infrastructure Protection – Key Private and Public Cyber Expectations Need to Be Consistently Addressed (GAO-10-628)', Government Accountability Office, 15 July 2010, www.gao.gov/products/GAO-10-628 (accessed 9 September 2013).

—(2011), 'Progress Made and Work Remaining in Implementing Homeland Security Missions 10 Years after 9/11 (GAO 11-881)', Government Accountability Office, 7 September 2011, www.gao.gov/products/GAO-11-881 (accessed 9 September 2013).

Gellman, B. and L. Poitras (2013), 'US, British Intelligence Mining Data from Nine US Internet Companies in Broad Secret Program', *The Washington Post*, 6 June 2013, http://articles.washingtonpost.com/2013-06-06/news/39784046_1_prism-nsa-u-s-servers (accessed 10 September 2013).

Gorman, S. (2007), 'NSA to Defend Against Hackers: Privacy Fears Raised as Spy Agency Turns to System Protection', *The Baltimore Sun*, 20 September 2007, http:// articles.baltimoresun.com/2007-09-20/news/0709200117_1_homeland-national-security-agency-intelligence-agencies (accessed 10 September 2013).

—(2010), 'US Plans Cyber Shield for Utilities, Companies', *Wall Street Journal*, 8 July 2010, http://online.wsj.com/article/SB10001424052748704545004575352983850463108.html (accessed 10 September 2013).

Greenwald, G. and E. MacAskill (2013), 'NSA Prism Program Taps in to User Data of Apple, Google and Others', *The Guardian*, 6 June 2013, www.theguardian.com/world/2013/jun/06/us-tech-giants-nsa-data (accessed 10 September 2013).

Harknett, R. J. and J. A. Stever (2011), 'The new policy world of cybersecurity', *Public Administration Review*, May/June, 455–60.

Juniper Networks (2008), 'Juniper Networks Trusted Internet Connection (TIC) Solution', Technical document, www.juniper.net/us/en/local/pdf/solutionbriefs/3510299-en.pdf (accessed 10 September 2013).

Klein, M. (2009), *Wiring Up The Big Brother Machine ... And Fighting It*, North Charleston, SC: BookSurge Publishing.

Kuehn, A. (2013), 'Extending Cybersecurity, Securing Private Internet Infrastructure: The US Einstein Program and its Implications for Internet Governance', in R. Radu, J. M. Chenou, R. H. Weber (eds), *The Evolution of Global Internet Policy: New Principles and Forms of Governance in the Making?*, Zürich: Schulthess, Publikationen aus dem Zentrum für Informations- und Kommunikationsrecht der Universität Zürich.

Kuehn, A. and M. Mueller (2012), 'Profiling the Profilers: Deep Packet Inspection and Behavioral Advertising in Europe and the United States', http://dx.doi.org/10.2139/ssrn.2014181 (accessed 10 September 2013).

Kuerbis, B. and M. Mueller (2011), 'Negotiating a new governance hierarchy: an analysis of the conflicting incentives to secure internet routing', *Communications & Strategies*, 81: 125–42.

Landau, S. (2010), *Surveillance or Security?*, Cambridge, MA: MIT Press.

Lockheed, Martin (2013), 'Lockheed Martin Named as a Commercial Cyber Security Provider by Dept. of Homeland Security', Media release, 28 February 2013, www.lockheedmartin.com/us/news/press-releases/2013/february/isgs-dhs-cyber-0228.html (accessed 10 September 2013).

Menn, J. (2013), 'US to Protect Private Sector from Software Attacks', Reuters, 15 May 2013, http://www.reuters.com/article/2013/05/15/us-cyber-summit-flaws-idUSBRE94E11B20130515 (accessed 10 September 2013).

Miller, J. (2011), 'Budget Request for U.S. Cyber Command', Statement, 16 March 2011, before Committee on Armed Services, Subcommittee on Emerging Threats and Capabilities, House of Representatives, www.fas.org/irp/congress/2011_hr/cybercom.pdf (accessed 10 September 2013).

Mossavar-Rahmani, S. (2008), 'The protect America act: one nation under surveillance', *Loyola of Los Angeles Entertainment Law Review*, 29(1).

Mueller, M. L. and H. Asghari (2012), 'Deep packet inspection and bandwidth management: battles over bittorrent in Canada and the United States', *Telecommunications Policy*, 36: 462–475.

Mueller, M. L., A. Kuehn and S. M. Santoso (2012), 'Policing the network: using DPI for copyright enforcement', *Surveillance and Society*, 9(4).

Nakashima, E. (2011), 'NSA Allies with Internet Carriers to Thwart Cyber Attacks Against Defense Firms', *Washington Post*, 16 June 2011, www.washingtonpost.com/national/major-internet-service-providers-cooperating-with-nsa-on-monitoring-traffic/2011/06/07/AG2dukXH_story.html (accessed 11 September 2013).

Napolitano, J. (2013), 'The Cybersecurity Partnership Between the Private Sector and Our Government: Protecting Our National and Economic Security', Testimony of DHS Secretary, 7 March 2013, before Committee on Commerce, Science, and Transportation and Committee on Homeland Security and Governmental Affairs, Senate, hwww.dhs.gov/news/2013/03/07/written-testimony-dhs-secretary-janet-napolitano-senate-committee-homeland-security (accessed 11 September 2013).

Northrop Grumman (2013), 'Northrop Grumman Joins Department of Homeland Security Program to Bolster Cyber Protections for U.S. Critical Infrastructure', Media release, 13 May 2013, http://investor.northropgrumman.com/phoenix.zhtml?c=112386&p=irol-newsArticle&ID=1818734 (accessed 11 September 2013).

NSA (2010), 'A Framework for Assessing and Improving the Security Posture of Industrial Control Systems (ICS)', National Security Agency, Systems and Network Analysis Center, Version 1.1, 20 August, www.nsa.gov/ia/_files/ics/ics_fact_sheet.pdf (accessed 11 September 2013).

—(2012), 'FOIA Case 62332B, 'Statement of Work for (U) PERFECTCITIZEN. September 8, 2009', National Security Agency, 18 December, http://epic.org/foia/nsa/NSA-PerfectCitizen-FOIA_Docs.pdf (accessed 11 September 2013).

OMB (2007), 'Memorandum M-08-05, Implementation of Trusted Internet Connections (TIC)', Office of Management and Budget, 20 November 2007, http://georgewbush-whitehouse.archives.gov/omb/memoranda/fy2008/m08-05.pdf (accessed 11 September 2013).

Perera, D. (2013), 'Cybersecurity Framework Could Be Mandatory for Some Companies', FiecreGovernmentIT, 14 February 2013, www.fiercegovernmentit.com/story/cybersecurity-framework-could-be-mandatory-some-companies/2013-02-14 (accessed 11 September 2013).

Raytheon (2013), 'Raytheon Collaborates with DHS To Bolster Cyber Resiliency for Nation's Most Critical infrastructure', Media release, 1 March 2013, http://investor.raytheon.com/phoenix.zhtml?c=84193&p=irol-newsArticle&id=1791437 (accessed 11 September 2013).

SAIC (2013), 'SAIC Signs Agreement With Department of Homeland Security To Be A Commercial Service Provider', Media release, 15 May 2013, http://investors.saic.com/phoenix.zhtml?c=193857&p=RssLanding&cat=news&id=1820622 (accessed 11 September 2013).

Singel, R. (2010), 'NSA Denies It Will Spy on Utilities', Wired, Threat Level, 9 July 2010, www.wired.com/threatlevel/2010/07/nsa-perfect-citizen-denial (accessed 11 September 2013).

Skinner, R. L. (2010), 'Cybersecurity: DHS' Role, Federal Efforts, And National Policy', Statement of DHS Inspector General, 16 June 2010, before Committee on Homeland Security, House of Representatives, http://www.gpo.gov/fdsys/pkg/CHRG-111hhrg64697/pdf/CHRG-111hhrg64697.pdf (accessed 11 September 2013).

Sourdis, I. (2007), 'Designs and algorithms for packet and content inspection', PhD Dissertation, Delft: TU Delft.

US House of Representatives (2008), 'The Cyber Initiative. Homeland Security Committee', Hearing, 28 February 2008, http://web.archive.org/web/20080326202649/http://homeland.house.gov/Hearings/index.asp?id=118 (accessed 11 September 2013).

US Senate (2008), 'NSPD-54/HSPD-23 and the Comprehensive National Cybersecurity Initiative', Homeland Security and Governmental Affairs Committee, Classified Hearing, 4 March 2008, http://web.archive.org/web/20080325202700/http://hsgac.senate.gov/index.cfm?Fuseaction=Hearings.Detail&HearingID=528 (accessed 11 September 2013).

Warner, M. E. and A. Hefetz (2012), 'In-sourcing and outsourcing: the dynamics of privatization among US municipalities 2002–2007', *Journal of the American Planning Association*, 78: 313–27.

White House (The) (2009a), 'Remarks by the President on Securing our Nation's Cyber Infrastructure', Washington, DC, 29 May 2009, http://www.whitehouse.gov/the_press_office/Remarks-by-the-President-on-Securing-Our-Nations-Cyber-Infrastructure (accessed 11 September 2013).

—(2009b), 'Cyberspace Policy Review. Assuring a Trusted and Resilient Information and Communications Infrastructure', Washington, DC, 29 May 2009, www.whitehouse.gov/assets/documents/Cyberspace_Policy_Review_final.pdf (accessed 11 September 2013).

—(2010), 'The Comprehensive National Cybersecurity Initiative', Washington, DC, 2 March 2010, www.whitehouse.gov/sites/default/files/cybersecurity.pdf (accessed 11 September 2013).

—(2013), 'Executive Order – Improving Critical Infrastructure Cybersecurity', Washington, DC, 12 February 2013, www.whitehouse.gov/the-press-office/2013/02/12/executive-order-improving-critical-infrastructure-cybersecurity (accessed 11 September 2013).

Williamson, O. E. and S. G. Winter (1993), *The Nature of the Firm: Origins, Evolution, and Development*, New York: Oxford University Press.

Wolfson, S. (2007–8), 'The NSA, AT&T, and the secrets of room 641A', *I/S: A Journal of Law and Policy for the Information Society*, 3 Winter.

Wu, T. (2010), *The Master Switch: The Rise and Fall of Information Empires*, New York: Alfred A. Knopf.

Yin, R. K. (2008), *Case Study Research: Design and Methods*, 4th edn, Thousand Oaks, CA: Sage.

Appendix A: Sample flow record

Sample flow record and explanation as provided in DHS Privacy Impact Assessments for Einstein 1and 2. Source: DHS (2010a).

Sample Flow Record

127.0.0.1|192.168.0.20|52119|25|6|10|600|S|2008/04/28T00:02:47.958|44.9
85|2008/04/28T00:03:32.943|SENSOR1|out|S|
sIP|dIP|sPort|dPort|protocol|packets|bytes|flags|sTime|dur|eTime|sensor
|type|initialFlags|

Explanation of sample flow record

- 127.0.0.1 (sIP) IP of Computer who is the source of the connection
- 192.168.0.20 (dIP) IP of the computer who is the destination of the connection
- 52119 (sPort) Port the connection was initiated on by the source computer
- 25 (dPort) Port the connection was received on by the destination computer
- 6 (protocol) Protocol number, the number is based on the protocol being used to transport the data (6 = TCP, 1 = ICMP, 17 = UDP)
- 10 (packets) Count of total number of packets seen in this single connection (calculated by the sensor)
- 600 (bytes) Count of total number of bytes seen in this single connection (calculated by the sensor)
- S (flags) Aggregation of all flags seen in this single connection. Flags describe what happened in the connection
- 2008/04/28T00:02:47.958 (sTime) Start time of the connection, Universal Timestamp added by sensor to indicate when the connection was started
- 44.985 (dur) Duration of the connection, this field is calculated (dur = eTime – sTime)
- 2008/04/28T00:03:32.943 (eTime) End time of the connection, Universal Timestamp added by sensor to indicate when the connection was ended

- SENSOR1 (sensor) Name of the Sensor that collected the data, this field is added by the sensor
- out (type) Direction of the traffic (types include 'in, inweb, inicmp, out, outweb, outicmp, int2int, ext2ext')
- S (initialFlags) First flag seen in the connection, this is only based on the first packet of the connection

Flag Markers and their meanings:

- C = CWR – Congestion Window Reduced; E = ECE – Explicit Congestion Notification echo; U = URG – Urgent; A = ACK – Acknowledgement; P = PSH – Push; R = RST – Reset; S = SYN – Synchronize; F = FIN – Finished

Appendix B: Sample signature

Sample signature and explanation as provided in DHS Privacy Impact Assessment for Einstein 3. Source: DHS (2010b).

For illustrative purposes only, the following is an example of a commercially available signature. (This is not a signature the US-CERT intends to use.)

Signature:

alert tcp any any -> $HOME_NET 443 (msg: "DoS Attempt";
flow:to_server, established; content:"'|16 03 00|'"; offset:0; depth:3;
content:"'|01|'"; within:1; distance:2; byte_jump:1,37,relative,align;
byte_test:2,>,255,0,relative; reference:cve; classtype:attempted-dos;
sid:2000016; rev:5;)

Explanation of Signature:

- Alert: Type of IDS Event
- tcp: Protocol being examined
- any: Any source IP
- any: Any source port
- ->:   Direction (points to @HOME_NET which indicates inbound)
- $HOME_NET: A variable which is defined by the IDS as the subnets that make up the internal network
- 443:   Destination port traffic is bound for

- msg: 'DoS Attempt':   Name of the alert that is sent to the console (for humans reading the alert console)

The remaining fields of the string tells the IDS what to look for, the breakdown of the commands and instructs the IDS where in the packet to look for the text.

This signature example tells the IDS to alert on any external IP on any external port that sends traffic to the home network, on port 443, with the text – '|16 03 00|', and the text – '|01|' within certain parameters and offsets. The alert name is defined as – 'DoS Attempt' and references CVE, SID:2000016, revision 5.

Appendix C: Timeline

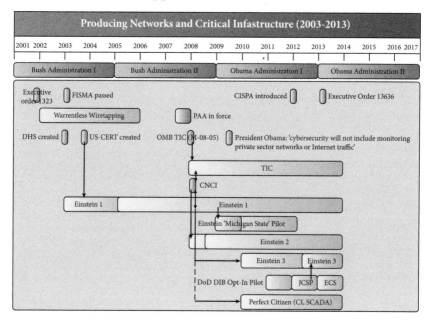

Figure 6.2 Timeline

7

Artificial or 'Legitimate' Barriers to Internet Governance?

Francesco Giacomini and Laura Cordani

Since times past the fates of people and their endeavours have been significantly affected by the geographical, historical and political characteristics of the territories where they lived or carried out their business. People, goods, ideas and technologies can only move along routes free of obstacles, be they natural or artificial. This exchange in turn fosters economic and social progress, which often leads to better state organization, improved democracy and more respect for human rights.

In *Guns, Germs and Steel: The Fates of Human Societies,* Diamond (1997) shows how the long East-West distance of the Eurasian continent and the lack of significant geographic or climatic barriers, such as mountains, deserts or different cycles of seasons, favoured the spread of agriculture and domestication of animals, which were the first steps toward civilization of the people settled there. By contrast, those barriers characterize the African and the American continents, which developed along a North-South axis and agriculture and the domestication of animals, with subsequent civilization, moved very slowly, if at all.

Diamond also cites situations where politics raised artificial barriers to the free flow of knowledge and technology, with negative long-term effects for the affected countries. For example, in the fifteenth century China practically destroyed its technological advantage over medieval Europe when it decommissioned its treasure fleet and dismantled its shipyards as the result of a local power struggle, isolating itself from the rest of the world. Another example involves Japan, which had an advanced industry of guns until the end of the sixteenth century, when the government, controlled by samurais, a warrior class who based their power on swords, started to restrict that strategic production, until Japan remained almost without guns.

People have always tried to circumvent natural barriers and, where already in place, artificial obstacles. Once the necessary technology is available, people have built roads, bridges, tunnels, channels, and aeroplanes. And many international organizations have been created so that goods and people could move more freely beyond country borders: the EEC, which became the EC and then the EU, the Association of Southeast Asian Nations (ASEAN), the Mercado Común del Sur (MERCOSUR), the World Trade Organization (WTO) and many others.

Then came the Internet and, on top of it, the World Wide Web, which all of a sudden, created a space that everybody could join, a space without intrinsic barriers, where information could flow between geographically distant locations at almost the speed of light (Berners-Lee, 1989).

> When the Internet was conceived in the early 1970s, the notion of openness lay at the heart of its architecture, philosophy and technical protocols. … When Tim Berners-Lee invented and released the World Wide Web (WWW) design in late 1991, he found an open and receptive Internet in operation onto which the WWW could be placed. The WWW design, like the design of the Internet, was very open. (Cerf, 2013)

Indeed, the popularity of the Internet exploded and its usage grew at an exponential rate, until some started to worry. The Internet could allow the exchange of any type of information, often in an anonymous way, and this possibility could undermine many established interests and disrupt existing stable practices.

Today, content providers tend to be bound to a business model rooted in the 'analogue' world and are sceptical about (independent), 'alternative' models that may emerge. Law-enforcement agencies may feel the risk of 'going dark' and, thanks to the technological advancements, have the temptation to deploy large surveillance initiatives to filter all communications, with the stated goal to make us all safer against criminals and terrorists. Governments and militaries are worried about attacks to national strategic infrastructures, which rely more and more on computer systems and network connectivity.

On the other hand those who were quick to embrace the new technology and to found successful businesses on top of it want to keep their dominance. Service providers love to profile their users, collecting personal information, for example for marketing purposes, or they place barriers around their customers to prevent them from moving to the competition.

There is a serious risk that the solutions devised to address the above concerns, if left only to the players mentioned, would converge towards a strictly controlled model of Internet governance, introducing artificial barriers into a world almost devoid of them. Should we, as a society, take a step back in the exploitation of the full potential of the Internet and indeed grant some protection to those interests and accept business practices that limit our rights? That is certainly a difficult question to answer and no single answer can exist for all the diverse situations that touch many aspects of our life, including our basic consumer and civil rights such as liberty and privacy, but also, for example, national security and economics. An effort is needed to understand, with a public and transparent process, which concerns are really legitimate and to address them in such a way that the benefits for society are greatest.

The economic perspective

In the following section, we will present different perspectives, all affecting the Internet and cyberspace at large, trying to understand what expectations are at stake, if they are legitimate, and how we can move forward with acceptable compromises, keeping however in mind that the ultimate goal of the old and new policies governing the Internet and its use is to preserve the potential that the Internet provides to promote the progress of humankind.

Let us start from the economic perspective. The Internet is at the roots of the success of many companies, both new and old. It is the keystone of the business models of giants like Google, Facebook, eBay, Yahoo!, Amazon, all founded in the late 1990s or early 2000. But also old giants in the IT industry, like IBM, Microsoft, and Apple, profited heavily from the new technology and restructured their respective business to adapt to it. 'Although it is probably not possible to produce a precise estimate of the growth in global GDP that can be attributed to the Internet and the World Wide Web, it seems likely to run into the hundreds of billions if not trillions of dollars' (Cerf, 2013). The Internet has entered the lives of billions of people worldwide. Can we imagine our daily life without being able to browse, buy, play, mail, chat, talk, listen to music, watch videos or read the latest news online?

However, not everybody is happy with this evolution. Consider the media companies, for example, whose business consists of producing and distributing music, films, and other creative works. They started to worry when analogue supports (LPs and cassette tapes) were replaced by digital supports (compact discs), because copying a song or a film could finally be done an indefinite number of times without any loss of quality. Things became much worse when the digital content could be spread an indefinite number of times at no practical cost, thanks to the Internet. So the media companies, through their associations (for example, the Recording Industry Association of America and the Motion Pictures Association of America in the USA) reacted. Unfortunately, instead of reviewing their business model in depth, still based on the selling of physical supports on which content happened to be stored, and transforming it into something that could leverage the new opportunities offered by the Internet, they reacted strongly against those who tried to do so.

Examples abound, but a quick reminder of just the first victim illustrates the point well. Napster was an Internet service that allowed people to share music, encoded in the MP3 format, easily and efficiently. It came online in 1999 and operated for a couple of years; at its peak it had almost 80 million registered users, clearly demonstrating that consumers appreciated such a service. Its problem was that all that music exchange did not generate any royalties for the copyright owners of the music being exchanged. This was very disruptive for a business model that used to work in a very different way. To shorten a long story, at the end of a legal battle Napster was forced to close.

The legal battle relied on a law approved by the US Congress in 1998, the Digital Millennium Copyright Act (DMCA),[1] whose purpose was to restrict the production and distribution of techniques aimed at circumventing the digital rights management (DRM) systems that protect against the unauthorized reproduction of copyrighted works. As the Electronic Frontier Foundation documents with examples in a periodic report (2013b), the law has had serious unintended consequences: 'the DMCA has become a serious threat that jeopardizes fair use, impedes competition and innovation, chills free expression and scientific research and interferes with computer intrusion laws.' Of particular interest, in view of the subsequent discussion of strategic infrastructures, are the situations where security research has suffered, with people even arrested, or threatened with arrest, for having disclosed vulnerabilities in DRM systems.

After Napster closed, many similar initiatives arose, because the basic idea of Napster was really good. They tried to avoid the technical shortcomings that had made Napster vulnerable, building on and improving the new paradigm that Napster had popularized for the distribution of files on the Internet and that can be considered its primary legacy: the peer-to-peer protocol. In peer-to-peer systems there is very little, if any, central coordination and consequently they are difficult, if not impossible, to stop. The bottom line here is, then, that if content is stored digitally, there is little chance that any copy-protection technology can survive for long.

On the other hand, any legislation aimed at controlling what people can do risks being very invasive and far-reaching, severely restricting consumer rights or even human rights, for example in terms of privacy (because of the invasive controls that would necessarily be put in place) or freedom of speech (because of the limits to publishing the results of certain research). A better route would be to fully embrace the Internet revolution and relax the copyright legislation. As Consumer Electronics Association CEO Gary Shapiro once said: 'The entire theme of the copyright community is that downloading off the Web is both illegal and immoral. It is neither' (Borland, 2002). Moreover, there is little evidence that a strict copyright regulation helps in the distribution of and access to creative works, on the contrary copyright 'seems to make books disappear' (Heald, 2013: 17).

There is also little evidence that unauthorized copying seriously harms traditional business; on the contrary there are studies showing that 'P2P file sharers, in particular, are heavy legal media consumers' (Karaganis and Renkema, 2013). But even if the profits of media were to fall with respect to the recent past, it would not be in the best interest of society to raise barriers in order to preserve old business models. And in any case, Apple iTunes[2] shows that it is possible to sell media content online and still be profitable. Even without abolishing copyright altogether, as some economists argue, there are sensible reform proposals, such as the Creative Commons initiative[3], that would be more in line with the purpose of copyright – 'To promote the Progress of Science and useful Arts' (US Constitution, Art. 1, Sect. 8) – that would encourage wide and cheap distribution of culture and still provide enough incentive for the production of creative works, at the same time fostering innovation in business models without jeopardizing fundamental rights (Boldrin and Levine, 2008). Relaxing copyright law would also bear a positive side effect in terms of reduced resources spent on controls by law-enforcement agencies and ISPs. Those resources could be better spent on fighting more dangerous forms of crime.

The law-enforcement perspective

Let us now move to the law-enforcement perspective. Law enforcement is one of the reasons typically advocated by governments to justify restrictions and constraints to the free use of the Internet. Unfortunately the level of control that is exerted on citizens often reaches levels that go well beyond what is needed to counter crime. This is all well documented in the annual report 'Freedom on the Net', published by Freedom House (2012), an independent watchdog organization dedicated to the expansion of freedom around the world. The report includes comprehensive studies of Internet freedom around the world. According to the latest issue, covering the developments in 47 countries in the period from January 2011 to May 2012, 'This year's findings indicate that restrictions on Internet freedom in many countries have continued to grow, though the methods of control are slowly evolving, becoming more sophisticated and less visible'.

Brutal attacks against bloggers, politically motivated surveillance, proactive manipulation of Web content, and restrictive laws regulating speech online are among the diverse threats to Internet freedom emerging over the past two years. Nevertheless, several notable victories have also occurred as a result of greater activism by civil society, technology companies, and independent courts, illustrating that effort to advance Internet freedom can yield results' (Freedom House, 2012). The last sentence underlines, and correctly so, how the role of the public can lead to important steps to improve on the current situation. Notable examples are the reactions to the ratification of the Anti-Counterfeiting Trade Agreement (ACTA) by the EU and the approval of the Stop Online Piracy Act (SOPA) and the Protect IP Act (PIPA) in the United States, which were all blocked by the fierce opposition of the civil society, worried by the potential threats to fundamental rights including freedom of expression and privacy.

Unfortunately, even in democratic countries, some secret programs are established in order to collect wide-ranging information on people's private communications. These programs are considered by many at the edge or even beyond what a government can lawfully do. Taking the United States as an example, sometimes the existence of such programs and how they work are exposed through a Freedom of Information Act request, such as the ample use of so-called National Security Letters, which 'served on communications service providers like phone companies and ISPs allow the FBI to secretly demand data about ordinary American citizens' private communications and Internet activity without any meaningful oversight or prior judicial review. Recipients of NSLs are subject to a gag order that forbids them from ever revealing the letters' existence to their coworkers, to their friends or even to their family members much less the public' (Electronic Frontier Foundation, 2013a). For example, in its annual Transparency Report,[4] Google only mentions a range for how many NSLs they have received and how many people and accounts are involved, not a precise number.

Sometimes the existence of secret surveillance programs is made public thanks to whistleblowers (Chapter 3 and 4), like William Binney (2012), who exposed a domestic surveillance program by the NSA and, more recently, Edward Snowden, who released classified information about another NSA program, called PRISM, to obtain direct access to the computer systems of Google, Apple, Facebook, Microsoft and other US Internet giants (Greenwald and MacAskill, 2013). Although in a democracy whistleblowers should be encouraged, thanked and protected, at this moment they are apparently not well received by the US administration,[5] as the story of Bradley Manning and Julian Assange, who released classified documents on the war on terror in Iraq through WikiLeaks, shows (Schneier, 2013c) and is well described in Chapters 3 and 4.

But, one may ask, what is the problem with the government spying on every citizen in order to fight crime or terrorism? After all, as UK Foreign Secretary William Hague argues, 'if you are a law-abiding citizen of this country going about your business and personal life, you have nothing to fear about the British state or intelligence agencies listening to the content of your phone calls or anything like that' (Corera, 2013). There are two counter-arguments to this attitude. The first one can be summarized with the Latin phrase *Quis custodiet ipsos custodes?* ('Who watches the watchmen?'). History has taught us about corruption; and the more powerful a person or an organization is, the higher the risk that they could be corrupted. That is the reason why the constitution of every reasonably democratic country provides checks and balances between the various institutional powers and why, for example, 'The right of the people to be secure in their persons, houses, papers, and effects, against unreasonable searches and seizures, shall not be violated, and no Warrants shall issue, but upon probable cause, supported by oath or affirmation, and particularly describing the place to be searched, and the persons or things to be seized' (US Constitution, Fourth Amendment).

The second counter-argument concerns the capability of a society to make progress if subjected to a constant and pervasive surveillance (or perception there of). Neil M. Richards, Professor of Law at the Washington University in St. Louis, in his paper 'The Dangers of Surveillance' offers an answer arguing about the harm that large-scale surveillance does to what he calls *intellectual privacy.* The 'theory [of intellectual privacy] suggests that new ideas often develop best away from the intense scrutiny of public exposure; that people should be able to make up their minds at times and places of their own choosing; and that a meaningful guarantee of privacy – protection from surveillance or interference – is necessary to promote this kind of intellectual freedom. It rests on the idea that free minds are the foundation of a free society, and that surveillance of the activities of belief formation and idea generation can affect those activities profoundly and for the worse' (Richards, 2013).

Richards also claims that 'surveillance inclines us to the mainstream and the boring. It is a claim that when we are watched while engaging in intellectual activities, broadly defined – thinking, reading, web-surfing, or private communication – we are deterred from engaging in thoughts or deeds that others might find deviant.' Would a society built on top of surveillance be very different from the Panopticon, 'A new mode of obtaining power of mind over mind', as its proponent Jeremy Bentham presented it? Professor Richards also warns about the disparity that surveillance induces between the watched and the watcher: it 'creates the risk of a variety of harms, such as discrimination, coercion, and the threat of selective enforcement, where critics of the government can be prosecuted or blackmailed for wrongdoing unrelated to the purpose of the surveillance' (Richards, 2013). Again, who watches the watchmen?

Security researcher Moxie Marlinspike uses similar arguments. In 'Why "I Have Nothing to Hide" Is the Wrong Way to Think About Surveillance' he starts with noticing how many unknown and obscure laws are in effect, so that at any given time there is a high probability that everyone is violating one of them. As a consequence, 'if everyone's every action were being monitored, and everyone technically violates some obscure law at some time, then punishment becomes purely selective. Those in power will essentially have what they need to punish anyone they'd like, whenever they choose, as if there were no rules at all.' He goes on to notice that in many cases, changes in legislation track progress in the rules that govern society by legitimizing established practices that were illegal before the change. 'A world where law enforcement is 100% effective', thanks to pervasive surveillance, eliminates 'the possibility to experience alternative ideas that might better suit us' (Marlinspike, 2013).

Richards concludes his article by suggesting four sensible principles that should guide the future development of surveillance law. First, surveillance transcends the public/private divide: although we are ultimately more concerned with governmental surveillance, all of us spontaneously give much personal information to private companies, for example through social networks. As it has been demonstrated, this wealth of information is easily made available to governments, often with very little, if any, judicial oversight. And new legislative initiatives are underway to expand this 'collaboration' (Schneier, 2013a).

Second, we must recognize that secret surveillance is illegitimate, at least in a democracy: the people, and not the state apparatus, are sovereign and have the right to know what their representatives do in their name and how, not the opposite. Third, total surveillance is illegitimate: there is an enormous potential for massive abuse in the government recording, directly or indirectly, all Internet activity without authorization. Finally and most important, we must recognize surveillance is harmful, because it threatens our intellectual privacy and creates a potentially dangerous imbalance between the watcher and the watched.

Translating those four principles into actual legislation and practices will surely take some time, because the current inertia of the system is in the opposite direction: secret and pervasive surveillance programs are flourishing, involving governments and private companies, and many people, who 'don't have anything to hide', wilfully trade privacy for convenience and alleged safety. In the meantime there are some effective actions that individuals can adopt to protect to some extent their privacy while using the Internet, ranging from using encrypted communication to blocking tracking systems to relying on anonymization techniques.

Would these limitations to the surveillance capabilities of law-enforcement agencies cause them to 'go dark' and allow criminals to prepare and perpetrate their crimes undisturbed? That is a very legitimate question, because law-enforcement agencies must be provided with the necessary tools to conduct their mission and one of those tools is the possibility to monitor a suspect. Peter Swire and Kenesa Ahmad argue, however, that we live in a golden age of surveillance: 'Compared with earlier periods, surveillance capabilities have greatly expanded'.

Consider three areas where law enforcement has far greater capabilities than ever before: (1) location information; (2) information about contacts and confederates; and (3) an array of new databases that create 'digital dossiers' about individuals' lives. This information about any individual suspect is made even more useful because of the way data mining can help identify suspects' (Swire and Ahmad, 2011). They also suggest a simple test to help decide between the 'going dark' and the 'golden age of surveillance' hypothesis: which situation is more favourable for a law-enforcement agency, being simply able to wiretap unencrypted communication (as it was the case 20 years ago) or having access to current capabilities such as location information, information about contacts, large databases and data mining tools? If the answer is the latter, then there is no need to call for total surveillance programs, for artificially weakened forms of encryption or, worse, any system can be made more vulnerable to eavesdropping by adding a back door to it.

This latter proposal, which is advanced periodically, would have at least two nefarious side effects: it would cause a serious competitive disadvantage to the software or hardware vendors who are subject to such a rule and it would make those systems more vulnerable (Schneier, 2013b). This point introduces the final perspective of this chapter: the argument that stricter controls on Internet use are needed in order to defend national and international strategic infrastructures.

The cyberspace perspective

In developed countries the use of advanced ICTs is pervasive in many areas of society, including activities that are strategic for the correct functioning of critical infrastructures, such as health, finance, energy distribution, communications. Undoubtedly ICTs have introduced convenience and efficiency in many situations; however, very often the security of those technologies or, more precisely, of their use in a specific application has not been properly thought out, leading to latent vulnerabilities that can manifest when certain events occur. Sometimes the effect is minimal (a website becomes unavailable), sometimes it is significant (important data are stolen), sometimes, it is simply catastrophic (the power grid goes down). Those unfortunate events can happen just by bad luck, but they might also be triggered by a malicious attack, perpetrated by an individual, an organization, or a state, for many reasons: crime, espionage, surveillance, sabotage, terrorism, politics, nationalism, retaliation and so on.

The possibility to provoke or influence events in cyberspace is in fact a form of power, which Kuehl calls cyber-power, defined as 'the ability to use cyberspace to create advantages and influence events in other operational environments and across the instruments of power' (Kuehl, 2009). Sheldon identifies three main characteristics of cyber-power: ubiquity, complementarily and stealthiness. First, cyber-power can generate effects in any other domain (land, sea, air and space), possibly in a simultaneous way. Second, it is a complementary instrument because it has a limited coercive ability, at least for the time being. For example the cyber-attacks against Estonia (2007) and Georgia (2008) caused disruption and inconvenience but were largely circumstantial on the final outcome of the events. Even the attack discovered in 2010 against an Iranian nuclear facility through the Stuxnet malware (see below) did not stop Iran's nuclear program. Cyber-attacks provoke damage and noise but they are not coercive, at least not yet. Finally, cyber-attacks can be difficult to attribute to a perpetrator who wants to act anonymously and can stay hidden or go unnoticed for a long time (Sheldon, 2011).

In particular the stealthiness of a cyber-action is very attractive for an attacker and the low-entry barrier to exploit cyberspace, both in terms of resources and of knowledge, has allowed even single individuals to cause havoc, for example through a denial of service attack against a website, accomplished with a piece of software downloaded from the Net, without any specific knowledge on how it works. The fact that the entry barrier is low does not mean that any attack can be mounted in a cheap way; on the contrary huge investments may be needed to design, implement, and deploy a piece of malware, as was the case for example with the already mentioned Stuxnet malware, allegedly produced jointly by the US and Israel. And indeed more and more states are engaging in the development of software and hardware tools that could be aimed against adversary infrastructures if needed. For some scholars, cyberspace 'by now could represent a non-conventional weapon able to produce conventional effects' (Siroli, 2012).

We could then consider the possibility that in the near future a cyber-war, a war conducted only through cyber-weapons, could replace a traditional kinetic war. This seems unlikely, however. If a war is to be cyber, it has to represent 'a potentially lethal, instrumental, and political act of force conducted through malicious code' but past known cyber-attacks were, in fact, only advanced variations of sabotage, espionage, or subversion (Rid, 2012). Some scholars, like Thomas Rid and Howard Schmidt, conclude that there has never been a cyber-war and there will never be one. However 'Future wars and the skirmishes that precede them will involve a mixture of conventional or kinetic weapons with cyberweaponry acting as a disrupter or force multiplier' (Sommer and Brown, 2011).

Stuxnet

Even if a pure cyber-war is not on the horizon, cyber-attacks are a reality and represent a clear threat to strategic infrastructures need to be defended and it is the dependability of such infrastructures that should be preserved if disruptive events happen in cyberspace, independently of who generates them. How can this be achieved? The Stuxnet event can teach some lessons and indicate the way forward.

Stuxnet is the most notable example of a cyber-action resembling very closely an act of war. It is a sophisticated and complex malware discovered in 2010. Its attribution and exact purposes are still unclear but it is generally attributed to the United States and Israel as an alternative to a traditional bombing attack, in order to delay the Iranian nuclear program by seriously damaging the centrifuges used to enrich uranium at the Iranian nuclear facility of Natanz, which in fact it did (Sanger, 2012). It is estimated that the attack has delayed the Iranian nuclear program by a couple of years. Its *modus operandi* was to change intermittently the rotation speed of the centrifuges beyond the safety range, slowly deteriorating them. It ran for several months, during which it went unnoticed because it also managed to produce fake monitoring data showing normal behaviour.

Stuxnet entered the facility on an infected USB memory stick and it started to spread over the internal network, which was physically separate from the outside network (i.e. there was an air gap between the two), when someone attached that stick to a computer. It replicated from computer to computer, exploiting several zero-day vulnerabilities (i.e. vulnerabilities that were still unknown even to the software maker and, consequently, not corrected) until it infected the control systems governing the centrifuges, where it operated covertly. Stuxnet at some point escaped the target site and spread in the wild, infecting at least 100,000 computers around the world, including the USA (Zetter, 2011).

Some facts about the Stuxnet event are worth noting.

1. Any target is vulnerable. From an attack point of view, if enough resources are invested (knowledge, people, hardware, software, testing infrastructure, agents on the field, etc.), any target can be violated. From a defence point of view, absolute security is not possible. The Iranians certainly considered the possibility of a cyber-attack, and in fact the internal network of the plant was separated from the general Internet; nonetheless the attack succeeded.

2. All hardware and, especially, software systems have defects, and defects can become security vulnerabilities.

3. The more complex a system is, the larger the attack surface it presents. The hardware and software infrastructure of the plant had many components and some of them inevitably had bugs, possibly manifesting only when components interacted with each other.

4. IT systems often are not designed with security in mind. Industrial control systems (ICS) and supervisory control and data acquisition (SCADA) systems – IT systems whose specific purpose is to monitor and control industrial processes that exist in the physical world – are particularly fragile in this respect, simply because functionality, not security, was the focus of the system design. Things are changing though.[6]

5. Security infrastructures themselves are not foolproof. Parts of the Stuxnet code were digitally signed with valid certificates so that installation would not generate any warning. Even vendors of security products and services are not immune to violations. Here are a few telling examples: VeriSign, a leading Internet infrastructure company, suffered repeated breaches in 2010 (Menn, 2012). DigiNotar, a now-bankrupt Certificate Authority, was fully compromised in 2011 (Fisher, 2012). RSA Security was infiltrated in 2011.[7]

6. 'Security is a chain; it's only as secure as the weakest link' (Schneier, 2000a). Moreover, very often the weakest link is a human,[8] the one who opens an attachment from an unknown source, chooses a guessable password, or inserts a USB memory stick found in the parking lot into a computer.

7. Malware can spread and cause damage beyond the intended target. Although the intention was probably to keep it confined within the Natanz facility, Stuxnet was discovered only after it went wild. Fortunately it did not cause much harm.

8. The operation was not conducted exclusively via the Internet, namely connecting from a remote location to one of the computers within the Natanz site, but required the involvement of field agents.

9. The attribution of the attack is not certain, despite informed speculation that indicates that the United States and Israel were behind it. A retaliation, by any means, could have missed the actual responsible party and caused an escalation with the involvement of other countries, possibly moving from the cyber space to the real world. The US 'International Strategy for Cyberspace'[9] itself states that 'When warranted, the United States will respond to hostile acts in cyberspace as we would to any other threat to our

country [...] We reserve the right to use all necessary means – diplomatic, informational, military, and economic – as appropriate and consistent with applicable international law, in order to defend our Nation, our allies, our partners, and our interests.'

Cyber-attacks

In light of the above considerations, what can be done to defend the IT infra-structures on which society more and more relies upon? A complex problem rarely has a simple solution, and securing a strategic infrastructure is no exception. 'Some of the solutions call for changes in user behaviours, some for changes in technology, some for changes in business practice and the practice of domestic and international law enforcement' (Cerf, 2013). Some of the solutions are suggested below.

We must realize that sooner or later, maybe by accident, maybe due to an attack, some system will fail and we have to be prepared to manage that situation, investing in emergency and mitigation responses. The end goal is to have a resilient society, not necessarily a resilient IT infrastructure. Not all IT systems and infrastructures are equally important. We can easily survive if a government or bank website is defaced, but a failure of the control system of an industrial plant can have serious consequences. Since resources are limited, they should be spent primarily on reinforcing the most critical systems.

Moreover, attackers are not equal. There are so-called script-kiddies, unskilled individuals who simply download attack tools from the Net and launch them against more or less random targets; there are criminals, more or less organized, who are able to invent new attack tools and then sell them or use them for their own criminal purposes; there are states or state-sponsored actors, who have access to significant resources and are very determined to achieve their goals. Defences that work against a script-kiddie do not necessarily work against a determined individual or organization; in the former case some straightforward technical solutions (a firewall, a good anti-virus, an enforced good password policy, an effective system update policy) may be enough, in the latter additional measures, involving the overall organization or even law-enforcement agencies and international cooperation, are necessary.

More attention should be devoted to the quality of the large amount of software that now governs our lives. Although it is true that certain sophisticated attacks (the so-called Advanced Persistent Threats (APT)) rely also on social engineering techniques that profit from human weakness almost all attacks exploit one or more software defects (Hadnagy, 2010). The current poor situation in this field derives from the historically prevalent attitude to focus on functionality rather than security, because the latter 'is all about placing obstacles in the way of attackers, but (despite the claims of security vendors) those same obstacles can get in the way of users, too'.[10] Moreover, security is not simply a product that can be included in a system at the end; rather, it is a process that needs to be followed from the very inception of a software product. In fact currently there are really no compelling reasons, for software vendors, to change their attitude because the probability of a security incident is, after all, rather low and, even if that happens, there is no liability for the damages caused.

'Real security is harder, slower, and more expensive, both to design and to implement. Since the buying public has no way of differentiating real security from bad security, the way to win in this marketplace is to design software that is as insecure as you can possibly get away with' (Schneier, 2000b). Some guidelines have already been recognized as useful in order to encourage real security, although they have not yet reached a sufficiently wide adoption: the use of software components and protocols that have been designed and implemented openly, with the contribution of recognized experts; the timely update of software components installed on computers; the responsible disclosure of software vulnerabilities, whereby a software vendor is notified of a discovered vulnerability and given some time to correct it before making it public. Additionally the introduction into the legislation of some form of liability for damages caused by software defects would be welcome, because it would encourage vendors to dedicate more resources to the security-related aspects of software.

Other initiatives will probably be necessary shortly in order to address new emerging issues, such as discouraging a market for zero-day exploits, that seem to grow day after day and extending effectively the software update service to mobile devices, such as smartphones and tablets, that have become as powerful as personal computers and are often permanently network-connected, but at the same time are often managed carelessly (Schneier, 2012b).

Then there are people, who should be educated, starting from school, to be more security-conscious. Although demanding for the general public, something more than basic digital hygiene would be too much. It is not too much for software developers and engineers, who are ultimately responsible for the design and implementation of what runs on our computers, nor for those who design and implement the overall IT systems that control the various infrastructures on which we rely upon.

Finally there could be agreements among states to refrain from attacking each other. Often the model used to describe the current situation in cyberspace is borrowed from the Cold War, with the United States and the Soviet Union, with their respective allies, on opposite sides, building up huge arsenals of nuclear bombs, sufficient to destroy the whole Earth over and over again. Such situation reached at some point an equilibrium based on the paradigm of mutually assured destruction.

Alternative views exist, though: 'Much like the Internet is becoming today, in centuries past the sea was a primary domain of commerce and communication upon which no one single actor could claim complete control. What is notable is that the actors that related to maritime security and war at sea back then parallel many of the situations on our networks today. They scaled from individual pirates to state fleets with a global presence like the British Navy. In between were state-sanctioned pirates, or privateers. Much like today's 'patriotic hackers' (or NSA contractors), these forces were used both to augment traditional military forces and to add challenges of attribution to those trying to defend far-flung maritime assets' (Shachtman and Singer, 2011). Independent of the model, an international treaty is universally recognized as the preferred way forward, both to regulate what states can do and to foster cooperation to fight criminal activities conducted fully or in part on the Internet (Schneier, 2012a).

Concerning cyber-crime, the first step of cooperation between states regulating the digital space is the Convention on Cyber-crime,[11] which entered into force in July 2004. This is a European Council regional agreement that tries to address the rapid increase of cyber threats against legitimate interests in the use and development of information technologies. The agreement includes guidelines that every country should adopt into national legislation to tackle unlawful activities on the Internet. The Convention is complemented by an additional protocol related to racist and xenophobic acts committed with digital systems.

However, addressing threats to peace, security and international stability, requires a move from states that have an important role in these fields, such as Russia and the United States, among others. Unfortunately Russia and the United States do not agree on a basic approach to cybersecurity: the former is in favour of a binding international regime, whereas the latter prefers to tackle the issue with law-enforcement systems at national and international levels. In addition, Russians refer to information security, a broader concept than cyber security, including protection against 'spreading disinformation or creating a virtual picture partially or totally misrepresenting reality in the communications sphere; or producing disorientation, loss of will power or temporary destabilization among the population' (Streltsov, 2007).

With respect to a safe and open Internet, the United States does not accept the idea of a restricted cyberspace: it could be a limit that runs against democratic principles and could be used to justify the limitation of the free flow of information. 'The United States [...] remains sceptical toward Russian ideas such as an international agreement, since it could provide cover for totalitarian regimes to censor the Internet' (Gady, 2010).

In September 2011, Russia surprised the international community by advancing a proposal for an International Code of Conduct for Information Security.[12] China, Tajikistan and Uzbekistan also subscribed to the proposal. The Code of Conduct addresses the security challenges in cyber space and recommends that the rights and responsibilities of a state in the protection of IT systems and networks should in any case respect that state's national laws and sovereignty. The principles of the Code 'stipulate that countries shall not use such information and telecommunication technologies as the network to conduct hostile behaviours and acts of aggression or to threaten international peace and security and stress that countries have the rights and obligations to protect their information and cyberspace as well as key information and network infrastructure from threats, interference and sabotage attacks.' Cyber-experts believe that China and Russia consider free flow of information of social networks, such as Facebook and Twitter, a real threat to their own governments. 'Apparently in response to the Arab Spring, the two countries are tightening access to many of the social networks used by the demonstrators' (Farnsworth, 2011).

The way forward

Evidence suggests that at present a definitive agreement on the matter would be premature. We are still in a phase where diplomacy should adopt transparency and confidence-building measures (TCBM), increasing debate and discussion and reducing the risk of escalation in case a cyber-attack actually happens, as, for example, Patryk Pawlak shows in Chapter 4 of this book. In the past, TCBMs have been used to control and regulate other domains and other weapons; its success in those situations is a good omen to develop similar measures for cyberspace.

Several multilateral discussion forums have taken place in these crucial years. One of these was the 'Challenges in Cybersecurity' Conference in Berlin, Germany, in December 2011, where the benefits of confidence-building measures were underlined. 'The need for CBMs is greater than ever, and states have a legal obligation as well as a political responsibility to work faster towards creating them for cyberspace'. In this forum cyber-diplomacy and preventive diplomacy were pointed out as a means to establish international cooperation aimed at the improvement of cybersecurity, thanks to the development of confidence measures in six categories: 'cyber security conference; military CBMs such as exchanging information on cyberdoctrines; joint training; 'hotlines'; law enforcement and economic measures [...]; network CBMs and CERT [Computer Emergency Response Teams] protocols' (Conference 'Challenges on Cybersecurity' Berlin, December 2011).

Indeed, measures that could be adopted to strengthen security, reduce or remove mistrust, misunderstanding and miscalculation on other states' intentions include: developing and sharing cyber policies; declaring the real purpose of current cyber activities; creating early-warning mechanisms; improving the cooperation among Computer Emergency Response Teams (CERTs); creating communication channels in case of crisis; implementing capacity-building in developing countries; increasing the resilience of critical infrastructures. In the short term four areas of concrete cooperation, in particular between the United States and Russia, have been suggested: an international system, defined within the International Telecommunication Union (ITU), of trusted identities based on public key infrastructure (PKI); a global framework of 24/7 points of contact to respond to cyber-crime emergencies; the definition of an international cyber-law, for example under the umbrella of the OSCE, especially in the domains of critical infrastructures and 'rules of engagement'; and NATO-Russia cyber-military exercises and exchanges (Gady, 2010). For the time being, the various conferences, summits and meetings are essential steps to encourage debate on cybersecurity, implement transparency, build confidence, find a common language and elaborate a shared security model upon which an international treaty can be based in the future.

In summary, we have in our hands a wonderful technology that has the potential to boost progress for all humankind, in developed and developing countries. Like all revolutionary technologies in history, the Internet has shaken the foundations upon which many interests and practices were standing, and many worries exist around its full exploitation. Some worries are very legitimate, for example those concerning the vulnerability of strategic infrastructures or the capabilities available to law-enforcement agencies; some worries are partially legitimate, for example those related to how to keep promoting the production of creative works; some worries instead are plainly unacceptable, such as those related to being less able to restrict the free expression of opinions. No simple single solution exists to address all the legitimate worries, however a set of solutions, probably incomplete and imperfect, consisting of a mixture of technical, political, diplomatic actions, is available that could move us in the right direction, without affecting the values on which democratic societies are founded.

Notes

1 Digital Millennium Copyright Act, Pub. L. 105-304, www.gpo.gov/fdsys/pkg/PLAW-105publ304/pdf/PLAW-105publ304.pdf (accessed 23 July 2013).

2 Apple Press Info, iTunes U Content Tops One Billion Downloads, 28 February 2013, www.apple.com/pr/library/2013/02/28iTunes-U-Content-Tops-One-Billion-Downloads.html (accessed 23 July 2013).

3 https://creativecommons.org/ (accessed 23 July 2013).

4 Google, *Transparency Report*, www.google.com/transparencyreport/userdatarequests/US/ (accessed 23 July 2013).

5 http://cartome.org/panopticon2.htm (accessed 23 July 2013).

6 www.blackhat.com/presentations/bh-federal-06/BH-Fed-06-Maynor-Graham-up.pdf (accessed 29 August 2013).

7 https://blogs.rsa.com/anatomy-of-an-attack (accessed 29 August 2013).

8 https://xkcd.com/538/ (accessed 29 August 2013).

9 www.whitehouse.gov/sites/default/files/rss_viewer/international_strategy_for_cyberspace.pdf (accessed 29 August 2013).

10 www.macworld.com/article/2041724/apples-security-strategy-make-it-invisible.html (accessed 29 August 2013).

11 www.coe.int/t/DGHL/cooperation/economiccrime/cybercrime/default_en.asp (accessed 29 August 2013). See also Chapter 8 in this book.

12 www.fmprc.gov.cn/eng/zxxx/t858978.htm (accessed 29 August 2013).

References

Berners-Lee, T. (1989), 'Information Management: A Proposal', CERN, Geneva, https://cds.cern.ch/record/369245?ln=en (accessed 23 July 2013).

Binney, W. (2012), 'Sworn Declaration of Whistleblower William Binney on NSA Domestic Surveillance Capabilities', https://publicintelligence.net/binney-nsa-declaration/ (accessed 23 July 2013).

Boldrin, M. and D. K. Levine (2008), *Against Intellectual Monopoly*, New York: Cambridge University Press, www.dklevine.com/general/intellectual/againstfinal.htm (accessed 23 July 2013).

Borland, J. (2002), 'Trade group: P2P not illegal or immoral', CNET News, 17 September 2002, http://news.cnet.com/2100-1023-958324.html (accessed 23 July 2013).

Cerf, V. G. (2013), 'The Open Internet and the Web', Geneva, CERN, 30 April 2013, http://home.web.cern.ch/cern-people/opinion/2013/04/open-internet-and-web (accessed 23 July 2013).

Corera, G. (2013), 'Hague: Law-abiding Britons Have Nothing to Fear From GCHQ', BBC News, 9 June 2013, http://www.bbc.co.uk/news/uk-22832263 (accessed 23 July 2013).

Diamond, J. (1997), *Guns, Germs and Steel: The Fates of Human Societies*, New York: Norton.

Electronic Frontier Foundation (2013a), 'National Security Letters', www.eff.org/issues/national-security-letters (accessed 23 July 2013

—(2013b), 'Unintended Consequences: Fifteen Years under the DMCA', www.eff.org/pages/unintended-consequences-fifteen-years-under-dmca (accessed 23 July 2013).

Farnsworth, T. (2011), 'China and Russia Submit Cyber Proposal', www.armscontrol.org/act/2011_11/China_and_Russia_Submit_Cyber_Proposal (accessed 29 August 2013).

Fisher, D. (2012), 'Final Report On Diginotar Hack Shows Total Compromise of Ca Servers', https://threatpost.com/final-report-diginotar-hack-shows-total-compromise-ca-servers-103112 (accessed 29 August 2013).

Freedom House (2012), 'Freedom on the Net', 2012 Edition Release, www.freedomhouse.org/report-types/freedom-net (accessed 23 July 2013).

Gady, F. S. and G. Austin (2010), *Russia, the United States, and Cyber Diplomacy: Opening the Doors*, New York: East-West Institute, www.ewi.info/system/files/USRussiaCyber_WEB.pdf (accessed 14 September 2013).

Greenwald, G. and E. MacAskill (2013), 'NSA Prism Program Taps in to User Data of Apple, Google and others', *The Guardian*, 7 June 2013, www.guardian.co.uk/world/2013/jun/06/us-tech-giants-nsa-data (accessed 23 July 2013).

Hadnagy, C. (2010), *Social Engineering: The Art of Human Hacking*, Hoboken, NJ: John Wiley & Sons, Inc.

Heald, P. J. (2013), 'How Copyright Makes Books and Music Disappear (and How

Secondary Liability Rules Help Resurrect Old Songs)', Illinois Program in Law, Behavior and Social Science Paper, http://ssrn.com/abstract=2290181 (accessed 23 July 2013).

Karaganis, J. and L. Renkema (2013), *Copy Culture in the US and Germany*, *The American Assembly*, New York: Columbia University, http://piracy. americanassembly.org/copy-culture-report/ (accessed 23 July 2013).

Kuehl, D. T. (2009), 'From Cyberspace to Cyberpower: Defining the Problem', in F. D. Kramer, S. Starr and L. K. Wentz (eds), *Cyberpower and National Security*, Washington, DC: National Defense University Press/Potomac Books.

Marlinspike, M. (2013), 'Why "I Have Nothing to Hide" Is the Wrong Way to Think About Surveillance', *Wired*, 13 June 2013, www.wired.com/opinion/2013/06/why-i-have-nothing-to-hide-is-the-wrong-way-to-think-about-surveillance/ (accessed 29 August 2013).

Menn, J. (2012), 'Key Internet operator VeriSign hit by hackers', Reuters, 2 February 2012, www.reuters.com/article/2012/02/02/us-hacking-verisign-idUSTRE8110Z820120202 (accessed 29 August 2013).

Richards, N. M. (2013), 'The Dangers of Surveillance', Boston: Harvard Law Review, http://ssrn.com/abstract=2239412 (accessed 23 July 2013).

Rid, T. (2012), 'Cyber war will not take place', *Journal of Strategic Studies*, 35: 5–32.

Sanger, D. (2012), 'Obama Order Sped Up Wave of Cyberattacks Against Iran', *The New York Times*, 1 June 2012, www.nytimes.com/2012/06/01/world/middleeast/obama-ordered-wave-of-cyberattacks-against-iran.html?_r=0 (accessed 29August 2013).

Schneier, B. (2000a), *Secrets and Lies: Digital Security in a Networked World*, New York: John Wiley & Sons, Inc.

—(2000b), 'Computer Security: Will We Ever Learn?', Crypto-gram Newsletter. www. schneier.com/crypto-gram-0005.html#1 (accessed 29 August 2013).

—(2012a), 'An International Cyberwar Treaty Is the Only Way to Stem the Threat', www.usnews.com/debate-club/should-there-be-an-international-treaty-on-cyberwarfare/an-international-cyberwar-treaty-is-the-only-way-to-stem-the-threat (accessed 29 August 2013).

—(2012b), 'The Vulnerabilities Market and the Future of Security', Forbes, www.forbes. com/sites/bruceschneier/2012/05/30/the-vulnerabilities-market-and-the-future-of-security/ (accessed 29 August 2013).

—(2013a), 'Do You Want the Government Buying Your Data From Corporations?', *The Atlantic*. www.theatlantic.com/technology/archive/13/04/governments-wont-need-to-issue-ids-data-brokers-will-identify-you-for-them/275431/ (accessed 29 August 2013).

—(2013b), 'The FBI's New Wiretapping Plan Is Great News for Criminals', *Foreign Policy*, www.foreignpolicy.com/articles/2013/05/29/the_fbi_s_new_wiretapping_plan_is_great_news_for_criminals (accessed 29 August 2013).

—(2013c), 'What We Don't Know About Spying on Citizens: Scarier Than What We Know', *The Atlantic*, http://www.theatlantic.com/politics/archive/2013/06/what-we-dont-know-about-spying-on-citizens-scarier-than-what-we-know/276607/ (accessed 23 July 2013).

Shachtman, N. and P. W. Singer (2011), 'The Wrong War: The Insistence on Applying Cold War Metaphors to Cybersecurity Is Misplaced and Counterproductive', Government Executive, Brookings, 15 August 2011, www.brookings.edu/research/articles/2011/08/15-cybersecurity-singer-shachtman (accessed 14 September 2013).

Sheldon, J. B. (2011), 'Deciphering cyberpower – strategic purpose in peace and war', *Strategic Studies Quarterly*, Summer, 95–112.

Siroli, G. P. (2012), 'Cyberspazio e Cyberwar', in G. Giacomello and A. Pascolini (eds), *L'ABC del Terrore. Le Armi di Distruzione di Massa del Terzo Millennio*, Milan: Vita e Pensiero.

Sommer, P. and I. Brown (2011), 'Reducing Systemic Cybersecurity Risks', OECD, OECD/IFP Project on 'Future Global Shocks'.

Streltsov, A. A. (2007), 'International information security: description and legal aspects', *Disarmament Forum*, 3: 5–13.

Swire, P. and K. Ahmad (2011), 'Going Dark Versus a Golden Age for Surveillance', CDT, 28 November 2011, www.cdt.org/blogs/2811going-dark-versus-golden-age-surveillance (accessed 29 August 2013).

Zetter, K. (2011), 'How Digital Detectives Deciphered Stuxnet, the Most Menacing Malware in History', *Wired*, www.wired.com/threatlevel/2011/07/how-digital-detectives-deciphered-stuxnet/ (accessed 29 August 2013).

8

Public-Private Partnerships: A 'Soft' Approach to Cybersecurity?

Views from the European Union

Maria Grazia Porcedda

Introduction

The real, or perceived,[1] relevance of CII to the economy and national security (Dunn Cavelty, 2009) has spurred the adoption of cybersecurity policies in most economically developed countries, and the creation of dedicated units or offices in public institutions, not least in the army (The White House, 2009, 2011; European Network and Information Security Agency (ENISA), 2012a; European Commission and High Representative of the European Union for Foreign Affairs and Security Policy, 2013).

However, since the key resources are shared between the public and the private sector, governmental intervention, particularly in the form of regulation, may be insufficient to address the growing need for cybersecurity. A solution has been found in the so-called public-private partnerships (PPPs), whereby the government and the key ICT operators (two fundamental actors in network and information security) pool their resources and know-how to tackle (a) CIIP and (b) the fight against cybercrime. The nature and functioning of these partnerships raise a number of questions. What are PPPs in practice and what is their rationale? Are they keeping up with their promise of increased security? Do they have any adverse impact on society?

This chapter offers answers to these three questions from a EU perspective. Sections 2 and 3 contain an analysis of the nature of PPPs. I first define the rationale for PPPs (section 2), and then, building on the taxonomy developed by the ENISA, I investigate examples of existing regional and international/transnational partnerships (section 3). National PPPs are too wide a subject for the purposes of this chapter; further scholarship should clarify their role.

Questions two and three are specular, and I address them jointly in section 4. I first review the question as to whether PPPs are keeping up with their promise of better addressing cyber-challenges. The dearth of workable metrics requires taking seriously into account PPPs' potential negative impact on society, which I label 'societal collateral damage'. The lack of a (binding) legal framework, a hallmark of all PPPs analysed, raises two additional questions. Is the lack of a binding legal framework necessary to allow for flexibility or, rather, is it conducive to collusion? Is the lack of a legal framework facilitating the violation of citizens' rights, and exposing companies to liabilities? I conclude (section 5) arguing that, in order to appraise the success and need for public-private partnerships, it is necessary to analyse the complex landscape of the PPPs as a whole, taking into account the risk of 'societal collateral damage' and the partnerships' contrasting objectives.

PPPs as a mode of 'soft' cybersecurity governance

The ensemble of network infrastructure (the Internet) and services supporting the World Wide Web (hereafter the Web), understood in this book as a three-layered structure of physical, syntactic and semantic strata, is part of CII. CII is defined as 'ICT systems that are critical infrastructures for themselves, or that are essential for the operation of critical infrastructures (telecommunications, computers/software, Internet, satellites, etc.)' (European Commission, 2005: 19). In turn, critical infrastructure (CI) is understood as:

> Those physical resources, services, and information technology facilities, networks and infrastructure assets that, if disrupted or destroyed, would have a serious impact on the health, safety, security or economic well-being of citizens or the effective functioning of governments. (European Commission, 2005: 20)

One of the three types of infrastructure assets is composed of 'public, private and governmental infrastructure assets and interdependent cyber and physical networks' (European Commission, 2005: 20). In countries where the provision of services previously run by the state has been liberalized and privatized, most of the CII is now privately owned (Dunn Cavelty, 2009). As a result, both the know-how and tools for securing CII are concentrated in the hands of the private sector. This presents challenges in terms of the most suitable approach to, or 'governance' of, the security in cyberspace, or 'cybersecurity', understood as a policy:

> Cyber-security commonly refers to the safeguards and actions that can be used to protect the *cyber domain*, both in the civilian and military fields, from those threats that are associated with or that may harm its interdependent networks and information infrastructure. Cyber-security strives to preserve the availability and integrity of the networks and infrastructure and the confidentiality of the information contained therein. (European Commission and High Representative of the European Union for Foreign Affairs and Security Policy, 2013: 3)

A policy option could consist in a 'hard' approach, whereby government and representative assemblies exercise vertical (top-down) decision-making, enforcing strict regulation of private stakeholders owning CII (who may or may not have been consulted in the process). In the EU, a patchwork of laws – addressing civil[2] and criminal aspects[3]– and non-binding resolutions[4] foster the security of CII at least at the physical and semantic levels (namely, the information infrastructure and Web-related services, from communications to e-commerce).

However, a purely regulatory approach is hindered by a number of challenges. First, being networked and nodal, Internet security requires multiagency cooperation: law enforcement agencies (LEAs) may not be able to police the cyberspace alone (Wall, 2011). Moreover, investigations and punishment are undermined by the problem of attribution (either of machine, human, or digital identity) (Landau, 2010) and the often insufficient training to master complex forensic techniques.[5]

Second, inefficient enforcement raises the incentives for offenders (Kshetri, 2005), and leads CII owners to the well-known and hard to resolve[6] problem of rational under-spending (Sommer and Brown, 2011) in security (European Commission, 2001; Anderson and Moore, 2006; Landau, 2010; The European Public-Private Partnership for Resilience (EP3R), 2010), which is costly[7] and reduces usability. Furthermore, liability for failure to provide sufficient security is addressed piecemeal by civil law,[8] of which sanctions are mild compared with criminal law penalties. Third, not only is regulation slower *vis-à-vis* technological advances (Lessig, 2006), but it may be unsuitable. The lack of reliable statistics on security failures and incidents (Kshetri, 2010) hampers an evidence-based approach to cybersecurity.

Finally, state actors themselves eschew the 'hard' approach. In some instances, governments have threatened to introduce legislation, but have actually preferred fostering industry's self- and co-regulation,[9] which appeared as more convenient and cost-effective solutions (McIntyre, 2011). Some have thus come to denounce the unsuitability of the regulatory/hard approach for tackling urgent security threats and a complex, constantly evolving reality, such as that of the Internet (The European Public-Private Partnership for Resilience (EP3R), 2010).[10]

Dunn Cavelty (2009: 218), in what could be an epitaph of the nation-state as monopolist of force and of the governance of security, states that countries 'Not only allowed nonstate (*sic*) actors to take on crucial roles, but [...] they actually *need* nonstate (*sic*) actors in order to provide one of the core tasks of the nation state: security for their citizens'. Although not going as far as rejecting regulation *per se*, the government itself invokes a 'soft' approach to cybersecurity made of self- and co-regulation, and the introduction of fora (for instance, the public-private partnerships) of cooperation for distributed responsibility (Dunn Cavelty, 2009). As the EU Commissioner for the Information Society in charge of Cybersecurity, Neelie Kroes (2012), stated: 'We all need to take responsibility ... act strategically, and ... work together. That includes the private and the public sectors cooperating'.

There are no agreed definitions of 'PPP'. ENISA (2011a: 10) defines a PPP as 'An *organised* relationship between public and private *organisations*, which establishes *common* scope and *objectives*, and uses defined roles and work methodology to achieve shared goals'. In other words, PPPs entail horizontal, egalitarian[11] decision-making by public authorities and private parties sitting together and sharing common goals. They represent a 'flexible' approach to cybersecurity, which is at odds with the idea of the state as monopolist of force. In fact, it is based on a *quid pro quo*: PPPs work on the basis of serving the interests of both types (public and private) of participants.

On the one hand, public authorities can reach the desired level of information sharing, cost-effectiveness and ensure the provision of security solutions. On the other hand, private parties gain leniency *vis-à-vis* existing security flaws, and ensure that the adoption of incentives, for example providing national security, do not damage them excessively (The European Public-Private

Partnership for Resilience (EP3R), 2010; ENISA, 2011a), for instance, by averting the adoption of negative regulation (ENISA, 2011b). Partnering is also presented as a means to open up business opportunities, since public authorities can share the risks of testing security solutions (Hoorens et al., 2012; European Commission, 2012a). As noted by Commissioner Kroes (2012), 'We will give the industry the opportunity to test out security solutions … with shared financial risks […]. We can create a new business opportunity: to supply private and public sectors alike with the tools they need to tackle online threats'.

The introduction of PPPs has been urged for some time. In the EU, it was suggested already in 2000 (European Commission, 2000), and the need has been reiterated in subsequent policy documents (European Commission and High Representative of the European Union for Foreign Affairs and Security Policy, 2013). Similarly, the creation of PPPs was recommended in the United States 2003 National Strategy to Cyberspace (The White House, 2003), and confirmed by subsequent policies (Sechrist, 2010). In particular, the 2008 Comprehensive National Cybersecurity Initiative (Pearlman, 2010), required the government to partner with the private sector to invest in high-risk and high pay-off solutions. Hence, it is particularly timely to discuss PPPs' nature and appraise their functioning.

What are PPPs? A complex landscape

The definition quoted above, whereby a PPP is 'An *organised* relationship between public and private *organisations*, which establishes *common* scope and *objectives*, and uses defined roles and work methodology to achieve shared goals', testifies to its complex nature (House of Lords, 2010). Indeed, there are no commonly agreed 'standards' on what constitutes a PPP. The ENISA recently built a taxonomy of the PPPs it surveyed within and outside the EU, which provides an interesting starting point for this analysis (ENISA, 2011a, 2011b). The taxonomy builds on eight criteria:

1. *Governance*: organizational structure and duration.[12]
2. *Scope*: element of the security life cycle addressed: deterrence, protection, detection, response, or recovery.
3. *Services* offered to address the scope: audit, policy, standards, etc.

4. The *security threat* addressed within the life cycle:

   a Unintentional threats: natural hazards and systems failure (software and hardware failure),

   b Malicious acts: cybercrime (malicious acts) and terrorism/nation-state (aimed at creating panic),

   c All hazards.

5. *Geographic/thematic coverage*: national, European and international/ and specific sector or theme.

6. *Start-up*: evolution path followed and sustainability.

7. *Links*: relationship with other PPPs or organizations.

8. *Incentives*: reasons why members take part in the PPP.

ENISA grouped PPPs into three categories according to the aspect of the security life cycle they focused on. Prevention-focused PPPs address deterrence and protection,[13] thus they work on long-term objectives and have a strategic approach, and are composed of mature partner institutions.[14] Response-focused PPPs address disaster response and tackle recovery to the pre-event level. Thus,

Why	Who	How	What	When
Scope	**Coverage**	**Governance**	**Services**	**Start up/ sustainability**
• Deter • Protect • Deduct • Respond • Recover	Geographical • National • European • International • Protect	Activity type • Long term community • Working group • Rapid response • Combine activity • Overreaching strategy or advisory group	• Research/Analysis • Good practice guides • Early warnings • Exercises • Awareness raising • Etc	• Top down • Bottom up • Top down then grown bottom up • Bottom up then grown top down • Fire and forget • Split or merge
Scope • All hazards • Natural hazards • System failure • Cyber-crime • Terrorism	**Focus** • Geographical • Sector • Cross section • Thermal	**Leadership** • Run by one from within • Run by a coordinating entity • Democratically peer led	**Incentives** • Reduced exposure • Cost savings • Access to valuable knowledge • Influence regulation or national policies • Etc	
	Links • Across National boundaries • Within national boundaries • CERTS or CSIRTS • Regular bodies • Law enforcement bodies	**Funding** • Mandatory membership • Charging for value • Public pays all or some • Members own time and travel		
		Communication style • Face-to-face • Virtual but personal • Computer bad distribution		
		Rules • Formal membership rules • Formal information usage agreements • Trust building policies • Membership requires security clearance		

Figure 8.1 Taxonomy based on eight criteria

ENISA 2011b, p. 16

they usually operate in real time; sometimes they have been created in the wake of major disasters, and have evolved ever since (United Nations Interregional Crime and Justice Research Institute (UNICRI), 2009).[15] Umbrella PPPs focus on the full security life cycle, composed of deterrence, protection, detection, response and recovery.[16] The taxonomy developed by ENISA (2011a, 2011b) concerned national PPPs, whereas this chapter intends to focus on regional and transnational PPPs. In what follows, I analyse a sample of PPPs based on item 5 (geographic/thematic coverage) of the taxonomy, and taking also into account items 2 (element of the security life cycle addressed) and 4 (security threat addressed within the life cycle).

Regional (EU-based) PPPs

Examples of regional, EU-based partnerships include umbrella, prevention-focused and response-focused PPPs, as well as all hazards and thematic ones:

The *Future Internet Public Private Partnership*[17] *(FI-PPP)* is a prevention-focused PPP tackling all hazards. Set up in May 2011 by the European Commission and the European Industry under the so-called Digital Agenda[18] (European Commission, 2010a), its objectives are fostering the competitiveness of European industry with regard to Internet technologies, and the production of services and infrastructures serving areas of social and public interest (transport, health and energy). The EU has committed several hundred million euros in funds over five years. Some of these resources support the creation of a core platform called FI-WARE, 'a standardised and interoperable Internet service platform' that includes the provision of security, 'eight use case projects',[19] and 'infrastructure and programme support' (European Commission, 2011a; Hoorens et al., 2012: 3).

The *European Public-Private Partnership for Resilience* (EP3R) is an umbrella PPP tackling all hazards. It was set up as part of the European Commission 2009 CIIP Action Plan (European Commission, 2009). Its mission is to cooperate with national PPPs, the European Forum for Member States (EFSM) and, prospectively, international actors, to tackle security risks – man-made and natural – and resilience (prevention and preparedness) concerning the Internet and fixed and mobile communications. The first objective of the EP3R is the exchange of sensitive information on threats and vulnerabilities of CII, and the subsequent establishment of standards and guidelines. The EP3R covers five areas of action (European Commission, 2010b):

1. Risk assessment of key infrastructural assets and resources, and modalities of functioning, based on information sharing.
2. Risk management, consisting in the harmonization of the level of security provided, based on the development of metrics, and the overcoming of barriers in terms of competition law and national security provisions.
3. Preparedness, consisting in partners' cooperation to respond to large-scale disruptions or failures of the networks.
4. Security in the supply chain, which includes the development of requirements for security in hardware, software and services.
5. Developing the market and economic incentives to provide CIIP.

Participants[20] include relevant national PPPs, public authorities working on network and information security, providers of electronic communications networks, services and nodes, and European industry associations working in the field. The EP3R is expected to complement existing PPPs, foster trust among partners, especially regarding the exchange of personal information, provide value or bi-directional exchanges for public and private actors, include all relevant actors and be open and transparent. While flexible, the EP3R should have a long-term horizon and focus on the economic dimension of resilience and competitiveness – all while avoiding the distortion of market mechanisms and the creation of cartels.

The *2CENTRE* is an umbrella PPP tackling malicious acts (cybercrimes). It is a network of national Cybercrime Centres of Excellence for Training, Research, and Education.[21] It is composed of members of industry, academia, and LEAs, whose shared goal is to advance the fight against cybercrime, through training and, for instance, the creation of 'Forensic Software Tools ready for use and tool validation documentation' and 'IP specifications for parties involved' (Cybercrime Centres of Excellence Network for Training Research and Education (2Centre), 2010b).

Finally, the second *pan-EU cybersecurity exercise* was an *ad hoc*, response focused, all hazards PPP involving private actors. Whereas the industry liaised with national governments, the overall direction emanated from the EU level. The ENISA acknowledged the marked difference in national PPP approaches (ENISA, 2012), which supports the choice of this chapter to address national PPPs in a separate study.

Transnational[22] institutional and non-institutional PPPs

Transnational PPPs include umbrella, prevention-focused and detection-focused PPPs, as well as all hazards and thematic ones. Transnational PPPs can be further divided into institutional PPPs, which are hosted and fostered by international organizations (IMPACT and Octopus), and non-institutional PPPs, which have been created under the auspices of institutions, but do not belong directly to them and operate as 'independent' fora of cooperation (Global Alliance, the Virtual Global Task Force and the London Action Plan).

Institutional PPPs

The 'International Multilateral Partnership Against Cyber Threats' (IMPACT) is an umbrella PPP focused on malicious acts. It was founded in 2008 as a 'politically neutral' 'cybersecurity alliance against cyber threats' (IMPACT, 2013), gathering 145 governments, academia and industry stakeholders.[23] In particular, IMPACT is tasked, since 2008, with the operationalization of the United Nations specialized agency International Telecommunication Union's (ITU) Global Cybersecurity Agenda (GCA), which is a collection of recommendations aimed at increasing cybersecurity in the following five areas: legal, technical and procedural measures, organizational structures, capacity-building and international cooperation (ITU, 2009).

IMPACT became ITU's 'cybersecurity executing arm' (IMPACT, 2013) by means of a Memorandum of Agreement in 2011. Moreover, IMPACT also signed a Memorandum of Understanding with the United Nations Office on Drugs and Crime (UNODC) to support UNODC's member states in the fight against cybercrime with expertise, facilities and resources through its Global Response Centre (IMPACT, 2013).

Another umbrella partnership focused on malicious acts is the Council of Europe's PPP, called 'Octopus', which was established in 2007. It groups LEAs, industry and service provider associations from all over the world 'that participate in Octopus Conferences and other Council of Europe activities against cybercrime' (Council of Europe, 2013), as listed in the Cybercrime Convention. These include both crimes against the availability, integrity, and confidentiality of computer systems, as well as computer-related crimes, content-related crimes and copyright infringement. The Convention does not address cyber-attacks yet.

Non-institutional PPPs

The 'Global Alliance' is a detection-focused PPP combating child pornography (malicious act) fostered by the Working Group on Cybersecurity and Cybercrime, created in turn by the EU-US Summit (Council of the European Union, 2010; EU-US Working Group on Cybersecurity and Cybercrime; Porcedda, 2011). The Global Alliance (European Commission, 2012b) was established in cooperation with several governments at the end of 2012 with four operational goals:

1. Increasing the identification of victims, and ensuring their support.
2. Stepping-up investigations and prosecution of child sexual abuse online.
3. Raising public awareness; and
4. Reducing the availability of child porn material online and the re-victimization of children.

The Global Alliance aims to cooperate with the Virtual Global Taskforce (see below). The envisaged role of the private sector is clarified by goals two and four of the Guiding Principles (Global Alliance Partners, 2012). Goal two states that LEAs should cooperate with 'private sector actors, whose infrastructure and services may be used for the trade in child sexual abuse material, to facilitate effective investigations into these crimes, including all financial aspects' (Global Alliance Partners, 2012: 2). Goal four envisages an even more active role for the private sector. First, the industry should actively identify and remove known child pornographic material, also by augmenting the quantity of data analysed. To this end, governments should overcome possible legal hurdles, draft guidelines for the cooperation between LEAs and the private sector, and develop and deploy suitable technology. Second, industry should take part in the implementation of swifter procedures of notice and takedown. For instance, standardized interfaces should be built between hotlines and ISPs, regulated by memoranda of understanding overseeing the conduct of investigations and the expedite preservation of evidence (Global Alliance Partners, 2012).

The above mentioned 'Virtual Global Taskforce' (VGT), with which the Global Alliance should cooperate, is an international detection-focused partnership of LEAs, industry and non-governmental organizations (NGOs) established in 2003 to protect children from online abuse (malicious acts).[24] The objectives of the VGT are:

1. Making the Internet a safer place;
2. Identifying, locating and helping children at risk;
3. Holding perpetrators appropriately to account (Virtual Global Taskforce, 2011b).

The private sector is deemed to play 'a vital role ... in tackling online child abuse', and thus it is encouraged to join to 'publicly recognise good corporate citizenship, support innovative thinking and, ultimately, to reduce the incidence of child abuse online.' Several private partners work with VGT 'to help make the Internet safer by design', including companies such as Paypal, Microsoft Digital Crimes Unit, Research in Motion, and NGOs such as World Vision Australia (Virtual Global Taskforce, 2011a).[25] VGT publicized four operations ('Rescue', 'Basket', 'Elm' and 'Chandler') carried out in the last four years, which led to the uncovering of national and global paedophile networks, the dismantling of thousands of websites, the arrest of 250 criminals, the identification of almost a thousand suspects, and the protection of at least 250 children (Virtual Global Taskforce, 2011b).

Finally, and differently from the above, the 'London Action Plan' (International Cybersecurity Enforcement Network) is an umbrella PPP focused on malicious acts. It was created in 2004 to 'promote international spam enforcement cooperation and address spam related problems, such as online fraud and deception, phishing, and dissemination of viruses.' (International Cybersecurity Enforcement Network (London Action Plan), 2012). It includes public bodies and private companies[26] interested in developing anti-spam partnerships. The Action Plan:

> Is not intended to create any new legally binding obligations by or amongst the Participants [...]. Participants to (sic) this Action Plan recognize that cooperation pursuant to this Action Plan is subject to their laws and their international obligations, and that nothing in this Action Plan requires the Participants to provide confidential or commercially sensitive information. (International Cybersecurity Enforcement Network (London Action Plan), 2012).

Proposed international PPPs

New international PPPs are also being proposed. The 'Strategy for Partnerships between States and Businesses to Counter Terrorism', adopted at the end of 2006 by the Group of Eight (G8) (UNODC, 2012), fostered the creations of detection, malicious acts-focused PPPs to fight against the misuse of the Internet by terrorists for recruitment, training and incitement to commit terrorist acts, and inhibit radicalization (General Assembly of the United Nations, 2009).

Likewise, a report by UNODC advocated the introduction of detection, malicious acts-focused PPPs with Internet service providers (ISPs or access providers) for fighting the use of the Internet for terrorist purposes (UNODC, 2012). ISPs, in fact, are likely to hold information concerning propaganda, financing, training, planning, and execution of terrorist activities,[27] and should, according to UNODC (2012), perform content control, which is a controversial initiative as discussed below. While cyber-attacks were mentioned as one of the possible terrorist uses of the Internet, they were overlooked as being beyond the scope of the report. Recently, it was proposed to set up an umbrella PPP dealing with the security of undersea communication cables (Sechrist, 2010).

Contrasting objectives

What emerges from this non-exhaustive overview of existing and proposed partnerships is a fragmentary landscape that escapes systematization. It seems clear, though, that PPPs vary in focus. Existing and proposed international PPPs, with the exception of the London Action Plan and the proposed PPP for undersea cables, seem more concerned with cyber-threats at the semantic level (malicious acts), which affect neither the confidentiality of information, nor the physical or syntactic layers. The latter seem to pertain more to regional PPPs, perhaps unsurprisingly, as tackling them entails the disclosure of more sensitive information and industrial secrets.

A terminological clarification may be needed at this point. Different threats populate cyberspace: although commonly referred to as 'cybercrimes', such threats are essentially different from each other (and should rather be called 'cyberspace crimes') (Wall, 2011). The crimes against the integrity, availability and confidentiality of computer systems and networks are proper cybercrimes (or 'crimes against the machine') (Wall, 2011) and largely overlap with the notion of cybersecurity ('the availability and integrity of the networks and infrastructure and the confidentiality of the information contained therein'). Incitement to terrorism, copyright infringing material, and distribution of child pornography are 'broad' cybercrimes (or 'crimes in, and through, the machine')

(Wall, 2011), that is, offences relating to the distribution of content deemed unlawful (and thus, are regime-sensitive[28]).

Some of the proposed and existing regional and international PPPs reviewed address content-related cyberspace crimes, and focus on detection and removal (as well as prosecution of the offenders). The detection of unlawful content requires techniques that include mild forms of filtering (Anderson and Murdoch, 2008), but also intrusive deep packet inspection engines, which can cover a wide spectrum of layers of the Internet architecture (Mueller, 2011). On the one hand, this endangers civil liberties and undermines trust in the security provider, as I address below. On the other hand, it endangers CII by creating backdoors that could be exploited by malicious actors (Landau, 2010). Thus, state (and non-state) actors are engaged in contradictory activities of tackling CII protection with some PPPs, and undermining it with others.

What is the impact of PPPs on society?

PPPs can have both a positive impact, expressed in terms of increased cybersecurity, and a negative one, expressed in terms of harmful consequences on society, which I label 'societal collateral damage'. I start with the former.

Are PPPs offering higher cybersecurity?

In 2007, a joint report by the US Departments of Homeland Security and Defense acknowledged the lack of criteria to carry out impact assessments of PPPs (Talbot Jensen, 2011). The situation does not seem different now. 'Metrics for the success of a PPP are hard to identify, with the length of time in existence being often quoted' (European Network and Information Security Agency, 2011b: 41). It is hard to encounter data about the added value of existing PPPs, apart from those that tackle child pornography (for instance, Virtual Global Task Force's operations).

A recent report by Microsoft Trustworthy Computing tries to fill the gap. Membership of the PPP London Action plan is considered an indicator of overall performance in cybersecurity. Cybersecurity, in turn, is measured by proxy, through an indicator called 'computers cleaned per mille' (CCM), which 'represents the number of computers cleaned for every 1,000 times that the

Malicious Software Removal Tool is run' (Kleiner et al., 2013: 5). The Malicious Software Removal Tool, in turn, checks Windows computers and removes any (known) malware or infections found. The proposed metrics represents a promising beginning for PPPs, yet it covers only one aspect of cybersecurity. Consequently, it does not seem sufficient to appraise, at this stage, the success of PPPs in addressing the security of the physical, syntactic and semantic layer, and calls for further research. In the light of the limitedness of proposed metrics to evaluate the success of partnerships, discussing possible negative societal impacts of PPPs is particularly important.

Is the lack of a legal framework fostering flexibility, or is it conducive to collusion, liability and 'societal collateral damage'?

A common feature of the PPPs surveyed is the opaqueness of their legal basis (if any). This points to the lack of an underlying sound legal framework, and the preference for soft agreements, rather than hard regulation. As stated in the above mentioned UNODCs, PPPs are ideally understood as 'informal relationships' or 'understandings' with domestic or foreign ISPs: the establishment of 'formal channels' and the use of 'appropriate judicial authorizations' for the preservation of such data held by foreign ISPs should be pursued only if such informal alternatives do not exist (UNODC, 2012: 138). Two fundamental questions emerge: is the lack of a binding legal framework necessary to allow for flexibility, or is it conducive to collusion? Does it expose companies to liabilities, and society to the risk of 'collateral damage'?

The lack of a clear and binding legal framework could work as a double-edged sword. On the one hand, memoranda of understanding and codes of conduct may allow PPPs to have sufficient flexibility to respond to urgent, unforeseen and substantially novel events. On the other hand, though, the lack of binding rules overseeing the functioning of PPPs could expose private parties to liability, for at least three reasons.

First, potential members of PPPs fear to breach competition laws, in that they could be seen as creating cartels. In this respect, the involvement of the regulator may be viewed as either welcome or undesirable, due to possible conflict of interests (European Network and Information Security Agency, 2011b). This may depend, in turn, on the varying degree of institutional trust existing in different member states of the EU (Dunn Cavelty, 2009). Second, the industry fears the consequences related to the disclosure of information, in particular of industrial secrets, or encryption keys, deriving from the involvement of the regulator, or LEAs (House of Lords, 2010; European Network and Information Security Agency, 2011b). Finally, private actors are wary of the costs connected to the regulators' or LEAs' requests, and of introducing demanding procedures (Porcedda, 2011).

A binding legal framework would thus help relieving private parties of any liability, in particular as relates to collusion and anti-trust, and clarify issues pertaining to the protection of industrial secrets and cost sharing. But there is another important reason for supporting the adoption of a stringent legal framework. Some private actors, in fact, fear to lose their consumers' trust, as cooperation with the regulator and LEAs may lead to the monitoring of consumers' communications (House of Lords, 2010), and activities on the Internet. The protest sparked by the revelations relating to the US National Security Agency's 'Prism' program, and the UK GCHQ's 'Tempora' program is a case in point (MacAskill et al., 2013; Risen and Wingfield, 2013).[29]

LEA's actions to acquire evidence outside a binding legal framework may raise concerns. In fact, the expedited detection and preservation of evidence to investigate cyberspace crimes requires the analysis of content and metadata, which can be intrusive for the confidentiality of personal communications, enshrined in the fundamental rights to privacy (article 7, European Union, 2007), and personal data, enshrined in the fundamental right to data protection (article 8, European Union, 2007). The access to such communications and data, realized through intrusive deep packet inspection engines, can affect other civil rights, such as freedom of information, expression, religion, association, etc.

A loose cooperation may thus pave the way to the risk of 'societal collateral damage': the illegitimate, and unlawful, violation or destruction of civil liberties and the very rights that inform and protect democracy. As for the illegitimacy, such loosely defined PPPs may amount to state-corporate crime, namely, 'Illegal or socially injurious actions that occur when one or more institutions of political governance pursue a goal in direct cooperation with one or more institutions of economic production and distribution' (Kramer et al., 2002: 270).

As for unlawfulness, the limitations on civil and political rights for the sake of a legitimate aim such as cybersecurity cannot be unrestrained, but must conform to a number of criteria, including legality, compliance with the rule of law, necessity, proportionality, and oversight (Porcedda et al., 2013), which can only be established under a binding legal framework.[30] This is especially the case when defence is added to the equation, as the military is moving towards asserting control over Internet communications by using the same techniques of LEAs (Hoorens et al., 2012) – in a yet laxer regulatory framework.[31]

Thus, a more stringent framework is not only necessary for the sake of lawfulness, but would increase transparency and users' trustworthiness. Indeed, the guidelines issued by the Council of Europe to support LE and industry cooperation go in this direction (Council of Europe, 2008).

Conclusions: A 'soft' success for cybersecurity?

In this chapter, I surveyed a number of regional (EU-based) and transnational PPPs. More research is needed to complement existing taxonomies, systematize what appears a complex landscape (for instance, on the basis of their physical, syntactic or semantic focus), and build a valid metric to assess the efficacy of PPPs. Some elements, though, seem to emerge. PPPs addressing the physical and syntactic level seem to be concentrated at the (national and) regional level, possibly in connection with exigencies of national security and the preservation of industrial secrets. Transnational PPPs seem to focus more on detection/prosecution and

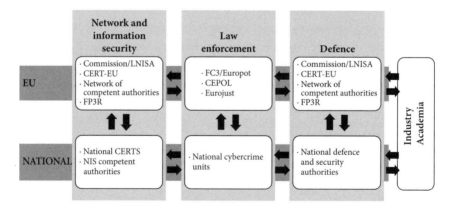

Figure 8.2 Integration between NIS, LEAs and defence

European Commission and High Representative of the European Union for Foreign Affairs and Security Policy (2013, p. 17)

on single security threats, mostly related to broad cyberspace crimes, such as child pornography and terrorism online (with the exception of spamming).

Thus, the surveyed PPPs focus on different threats to the cyberspace, and on clashing notions of cybersecurity: on the one hand, network and information security and proper cyberspace crimes, on the other, broad cyberspace crimes. Moreover, all PPPs seem to be developing outside clear and binding legal frameworks. Not only does this affect trust and efficacy; coupled with the different missions of PPPs, it may create unwanted – and incommensurable – outcomes for cybersecurity. The diverging focus and the lack of legal frameworks are connected: proper cybersecurity can only be achieved if interests and behaviours converge towards a common understanding of what we are trying to protect. Given the networked and nodal nature of security in cyberspace, PPPs probably represent the best tool available to date. Yet, given the inherent *quid pro quo* nature of PPPs, the decision as to what is a threat, and how to pursue it, cannot be left to them. Convenience and the pursuit of vested interests, rather than heightened cybersecurity, could easily be the outcome of PPPs, as a result of a habit of exchange.

Parliaments still represent the best arena to host the crucial discussion as to the objectives and means of cybersecurity, especially if one considers the possible collateral damage of PPPs on civil liberties and the organization of society at large. The 'silver bullet' may lie in a careful combination of 'hard' regulation and 'soft' PPPs, whereby the regulation defines objectives and procedures of PPPs, as well as convincing sanctions for those actors – whether public or private – which are liable for security failures at the physical, syntactic and semantic strata (for instance, faulty software).

Certainly, regulation is not resolutive, but is crucial to eliminate the ambiguity of technology (for instance, that used to pursue cybersecurity), and consolidate technological achievements that protect societal values (Nissenbaum, 2011). If the regulator failed in this respect, it would be legitimate to ask whether there still existed any division between the public and the private, and whether the former could be really regarded as the monopolist of force, and provider of security. PPPs, in fact, could be seen as a form of 'tilting', the shifting of the private actor between the state and the user that short-circuits 'the classical vertical state-citizen relationship on which [...] freedom [...] is founded' (McIntyre, 2011).[32] Such tilting would trigger questions about sovereignty and the organizations of our society – a more radical issue than both cybersecurity (however defined) and the role of PPPs. In order to make

PPPs the 'soft' key to cybersecurity, 'hard' safeguards must be in place to guide them, minimize contrasting objectives and liabilities, and to ward off societal collateral damage.

Notes

1   Dunn Cavelty (2009) argues that the fear of state actors for attacks against CIIs affects haves as well as 'have-nots' as a result of a generalized perception of risk, which is partly related to the inherent insecurity of CII (such as Supervisory Control and Data Acquisition systems, also known as SCADA), heightened by the phobias about new threats characterized by 'asymmetry' that emerged at the end of the Cold War.

2   This includes primarily the so-called Telecom Package (Directives 2009a, 2009b), which contains five Directives addressing the owners of infrastructure (see in particular articles 13 letters (a) and (b) of the revised Directive 2002/21/EC (Directive 2009b), providers of services, and controllers of data. As for the latter, article 4 of the e-Privacy Directive (European Parliament and European Council, 2002), for instance, obliges the providers of publicly available electronic communications to adopt appropriate technical and organizational measures to safeguard the security of their services in cooperation with the provider of public communications networks.

3   These are the Directive on attacks against information systems and replacing Council Framework Decision 2005/222/JHA (Directive 2013) and the Cybercrime Convention (Council of Europe, 2001), which addresses broader crimes in the cyberspace and has been signed by all EU members, and some non-members such as the United States, Canada, Australia and South Africa. The updated list of signatories is available at: http://conventions.coe.int/Treaty/Commun/ChercheSig. asp?NT=185&CM=&DF=&CL=ENG (accessed 15 February 2013).

4   These are the Council of the European Union (Council) resolutions on network and information security (Council, 2009, 2003, 2002).

5   Indeed, it seems that LEAs have long focused on 'known' crimes that are likely to end up in successful investigations (Sommer and Brown, 2011). Moreover, LEAs often lack appropriate tools, such as databases

on reported and prosecuted cybercrimes, which affects the availability of reliable statistics (Kshetri, 2010).

6 At the beginning of 2013, the European Commission published a proposal for a Directive containing measures to ensure a high level of network and information security across the EU (European Commission, 2013), which, if adopted in its current form, will address the issues of under-reporting and distorted incentives.

7 For instance, software companies prefer releasing new products as soon as possible in order to enjoy a first mover advantage, and compensate for security flaws, promptly exploited by viruses, with patches and updates only after the first release, in what has been dubbed the 'arms race' (House of Lords, 2008). Security fallacies have increased in proportion with the size of programs, measured in SLC (Source Lines of Code) (Sartor, 2010; Porcedda, 2012). Moreover, the new market for zero-day exploits could lead code writers to willingly add zero-day exploits to sell the information afterwards. See also Schneier (2013).

8 The recent introduction of mandatory reporting of security incidents breaches in the United States and the EU, accompanied by consistent pecuniary sanctions, tries to address this problem. However, in the EU, it is so far applicable only to few types of legal persons (Barcelo, 2009). Article 4.3 of the amended e-Privacy Directive (European Parliament and Council, 2009a) provides for the mandatory notification of data security breaches for the providers of publicly available electronic communications. The transposing laws adopted by the member states of the EU provide for liability and sanctions in case of transgressions. Some scholars, though, expressed doubts as to the efficacy of notification of data breaches (Edwards and Waelde, 2009).

9 For a discussion of the meaning of self- and co-regulation, see Ofcom (2008).

10 'Hard' regulation is defined as 'premature', 'inappropriate', and 'risky' by EP3R members (EP3R, 2010).

11 According to Mr Clinton, a representative of a US PPP interviewed by the ENISA, the PPPs should 'Be cooperative in nature, lacking punitive overtones characterized by regulatory models, so that trust and affirmative proactive steps are taken by both partners' (ENISA, 2011b: 52).

12 Some PPPs can only be formed one-off. This may be the case of the joint

cyber-exercises, like the Europe-wide one held at the end of 2012 (ENISA, 2012).

13 Prevention-focused PPPs may overlap with Computer Emergency Response Teams (CERTs), which collect and analyse data about existing and emerging security threats, and plan for forward-looking responses.

14 Slovenian Varni Na Internetu, British NSIE, and the US Information Technology- Information Sharing and Analysis Centre (IT-ISAC) are examples of this type of PPP.

15 The British EC RRG, the Dutch NCO-T, and the Polish CERT Polska are examples of this type of PPP.

16 The US National Security Telecommunications Advisory Committee (NSTAC) and German UPKRITS fall within this category.

17 'The aims of the FI-PPP are to increase the effectiveness of business processes and of the operation of infrastructures supporting applications in sectors such as transport, health, or energy and to derive possible innovative business models in these sectors, strengthening the competitive position of European industry in domains like telecommunications, mobile devices, software and service industries, content providers and media' (European Commission, 2011b).

18 The Digital Agenda is the Commission's plan for the development of a suistainable e-market.

19 Namely, CONCORD, ENVIROFI, FI-CONTENT, FI-WARE, FINEST, FINSENY, INFINITY, INSTANT MOBILITY, OUTSMART, SAFECITY, and SMARTAGRIFOOD. For the details of each, see at: http://www.fi-ppp. eu/about/ (accessed 15 September 2013).

20 The EP3R is double-layered. The high-level steering group is composed of executives and provides the necessary impetus. The strategic level encompasses senior experts addressing policy priorities and measures in various working groups.

21 See Cybercrime Centres of Excellence Network for Training Research and Education (2Centre) (2010a).

22 Some PPPs are hybrid, in that the government liaises with national industry operating abroad to exchange information about security. This is the case of the US Overseas Security Advisory Council (UNODC, 2012).

23 For the complete list of the 145 member countries and the list of partners, see IMPACT (2013) www.impact-alliance.org/home/index-countries.html

and at: www.impact-alliance.org/partners/introduction.html (accessed 15 September 2013).

24 Both the US Immigration and Customs Enforcement and Operation Predator are part of the Department of Homeland Security, the former being its investigative arm. The following authorities of member countries participate in the works: Australian Federal Police, National Child Exploitation Coordination Centre, Royal Canadian Mounted Police, Europol, Interpol, Italian Postal and Communication Police Service, New Zealand Police, Ministry of Interior for the United Arab Emirates, the United Kingdom Child Exploitation and Online Protection Centre, and the US Immigration and Customs Enforcement and Operation Predator.

25 For a complete list of partners, see Virtual Global Taskforce (2011a) at: www.virtualglobaltaskforce.com/who-we-are/industry-partners// (accessed 15 September 2013).

26 For a complete list of partners, see International Cybersecurity Enforcement Network (London Action Plan) (2012) at: http:// londonactionplan.org/members/ (accessed 15 September 2013).

27 Propaganda includes recruitment, radicalization and incitement to terrorism, whereas planning includes secret communication and the collection of open-source information.

28 For instance, in different countries the same crimes may consist in the provision of free information or incitement to democracy (Rid, 2012).

29 This chapter was almost entirely drafted before the disclosure of the Prism and Tempora programs. However, I believe that the revelations reinforce, rather than weaken, the arguments presented in these pages. The complexity of the two programs requires a dedicated analysis, but it should be noted that Prism (like Tempora) does not come as a surprise. The existence of a partnership between Google and the National Security Agency (NSA), reportedly to share information with a view to improving Google's (privately owned) networks' security negotiated after the attacks suffered by Gmail in 2010, was known for some time (Sommer and Brown, 2011), and the refusal to provide information had raised suspicion (Kravets, 2012). Prism is certainly not the first partnership of this type. A couple of years ago, the secret cooperation between the NSA and the telecommunication giant AT&T was also unveiled (Landau, 2010). Concerns such as those raised by Prism may apply to the 'Enduring Security Framework', made up of CEOs of information and

204 · Security in Cyberspace

communication technologies and defence companies, the heads of the Department of Homeland Security, the Department of Defence and the Office of the Director of National Intelligence (Lynn III, 2010; Armerding, 2012).

30 Recently, the European Data Protection Supervisor (2012) defined the lack of a clear scope and modalities relating to the PPPs foreseen by the European Cybercrime Centre (EC3), recently created within Europol and that 'will have child abuse material online as a main focus, of 'particular concern'. See also European Commission (2012a).

31 While initiatives in the EU have not been defined yet, the United States' Einstein 2 and 3 programmes provide an example in point (White House, 2012).

32 Quoting Lambers (2006).

References

Anderson, R. and T. Moore (2006), 'The economics of information security', Science, 314: 610–1.

Anderson, R. and S. J. Murdoch (2008), 'Tools and Technology of Internet Filtering', in J. Palfrey, R. Deibert, R. Rohozinski and J. Zittrain (eds), Access Denied: The Practice and Policy of Global Internet Filtering, Cambridge, MA: MIT Press, 57–72.

Armerding, T. (2012), 'Public vs. Private Cyberattack Responsibility Debate Heats Up', CSOonline, 14 May 2012.

Barcelo, R. (2009), 'EU: revision of the eprivacy directive', Computer Law Review International no. 31: 31.

Council of Europe (1950), 'Convention for the Protection of Human Rights and Fundamental Freedoms', as amended by Protocols No 11 and 14, 4 November 1950, Rome, Italy.

—(2001), 'Convention on Cybercrime', CETS n. 105, Budapest, originally signed on 23 November 2001.

—(2008), 'Guidelines for the Cooperation Between Law Enforcement and Internet Service Providers against Cybercrime', adopted by the Global Conference Cooperation against Cybercrime, Strasbourg, France, www.coe.int/t/informationsociety/documents/Guidelines_cooplaw_ISP_en.pdf (accessed 14 September 2013).

—(2013), 'Octopus Cybercrime Community 2013', http://octopus-web.ext.coe.int/ (accessed 8 February 2013).

Council of the European Union (2002), 'Resolution of 16 February 2002 on a Common Approach and Specific Actions in the Area of Network and Information security', Brussels, Official Journal C 043, 16 February 2002.

—(2003), 'Resolution of 18 February 2003 on a European Approach Towards a Culture of Network and Information Security', Brussels, Official Journal C 4, 28 February 2003.

—(2005), 'Council Framework Decision 2005/222/JHA of 24 February 2005 on "Attacks against Information Systems", Brussels, Official Journal L 69, 16 March 2005.

—(2009), 'Resolution of 18 December 2009 on a Collaborative European Approach to Network and Information Security', Brussels. Official Journal C 321, 29 December 2009.

—(2010), 'EU-US Summit Joint Statement', Lisbon, 16726/10, Presse 315, 20 November 2010, http://europa.eu/rapid/press-release_PRES-10-315_en.htm?locale=en (accessed 8 February 2013).

Cybercrime Centres of Excellence Network for Training Research and Education (2Centre) (2010a), http://www.2centre.eu/ (accessed 8 February 2013).

—(2010b), 'What are the expected outcomes of the project?' http://www.2centre.eu/node/60 (accessed 8 February 2013).

Directive (2002), 'Directive 2002/58/EC of the European Parliament and of the Council of 12 July 2002 concerning the processing of personal data and the protection of privacy in the electronic communications sector (Directive on privacy and electronic communications) (e-Privacy Directive)' Official Journal L 201, 31 July 2002.

—(2009a), 'Directive 2009/136/EC of the European Parliament and of the Council of 25 November 2009 amending Directive 2002/22/EC on universal service and users' rights relating to electronic communications networks and services, Directive 2002/58/EC concerning the processing of personal data and the protection of privacy in the electronic communications sector and Regulation (EC) No 2006/2004 on cooperation between national authorities responsible for the enforcement of consumer protection laws. Official Journal L 337, 18 December 2009.

—(2009b), Directive 2009/140/EC of 25 November 2009 amending Directives 2002/21/EC on a common regulatory framework for electronic communications networks and services, 2002/19/EC on access to, and interconnection of, electronic communications networks and associated facilities, and 2002/20/EC on the authorisation of electronic communications networks and services. Official Journal L 337, 18 December 2009.

—(2013), Directive 2013/40/EU of the European Parliament and of the Council of 12 August 2013 on attacks against information systems and replacing Council Framework Decision 2005/222/JHA. Official Journal L 218, 14 August 2013.

Dunn Cavelty, M. (2009), 'National security and the internet: distributed security through distributed responsibility', in J. Eriksson and G. Giacomello (eds), 'Who

Controls the Internet? Beyond the Obstinacy or Obsolescence of the State', The Forum, *International Studies Review* 11: 214–218.

Edwards, L. and C. Waelde (2009), *Law and the Internet*, Portland, OR: Hart Publishing.

EU-US Working Group on Cyber-Security and Cyber-Crime (2011), 'Concept Paper', www.huembwas.org/News_Events/20110408_cyber_conf/summary_elemei/ MD-018a-11-EU US WG – Concept paper – CL 201110413_US.pdf (accessed 15 September 2013).

European Commission (2000), 'Communication from the Commission to the Council, the European Parliament, the Economic And Social Committee and the Committee of the Regions: Creating a Safer Information Society by Improving the Security of Information Infrastructures and Combating Computer-Related Crime', Brussels, COM (2000) 890 final, 26 January 2000.

—(2001), 'Communication from the Commission to the Council, the European Parliament, the Economic and Social Committee and the Committee of the Regions – Network and Information Security: Proposal for a European Policy Approach', Brussels, COM (2001) 298, 6 June 2001.

—(2005), 'Green Paper on a European Program for Critical Infrastructure Protection', Brussels, COM (2005) 576 final, 17 November 2005.

—(2009), 'Communication from the Commission to the Council, the European Parliament, the Economic and Social Committee and the Committee of the Regions – Protecting Europe from large-scale cyber-attacks and disruptions: enhancing preparedness, security and resilience', Brussels, COM (2009) 149 final, 30 March 2009.

—(2010a), 'Communication from the Commission to the Council, the European Parliament, the Economic and Social Committee and the Committee of the Regions – A Digital Agenda for Europe', Brussels, COM (2010) 245 final, 19 May 2010.

—(2010b), 'Meeting of The European Public-Private Partnership for Resilience (EP3R)', Brussels, Summary Report, 29 June 2010.

—(2011a), 'Digital Agenda: Commission and European industry join forces to build the Internet of the Future', IP/11/525, Brussels, 3 May 2011. http://europa.eu/rapid/press-release_IP-11-525_en.htm?locale=en (accessed 8 February 2013).

—(2011b), 'Future Internet Public Private Partnership (FI-PPP), http://www.fi-ppp.eu/about/ (accessed 8 February 2013).

—(2012a), 'Communication from the Commission to the Council, the European Parliament, the Economic and Social Committee and the Committee of the Regions – Security Industrial Policy. Action Plan for an Innovative and Competitive Security Industry', Brussels, COM (2012) 417 final, 26 July 2012.

—(2012b), 'Declaration on the Launch of the Global Alliance against Child Sexual Abuse Online', Brussels, MEMO/12/944, 5 December 2012.

—(2013), 'Proposal for a Directive of the European Parliament and of the Council
Concerning Measures to Ensure a High Common Level of Network and
Information Security Across the Union', Brussels, (SWD (2013) 31 final) (SWD
(2013) 32 final), COM (2013) 48 final, 7 February 2013.

European Commission and High Representative of the European Union for Foreign
Affairs and Security Policy (2013), 'Joint Communication to the Council, the
European Parliament, the Economic And Social Committee and the Committee of
the Regions – EU Cyber Security Strategy: An Open, Safe and Secure Cyberspace',
Brussels, JOIN (2013) 01 final, 7 February 2013.

European Data Protection Supervisor (2012), 'Opinion on the Communication from
the European Commission to the Council and the European Parliament on the
establishment of a European Cybercrime Centre', Brussels 29 June 2012, https://
secure.edps.europa.eu/EDPSWEB/webdav/site/mySite/shared/Documents/
Consultation/Opinions/2012/12-06-29_European_Cybercrime_Center_EN.pdf
(accessed 15 September 2013).

European Network and Information Security Agency (2011a), 'Cooperative Models
for Effective Public Private Partnerships. Desktop Research Report', Luxembourg:
Publications Office of the European Union, www.enisa.europa.eu/activities/
Resilience-and-CIIP/public-private-partnership/national-public-private-
partnerships-ppps/copy_of_desktop-reserach-on-public-private-partnerships
(accessed 15 September 2013).

—(2011b), 'Good Practice Guide – Cooperative Models for Effective Public Private
Partnerships', Luxembourg: Publications Office of the European Union, www.
enisa.europa.eu/activities/Resilience-and-CIIP/public-private-partnership/
national-public-private-partnerships-ppps/good-practice-guide-on-cooperatve-
models-for-effective-ppps (accessed 15 September 2013).

—(2012a), 'National Cyber Security Strategies: Setting the Course for National
Efforts to Strengthen Security in Cyberspace', Luxembourg: Publications Office
of the European Union, www.enisa.europa.eu/activities/Resilience-and-CIIP/
national-cyber-security-strategies-ncsss/national-cyber-security-strategies-an-
implementation-guide (accessed 15 September 2013).

—(2012b), 'Cyber Europe 2012, Key Findings and Recommendations', Luxembourg:
Publication Office of the European Union, www.enisa.europa.eu/activities/
Resilience-and-CIIP/cyber-crisis-cooperation/cyber-europe/cyber-europe-2012/
cyber-europe-2012-key-findings-report-1 (accessed 15 September 2013).

European Union (2007), 'Charter of Fundamental Rights of the European Union',
Official Journal C 303/1, 14 December 2007.

General Assembly of the United Nations (2009), 'Resolution 19/1, Strengthening
Public-Private Partnerships To Counter Crime in All Its Forms and Manifestations',
Prepared by the Commission on Crime Prevention and Criminal Justice
A/61/606-S/2006/936', www.unodc.org/documents/commissions/CCPCJ/

CCPCJ-ECOSOC/CCPCJ-ECOSOC-00/CCPCJ-ECOSOC-10/Resolution_19-1.pdf (accessed 15 September 2013).

Global Alliance Partners (2012), 'Guiding principles on the Global Alliance against Child Sexual Abuse Online', Annex to the Declaration on Launching the Global Alliance against child sexual abuse online, http://ec.europa.eu/dgs/home-affairs/ what-is-new/news/news/2012/docs/20121205-declaration-anex_en.pdf (accessed 15 September 2013).

Hoorens, S., D. Elixmann, J. Cave, M. S. Li and G. Cattaneo (RAND) (2012), 'Towards a Competitive European Internet Industry. A Socio-economic Analysis of the European Internet Industry and the Future Internet Public-Private Partnership', Prepared for European Commission, Information Society and Media Directorate-General.

House of Lords (2008), 'Follow-up to the Personal Internet Security Report', Science and Technology Committee, 4th Report of Session 2007–08, London, 24 June 2008, www.publications.parliament.uk/pa/ld200708/ldselect/ldsctech/131/13102.htm (accessed 15 September 2013).

—(2010), 'Protecting Europe against Large-Scale Cyber-attacks', European Union Committee, 5th Report of Session 2009–10, London, 18 March 2010, www. publications.parliament.uk/pa/ld200910/ldselect/ldeucom/68/6802.htm.

International Cybersecurity Enforcement Network (London Action Plan) (2013), 'The London Action Plan 2012', http://londonactionplan.org/ (accessed 15 September 2013).

International Multilateral Partnership Against Cyber Threats (IMPACT) (2013), 'About Us: Who We Are. Mission and Vision', www.impact-alliance.org/aboutus/mission- &-vision.html (accessed 15 September 2013).

International Telecommunication Union (2009), 'The ITU Global Cybersecurity Agenda (GCA)', www.itu.int/osg/csd/cybersecurity/gca/pillars-goals/index.html (accessed 15 September 2013).

Kleiner, A., P. Nicholas and K. Sullivan (2013), 'Linking Cybersecurity Policy and Performance', Microsoft Trustworthy Computing.

Kramer, R. C., R. J. Michalowski and D. Kauzlarich (2002), 'The origins and development of the concept and theory of state-corporate crime', *Crime & Delinquency*, 48: 263–82.

Kravets, D. (2012), 'Court Upholds Google-NSA Relationship Secrecy', *Wired*, 11 May 2012.

Kroes, N. (2012), 'Public-Private Cooperation in Cybersecurity', Speech delivered at the Security and Defence Agenda dinner. SPEECH/12/47, Brussels 30 January. http:// europa.eu/rapid/press-release_SPEECH-12-47_en.htm (accessed 15 September 2013).

Kshetri, N. (2005), 'Information and communication technologies, strategic asymmetry and national security', *Journal of International Management*, 11: 563–80.

—(2010), *The Global Cybercrime Industry: Economic, Institutional and Strategic Perspectives*, London: Springer.

Landau, S. (2010), *Surveillance or Security? The Risk Posed by New Wiretapping Technologies*, Cambridge, MA: MIT Press.

Lessig, L. (2006), *Code: And Other Laws of Cyberspace, Version 2.0*, New York: Basic Books.

Lynn, W. J., III (2010), 'Defending a New Domain: the Pentagon's Cyberstrategy', *Foreign Affairs*, 89, 1 September 2010. www.foreignaffairs.com/articles/66552/william-j-lynn-iii/defending-a-new-domain (accessed 15 September 2013).

MacAskill, E., J. Borger, N. Hopkins, N. Davies and J. Ball (2013), 'GCHQ Taps Fibre-Optic Cables for Secret Access to World's Communications', *The Guardian*, 21 June 2013.

McIntyre, T. J. (2011), 'Child Abuse and Cleanfeeds: Assessing Internet Blocking Systems', https://papers.ssrn.com/sol3/papers.cfm?abstract_id=1893667 (accessed 25 June 2013).

Mueller, M. (2011), 'DPI Technology from the Standpoint of Internet Governance Studies: An Introduction', Syracuse University School of Information Studies, http://deeppacket.info (accessed 15 September 2013).

Nissenbaum, H. (2011), 'From preemption to circumvention: if technology regulates, why do we need regulation (and viceversa)?', *Berkeley Technology Law Journal*, 3: 1367–86.

Ofcom (2013), 'Identifying Appropriate Regulatory Solutions: Principles for Analysing Self- and Co-Regulation – Statement 2008', http://stakeholders.ofcom.org.uk/consultations/coregulation/statement/ (accessed 25 June 2013).

Pearlman, A. R. (2010), 'Cybersecurity Programs', New Federal Initiatives Project, 12 August 2010, www.fed-soc.org/publications/detail/federal-cybersecurity-programs (accessed 25 June 2013).

Porcedda, M. G. (2011), 'Transatlantic Approaches to Cyber-security: The EU-US Working Group on Cyber-security and Cybercrime', in P. Pawlak (ed.), *The EU-US Security and Justice Agenda in Action*, Paris: European Union Institute of Security Studies.

—(2012), 'Data Protection and the Prevention of Cybercrime: the EU as an AREA of Security?' EUI Working Paper no. 2012/25:90, Florence: European University Institute.

Porcedda, M. G., M. Vermeulen and M. Scheinin (2013), 'Report on Regulatory Frameworks Concerning Privacy and the Evolution of the Norm of the Right to Privacy', Deliverable 3.2, SurPRISE Project. Florence: European University Institute.

Rid, T. (2012), 'Think Again: Cyber War', *Foreign Policy*, 27 February 2010. www.foreignpolicy.com/articles/2012/02/27/cyberwar (accessed 25 June 2013).

Risen, J. and N. Wingfield (2013), 'Silicon Valley and Spy Agency Bound by Strengthening Web', *The New York Times*, 19 June 2013.

Sartor, G. (2010), *L'informatica Giuridica e le Tecnologie dell'Informazione: Corso di Informatica Giuridica*, Turin: Giappichelli Editore.

Schneier, B. (2013), 'The Vulnerabilities Market and the Future of Security', Cryptogram Newsletter, 15 June 2013, www.schneier.com/crypto-gram-1206.html (accessed 15 September 2013).

Sechrist, M. (2010), 'Cyberspace In Deep Water: Protecting Undersea Communication Cables, By Creating an International Public-Private Partnership', Harvard Kennedy School of Government, Policy Analysis Exercise, http://belfercenter.ksg.harvard. edu/publication/20710/cyberspace_in_deep_water.html?breadcrumb=%2Fexperts %2F2223%2Fmichael_sechrist (accessed 10 September 2013).

Sommer, P. and I. Brown (2011), 'Reducing Systemic Cybersecurity Risks', OECD/ IFP Project on Future Global Shocks, IFP/WKP/FGS(2011)3. www.oecd.org/ governance/risk/46889922.pdf (accessed 10 September 2013).

Talbot Jensen, E. (2011), 'Ten Questions, Responses to the Ten Questions: President Obama and the Changing Cyber Paradigm', William Mitchell Law Review, 37 (5049), http://papers.ssrn.com/sol3/papers.cfm?abstract_id=1740904 (accessed 10 September 2013).

United Nations Interregional Crime and Justice Research Institute (UNICRI) (2009), 'PublicPrivate Partnerships (PPPs) for the Protection of Vulnerable Targets against Terrorist Attacks: Review of Activities and Findings', www.un.org/en/terrorism/ctitf/ pdfs/web_protecting_human_rights.pdf (accessed 10 September 2013).

United Nations Office on Drug and Crime (UNODC) (2012), 'The Use of Internet for Terrorist Purposes', Vienna, September, www.unodc.org/unodc/en/frontpage/2012/ October/unodc-launches-report-to-assist-member-states-to-counter-the-use-of-the-internet-for-terrorist-purposes.html (accessed 10 September 2013).

Virtual Global Taskforce (2011a), 'Private Sector Partners', cited 8 February 2013, http://www.virtualglobaltaskforce.com/who-we-are/industry-partners// (accessed 15 September, 2013).

—(2011b), 'What We Do: Making the Internet Safer for Children', www. virtualglobaltaskforce.com/what-we-do/ (accessed 10 September 2013).

Wall, D. (2011), 'Policing cybercrimes: situating the public police in networks of security within cyberspace', *Police Practice and Research: An International Journal*, 8: 183–205.

White House (The) (2003), 'National Strategy to Cyberspace', Washington, DC, www. dhs.gov/national-strategy-secure-cyberspace (accessed 10 September 2013).

—(2009), 'President's Cyberspace Policy Review: Assuring a Trusted and Resilient Information and Communications Infrastructure', Washington, DC, www. whitehouse.gov/assets/documents/Cyberspace_Policy_Review_final.pdf (accessed 10 September 2013).

—(2011), 'International Strategy for Cyberspace. Prosperity, Security, and Openness in a Networked World', Washington, DC, www.whitehouse.gov/sites/default/files/

rss_viewer/international_strategy_for_cyberspace.pdf (accessed 10 September 2013).

—(2012), 'The Comprehensive National Cybersecurity Initiative', Washington DC, www.whitehouse.gov/cybersecurity/comprehensive-national-cybersecurity-initiative (accessed 10 September 2013).

9

Being Publicly Private: Extreme Nationalist User Practices on Social Networks

Andra Siibak

Introduction

Rapid changes in the dynamics of communication and information trans-mission are transforming the general understandings of what the society accepts as proper behaviour (Brown, 2012). Matthew Williams (2007: 60) for instance, argued that 'new technologies are facilitating traditional criminal activities and creating avenues for new and unprecedented forms of deviance'. Considering that there are numerous websites on the net which 'teach' 'both the classical offender and those previously ill-equipped potential offenders' (Williams, 2006: 60) how to make bombs and other weapons, or how to commit suicide, it is not surprising that the Internet may be referred to as the 'potential tinderbox of unguided anarchy' (Jaffe, 2000: 275, quoted in Cohen-Almagor, 2010: 94). In fact, numerous scholars have explored the role social media and social network sites (SNS) played as broadcasting and logistical tools in the events which led to the Arab Spring (Dellicastelli, 2011) or the riots in London (Baker, 2012; Briggs, 2012; Jurgenson, 2012).

Various authors (Barletta, 2007; Herzog, 2011) have analysed the course of events known as the Bronze Night or the April Unrest, namely the events that occurred on the streets of Tallinn in 2007 after the Estonian government's decision to relocate the 'Bronze Soldier', a Soviet era memorial to an unknown World War II Russian soldier. The riots left one person dead, 57 injured and more than 300 individuals arrested (Postimees Online, 2007), but it has been almost unacknowledged that the Estonian SNS Rate[1] was at the time actively used by both the ethnic Estonians and Russian-speaking individuals, not only in producing the narratives of hatred and violence and spreading information, but also in calling on people to take action. In fact, more than 200 moderators worked on the site to delete the accounts of users whose posts and comments contained hateful and violence-provoking messages (Pino, 2007).

Other service providers, for example, Facebook, are also known to employ a team of professionals whose task is to hunt down and remove content that contains actionable threats or other hateful materials that are in violation of the politics of the site. Nevertheless, even though a variety of technologies and metrics are available to support such surveillance ambitions, analysing all the materials gathered still needs to be carried out by individual experts so as to increase the 'so what?' value (see Naquin, 2007). Such expert teams are always made up of specialists who possess both the critical thinking skills and 'the insight and context' (Naquin, 2007: 5) for interpreting the data, but their knowledge and methodologies are continuously tested. I argue that due to the 'context collapse' (Marwick and boyd, 2011) on social media, it has become crucial for the experts and scientists to understand people's perceptions of their imagined audiences, namely the mental conceptualization of people with whom the users imagine themselves to be communicating in social media, and its alignment with the actual audience (see Litt, 2012).

This chapter aims to describe and analyse the changes of user practices that have occurred in the course of the last five years in the self-presentation strategies of the extreme-nationalist users on the Estonian SNS Rate, users who were very active in voicing their views and ideas at the time of the April Unrest in 2007. In the first part of the chapter I will explain why online extremism has become such a troubling phenomenon and give a short overview of the steps that different countries have taken to fight against it. The second part of the chapter is focused around the issue of imagined audiences (Marwick and boyd, 2010). I will also introduce a complex social privacy strategy known as social steganography (boyd and Marwick, 2010), which has become increasingly popular especially among young social media users. In the third part of the chapter, findings from an April 2007 empirical case-study about the self-presentation of the extreme-nationalist users on SNS Rate will be compared to the findings of a follow-up study from June 2011 so as to illustrate the changes that have occurred in the SNS Rate usage practices of profile owners who hold extreme right-wing or nationalist ideas. The chapter will end with my concluding thoughts.

Social media: A safe haven for extremist groups?

Because social media provides a cheap, instantaneous and uncensored platform it has become a popular asset for extremist and terrorist groups for intra-group communication and recruitment of new followers. Scholars have also argued that various extremist and white power activist platforms have become environments where like-minded individuals can express their adversarial or controversial ideas (Glaser et al., 2002). In fact, national governments in several countries, for instance, the United States (Obama, 2011), Denmark (Meret, 2012), Germany (Goodwin, 2012), Norway (Ravik Jupskås, 2012), and others have released strategies and country reports that emphasize the potential role of social media in sharing extremist propaganda and promoting radicalization. Furthermore, according to the 'First Report of the Working Group on Radicalization and Extremism that Lead to Terrorism: Inventory of State Programs' (2009: 15), 'many states have begun to place a high priority on curbing terrorist propaganda and recruitment through the Internet', for instance, by putting in place mechanisms that help to systematically monitor websites that facilitate and encourage violent extremist content.

Thus, in this area of 'public surveillance' (Nissenbaum, 2004), international security forces have started to invest more and more time, effort, and money in order to be able to monitor the traffic on social media. In other words, the surveillance systems different countries are adopting have become more complex and powerful. For example, in 2009 the CIA invested in Visible Technologies, a software firm that enables them to monitor millions of posts on SNS (Shachtman, 2009). In addition, the agents of the US Department of Homeland Security were allowed to create their own accounts on social media to monitor the traffic on these platforms (Triner, 2010). In 2013 it was revealed that the US government is targeting top Internet companies (for instance Facebook, Google, Yahoo) to monitor online activity in the context of the PRISM program (Fernback, 2013). Similar actions were also considered by the UK Home Office, which aimed to monitor the web communications of all UK citizens (Espiner, 2009). Although the main aim of these actions and strategies has been the fight against international terrorist organizations, that various domestic extremist groups that promote radicalization also actively use, social media is a fact recognized in these documents (cf. Obama, 2011).

In Estonia, the 'Annual Review' of the Security Police of the Republic of Estonia (2011) also takes note of this tendency, stating that social media play an increasingly important role in the self-radicalization of individuals with extremist worldviews. Even though classical, organized right- or left-wing extremism has not taken root in Estonia, data from the Estonian Security Police suggest that 'there are individuals who hold extremist views, and in certain circumstances, these views can influence their behaviour', and preventing those individuals from acting upon their ideas is a constant challenge for the police forces (Estonian Security Police, 2011: 7).

The above-mentioned trends indicate that 'surveillance has become a powerful, if dubious, symbol of national security' (Monahan, 2010: 8). Some authors, for example, argue that present day surveillance has become a 'central means for social sorting, of classifying and categorizing populations and persons for risk assessment (and its analogues) and management' (Lyon, 2001: 172). Such an approach also refers to the fact that 'surveillance involves not merely data collection, but creating social meaning from the data, and using that meaning to inform action' (Monahan et al., 2010: 110) because as suggested by David Lyon (2001) the main aim behind various surveillance mechanisms is to minimize the risk of possible harm for example someone breaking the law.

Creating secret messages for an ideal audience

It has been argued (cf. Fernback, 2013) that the motivations, powers and outcomes of these surveillance acts depend on the particular agent and hence tend to differ greatly. The never-ending tension between imagined audiences, actual receiving audiences, and invisible audiences (Marwick and boyd, 2010) is most visible in today's networked publics, namely 'publics which are restructured by networked technologies' (boyd, 2010: 1). This problem of invisible audiences is perhaps most apparent when creating content on various social media platforms where multiple audiences are blended into one (Marwick and boyd, 2010), and hence it has become increasingly difficult 'to determine what is socially appropriate to say or what will be understood by those listening' (boyd, 2010: 10). Therefore it is often claimed that people engaging in SNS, have not yet fully become used to the idea of 'omnopticon' of social media (Jensen, 2007) that is, the state of continuous mutual surveillance where every user acts both as agent and subject. Even though it is expected that the members of one's 'friends list' will keep an eye on one's profile, the fact that the information might also be collected by regulatory agencies, governments, the military and other institutions, is often left unnoticed.

The perceptions of one's online audience are closely connected to one's perceptions and understandings of privacy, because, in addition to choosing whether to share information, a right to privacy also includes the choice of with whom to share it (Rachels, 1975). A recent social privacy strategy, which especially young social media users have been found to implement (see boyd and Marwick, 2011; Oolo and Siibak, 2013), is social steganography, namely young people have become used to 'creating a message that can be read in one way by those who aren't in the know and read differently by those who are' (boyd, 2010).

Different sources from popular culture, for example, song lyrics, poems, aphorisms, and so on, but also inside jokes and phrases exchanged in offline context (cf. Oolo and Siibak, 2013), are often turned into social media posts that might seem meaningless to a public at large and be rightfully understood only by those who have the 'specific cultural awareness' (boyd, 2010) needed for interpreting the content. Hence, such a practice could be viewed as 'fairly extreme attempts to simultaneously maximize privacy and publicity' (Jurgenson and Rey, 2013: 7). On the one hand, the messages are sent on a public platform and can potentially be seen by thousands of viewers; on the other hand, the real meaning behind those messages is so private and hidden that only the 'ideal audience', i.e. 'the mirror image of the author' (Marwick and boyd, 2010: 7) who would share similar values, perspectives and cultural codes will be able to grasp it.

In other words, virtual environments and social media in particular help to create a hidden 'infrastructure of free spaces' (Simi and Futrell, 2004) where the extremist groups can share their worldviews and sustain the movement without the fear of downright public scrutiny or stigmatization. Such a tendency has also been noted in the Annual Review of the Estonian Internal Security Service (2012: 4) which states that the form of expression of the present day extremism has changed as 'a new generation of right-wing extremists, so-called autonomous nationalists, who do not make use of familiar extremist symbolism and keep their views hidden from the public, are gaining support'. Considering the above, I suggest that social steganography may serve as an important tool for different extremist groups, who also in offline contexts are known to constantly battle with the questions of 'how and when to conceal or reveal their identity' (Simi and Futrell, 2009: 93). At the same time, the sharing of these secret messages could create problems or lead to unwanted consequences in terms of the security and stability of the state.

In the following section I use the findings of a content analysis of the profiles of extreme-nationalist users on Rate, carried out two weeks after the April Unrest, to describe the main self-presentation practices of extreme-nationalist users on the site in 2007.

Self-presentation practices of the extreme-nationalist users of SNS Rate

Content analysis of the profiles of extreme-nationalist users on Rate[2] (N=174) indicates that such users often named aspects related to extreme nationalism, xenophobia, hatred, violence, and so on in the Interests section of their profiles. For instance, the analysis shows that 16–20 year old supporters of extreme nationalism included on average 5.3 interests that could be connected to this ideology. The most popular theme represented in the Interest section was that of racism (N=290), followed by interest in oi! music[3] (N=209) and xenophobia (N=135), different ideological messages (N=63), historical events (N= 36) and, – figures (N=21) as well as violence in general (N=43) (Pruul, 2007). In the majority of cases (N=448) the users made use of words, phrases, and slogans (for example, 'Heil Hitler!', 'White power worldwide', etc.) connected to their ideology to exhibit those particular interests.

The analysis of the content of the profiles from 2007 suggests that the extreme-nationalist users on Rate mainly relied on text when constructing their messages. Although acronyms (for example, WP, oi!, SS)[4] and secret number combinations (for instance, 14, 88, 85!)[5], could also be found on some of the profiles (217 and 132 cases respectively), these symbols represented only a very tiny fraction from the list of possibilities. In fact, the analysis detected only seven different acronyms and six different number combinations used on the profiles (ibid.). Hence, in comparison to the secret 'coded' messages, straight-forward hatred and violence-provoking slogans, song lyrics of old war-songs, or extracts from *Mein Kampf* could be found. The latter, however, can be much more easily interpreted by people without any specialist training, compared to those acronyms and secret number combinations which do require specialist knowledge about the symbols of skinheads, neo-Nazis and other radical groups.

Much of the popularity of Rate at the time was connected to the fact that the site offered its users a variety of opportunities for content creation, for instance, the users could upload photos or keep a blog, as well as communicate with other users in different forums and communities. The combination of such features not only created an opportunity to communicate with new people and thus to find new friends, but also to get acquainted with people who would share one's interests and hobbies. Both aspects were among the main reasons why youth had joined the site altogether – 55 per cent and 32 per cent respectively (Siibak, 2010).

The same reasons also motivated many young people to take part in forum discussions and to join various communities, an activity that was seen as a form of self-expression. In this context, it is important to note that according to the analysis of Simi, Futrell and Gottschalk (2006: 93) many activists who hold the white power ideals are concerned about 'how and when to conceal or reveal their identity as Aryans'. Therefore, Simi and Futrell (2004) argue, the online communities have become environments where, by sharing one's ideas with like-minded individuals, it has become possible for the extremists to sustain the movement. In fact, Simi et al.'s (2006: 93) ethnographic study among the white power activists in the United States revealed that the activists 'often live between a "virtual social identity" implied in the impressions they give off and their "actual social identity" comprised of the Aryan attributes they embrace'. In the light of the above, it could be argued that by having an opportunity to communicate with like-minded individuals and to join white power and nationalist communities, the users with extreme-nationalist views were provided with an opportunity to reveal an important part of their identity.

In 2007 there were 119 communities on Rate that were connected to spreading xenophobic, racist and radical worldviews, and 78 communities that were nationalist in their perspective (Pruul, 2007). The biggest number of users from our sample (N=34 in each) had joined a community called *Eestlane olen ja eestlaseks jään* ('I am an Estonian and will stay an Estonian') and *Suht OI!* ('Quite OI!'). In fact, communities built around the common taste in music were relatively popular among the extreme-nationalist users: 24 of them had joined a community named *Rock against Communism*, and nine users also belonged to a community that consisted of fans of the first Estonian skinhead music group, P.W.A. (Preserve White Aryans). Considering that 'the movement–music relationship in the WPM[6] scene is much more than the superficial stylistic behaviour devoid of political content or influence' (Simi et al., 2006: 295), such obvious popularity of oi! music amongst the extreme-nationalist Rate users was expected.

The analysis of profiles from 2007, however, reveals that the majority of the extreme-nationalist users of SNS Rate had not yet totally grasped the idea that one's interactions on online platforms tend to be public-by-default and private-through-effort (boyd and Marwick, 2011). I suggest there might be two possible explanations to their rather carefree and open communication on the site. On the one hand, the young extreme-nationalist users of Rate might have fallen victim to the general illusion of anonymity which young people tend to share on SNS, namely the young probably just did not expect strangers, and especially 'nightmare readers' (Marwick and boyd, 2010), like the police and government officials, to have any interest in their posts and profiles. On the other hand, being open and proud about one's beliefs might have helped to serve the purpose of recruiting new members and spreading their ideological messages (Asia News International, 2008).

Targeting one's ideal audience: Secret Codes from 2011

In the context in which various governments and security forces have taken steps to 'continue to closely monitor the important role the Internet and social networking sites play in advancing violent extremist narratives' (Obama, 2011: 6), the radicals using these sites are also continuously improving their strategies. For instance, extremist content is shared both on 'darknets' – private encrypted networks – that are difficult to detect and to disrupt (Dunn, 2011), but can also be spread on public social media platforms by means of secret codes.

Having monitored the profiles of extreme-nationalist users on Rate in June 2011, I argue that skinheads, neo-Nazis, and other individuals with radical views quite actively practise the use of social steganography in the site. My analysis indicates that in five years time, SNS usage practices and self-presentation techniques of the users will have changed so remarkably that the coding scheme used for the content analysis in 2007 had become totally useless in 2011. The biggest changes in this realm had to do with the increased variety of techniques and genres combined so as to indicate one's extreme-nationalist views on the profiles.

Although many of the users continued to make use of written text to express their worldviews, text was sometimes used in unconventional manner. For instance, I could detect practices that could be regarded as an illustration of the padonki or Olbanian counter-culture, a sub-culture mostly among the Russian-speaking Internet community, originating from a Russian skinhead online platform Udaff and characterized by erratic spelling and gratuitous use of profanity and obscene subjects.[7] The language also referred to as padonkaffsky jargon is based on the phonetic spelling of the Russian language and combines a complex orthography with a creative use of idioms and cultural slang, which is why it is difficult to translate.[8]

Another specialized form of symbolic writing visible on the profiles was Leet-speak (also known as eleet; 1337; elite; ieet; or l_££t). Leet-speak, which originated in the hacker community, is a form of netspeak where combinations of ASCII characters are used to replace letters of the Roman alphabet.[9] This 'secret language' has a unique but quite lax approach to orthography – 'anything that the *average* reader *cannot* make sense is valid'.[10] On occasions examples of computer text symbols and computer text art were visible on the profiles. By combining letters, numbers and symbols the extreme-nationalist users mainly emphasized white power and Nazi symbols (for instance, the swastika, and the 'SS' rune). Textual slogans like 'Whites will never fall!' were usually accompanying representations of a tank, a revolver or a fist.

In addition to making use of different cultures of netspeak, the profile owners had also broadened the scale and genres of their posts. In addition to song lyrics, nationalist poems and various slogans, short stories, for instance about Adolf Hitler, and personal diary entries were uploaded on the site under the Additional Information section. Furthermore, profile owners were also quite active in uploading different YouTube videos as well as various images representing symbols and other memorabilia, historical figures, oi! groups and other icons of the 'Aryan popular culture' (Back, 2002: 628) on their profiles. The continued popularity of white power music, or 'hate rock' in itself is not a surprise, as according to Chris Hale (2012: 9), it 'is becomingly an increasingly popular adolescent recruitment tool.' Other scholars have also noted that the extremist groups' ideals and worldviews are often spread through music and video content (O'Callaghan et al., 2012).

In comparison to the previous findings from 2007, the analysis of profiles from 2011 reveals that a multitude of new acronyms and number combinations had been employed as secret codes. Similar to the findings of Simi et al. (2006), the analysis of the profiles in Rate reveals that both the posts on the profiles as well as the comments sent to one another included various acronyms and phrases that would mark one's connection to white power or extreme-nationalist movements. Considering the fact that, according to research by Michael Weiss (Spiegel Online International, 2011), around 150 secret neo-Nazi codes have been found to be currently in use in Germany, the expansion of secret codes used by the Estonian neo-Nazis cannot be considered a huge surprise.

Some of the communities, for example, *Eesti Leegion* ('Estonian Legion'), *Eestlane olen ja eestlaseks jään!* ('I am an Estonian and will stay an Estonian!') and *Hoiame oma kodumaa väärika ja puhtana!* ('Let's keep our homeland dignified and clean!'), which had been most popular amongst the extreme-nationalist users in 2007, had disappeared. Although there were some communities that could be regarded as spreading nationalist or extreme right-wing worldviews, the majority of such communities were closed for the general public. In other words, one needed to get acceptance from the 'owner' of the community before being able to see and take part of its discussions. As the number of users in each of these nationalist or radical communities was small, it can be expected that skinheads and extreme nationalist users of Rate are making more active use of some other and more private online environments.

All of the above indicates that the extreme-nationalist users of Rate have not only broadened their scope in terms of strategies, but that these strategies have clearly become more sophisticated and not as easily interpretable as the ones from 2007. The secret codes and messages the profile owners are exchanging can be grasped and understood only by the 'ideal readers' (Marwick and boyd, 2010) of their posts, namely their peers supporting the same worldviews.

Conclusion

Social media and SNS in particular have played a crucial role in facilitating the events like the April Unrest, the Arab Spring, the London riots and the Occupy movement. Furthermore, social media platforms have become frequently used tools, not only in the hands of terrorists but also extreme nationalist users like Anders Behring Breivik who was responsible for the Norway attacks in July 2011 (Taylor, 2011). All the above-mentioned events also refer to the fact that as social media environments 'effectively *merge* the digital and the physical' into one we finally need to become accustomed to living in the conditions of 'augmented reality' (Jurgenson, 2012: 84). Furthermore, these extremist groups and individuals with radical worldviews have adapted quite quickly both to the changes occurring in the field of digital technologies but also to the changed social conditions brought along by the fact that numerous intelligence services and police forces are monitoring their actions.

This chapter has focused on to the changes that have occurred in the self-presentation practices of extreme nationalist users of Estonian language-based SNS Rate from 2007 to 2011. The analysis of the user profiles indicates that, in comparison to the results from 2007, the extreme nationalist users on Rate have started to use much more complex strategies for promoting their ideology. For instance, counter-culture versions of netspeak and examples of social steganography could be found on the profiles and the variety of acronyms and number combinations had grown remarkably. These changes indicate that the profiles and posts made by the extreme nationalist users are mainly targeted to their peers and those individuals who share and hence are able to interpret their worldviews. In this respect, my findings support the views of Simi et al. (2006) who have argued that white supremacists and other extremists often write and speak in code so as to build a community of like-minded individuals.

In the light of the above, I argue that we should not forget the fact that social media and SNS may serve both as a 'liberation technologies' (Dunn, 2011) but also have a potential of turning into a nasty 'double-edged-sword'. Hence, I agree with Kohlmann (2006) who has argued that governments and intelligence services need not only to develop their IT capacity to learn how to monitor the extremist activities in online environments, but they also need to continue developing their cultural and linguistic capacity for assessing online content.

Acknowledgement

The preparation of this article was supported by the research grant PUT 44 financed by Estonian Research Council.

Notes

1   In the year 2007, SNS Rate was by far the most popular social media platform in Estonia, with more than 300,000 active users. The site was most actively used by

young people – in 2007, 70 per cent of 11–18 year old students were users of Rate. Young users of Rate were also most active in voicing their extreme nationalist worldviews. See the website www.rate.ee

2   The overall profile features and applications offered on SNS Rate were similar to the ones on Facebook or any other SNS. The users were free to choose the content and the exact wording for describing their interests and hobbies, as well as to include all the other personal information they were willing to share.

3   Oi! is a subgenre of punk rock that originated from the United Kingdom and is often associated as a skinheads music style.

4   WP is a racist acronym which stands for White Power; Oi! is a subgenre of punk rock, often associated with skinheads; SS is an abbreviation of Schutzstaffel, a para-military organization within the Nazi Party www.britannica.com/EBchecked/topic/562059/SS (accessed 27 December 2013).

5   The number 14 represents the phrase '14 words' that has become a slogan for the white supremacist movement: 'We must secure the existence of our people and a future for white children', http://archive.adl.org/hate_symbols/numbers_14words.asp (accessed 14 September 2013); the number 88 is a Neo-Nazi symbol which represents the eighth letter in the alphabet 'H' and, when written twice, it signifies 'HH' a shorthand for the Nazi greeting 'Heil Hitler', http://archive.adl.org/hate_symbols/numbers_88.asp (accessed 14 September 2013); finally, it is hypothesized that the number combination „85!' stands for the greeting 'Heil Estland!' – number 8 represents the eighth letter in the alphabet 'H' and the fifth letter in the alphabet is 'E' (Pruul, 2007).

6   WPM stands for white power music.

7   http://en.wikipedia.org/wiki/Padonki (accessed 14 September 2013).

8   http://en.wikipedia.org/wiki/Padonkaffsky_jargon (accessed 14 September 2013).

9   http://en.wikipedia.org/wiki/Leet (accessed 14 September 2013).

10 Italics in the original; http://en.wikipedia.org/wiki/Leet (accessed 14 September 2013).

References

Asia News International (2008), 'Extremist Groups Using Facebook, MySpace, YouTube to "Recruit Members"', The Free Library, http://news.oneindia.in/2008/11/20/extremist-groups-facebook-myspace-youtube-recruit-members-1227161160.html (accessed 23 February 2013).

Back, L. (2002), 'Aryans Reading Adorno: Cyber-Culture and Twenty-First Century Racism', Ethnic and Racial Studies, 25: 628–51.

Baker, S. A. (2012), 'From the criminal crowd to the "mediated crowd": the impact of social media on the 2011 English riots', *Safer Communities,* 11: 40–9.

Barletta, W. A. (2007), 'Cyberwar or Cyber-Terrorism: The Attack on Estonia', in A. Zichichi and R. Ragaini (eds), *International Seminar on Nuclear War and Planetary Emergencies 38th Session,* Cambridge: World Scientific Publishing, 481–487.

boyd, d. (2010), 'Social Steganography: Learning to Hide in Plain Sight', danah boyd's blog, www.zephoria.org/thoughts/archives/2010/08/23/social-steganography-learning-to-hide-in-plain-sight.html (accessed 23 February 2013).

boyd, d. and A. Marwick (2011), 'Social Steganography: Privacy in Networked Publics', Boston, MA: International Communication Association.

Briggs, D. (2012), 'What we did when it happened: a timeline analysis of the social disorder in London', *Safer Communities,* 11: 6–16.

Brown, G. (2012), 'Business vs. Nobody's Business: Search of Employer-Issued Technology and the University Employee's Expectation of Privacy', www.princeton.edu/ogc/whats-new/EmployerTech.pdf (accessed 23 February 2013).

Cohen-Almagor, R. (2010), ' In Internet's Way', in M. Facler and R. S. Fortner (eds), *Ethics and Evil in the Public Sphere: Media, Universal Values & Global Development,* Cresskill: NJ: Hampton Press, 93–115.

Dellicastelli, C. (2011), 'Every tool is a weapon if you hold it right: the role of social media in the pro-democratic uprisings of the Arab spring', *Journal of Digital Research and Publishing,* 1: 52–60. http://ses.library.usyd.edu.au/bitstream/2123/8137/1/DRPJournal_5pm_S2_2011.pdf#page=29 (accessed 23 February, 2013).

Dunn, J. E. (2011), 'Extremists are Tech Early Adopters, Counter-Terror Report Notes', Computerworlduk, 14 July 2011, www.computerworlduk.com/news/security/3291197/extremists-are-tech-early-adopters-counter-terror-report-notes/ (accessed 23 February 2013).

Espiner, T. (2009), 'UK To Monitor, Store All Social-Network Traffic?' CNet, 18 March 2009, http://news.cnet.com/8301-1009_3-10199107-83.html (accessed 23 February 2013).

Estonian Internal Security Service (2012), 'Annual Review 2012', www.kapo.ee/cms-data/_text/138/124/files/kapo-aastaraamat-2012-eng.pdf (accessed 25 June 2013).

Fernback, J. (2013), 'In Context: Digital Surveillance, Ethics, and PRISM', Culture Digitally,http://culturedigitally.org/2013/06/in-context-digital-surveillance-ethics-and-prism/ (accessed 26 June 2013).

Glaser, J., J. Dixit and D. P. Green (2002), 'Studying hate crime with the internet: what makes racists advocate racial violence?', *Journal of Social Issues,* 58: 177–93.

Goodwin, M. (2012), 'Germany', in V. Ramalingam, A. Glennie and S. Feve (eds), *Preventing and Countering Far-Right Extremism: European Cooperation. Country*

Reports, Stockholm: Ministry of Justice, Sweden and Institute of Strategic Dialogue,
   www.strategicdialogue.org/FarRightEM.pdf (accessed 26 June 2013).

Hale, C. (2012), 'Extremism on the world wide web: a research review', *Criminal Justice
   Studies: A Critical Journal of Crime, Law and Society*, 25: 343–356.

Herzog, S. (2011), 'Revisiting the Estonian cyber attacks: digital threats and
   multinational responses', *Journal of Strategic Security*, 4: 49–60.

Jaffe, J. M. (2000), 'Riding the Electronic Tiger: Censorship in Global, Distributed
   Networks', in R. Cohen-Almagor (ed.), *Liberal Democracy and the Limits of
   Tolerance: Essays in Honor and Memory of Yitzhak Rabin,* Ann Arbor: University of
   Michigan Press, 275–294.

Jensen, J. L. (2007), 'The Internet Omnopticon: Surveillance or Counter-insurgency',
   in H. Bang and A. Esmark (eds), *New Publics with/out Democracy*, Frederiksberg:
   Samfundslitteratur, 351–80.

Jurgenson, N. (2012), 'When atoms meet bits: social media, the mobile web and
   augmented revolution', *Future Internet*, 4: 83–91.

Jurgenson, N. and P. J. Rey (2013), 'The Fan Dance: How Privacy Thrives in an Age of
   Hyper-Publicty', in G. Lovink and M. Rasch (eds), *Unlike Us Reader: Social Media
   Monopolies and Their Alternatives*, Amsterdam: Institute of Network Cultures, www.
   pjrey.net/documents/jurgenson_and_rey_the_fan_dance.pdf (accessed 5 March 2013).

Kohlmann, E. (2006), 'The Real Online Terrorist Threat', *Foreign Affairs*, 85: 115–24.

Litt, E. (2012), 'Knock, knock. who's there? The imagined audience, *Journal of
   Broadcasting & Electronic Media*, 56: 330–45.

Lyon, D. (2001), 'Facing the future: seeking ethics for everyday surveillance', *Ethics and
   Information Society*, 3: 171–81.

Marwick, A. and boyd, d. (2010), 'I tweet honestly, I tweet passionately: Twitter users,
   context collapse, and the imagined audience', *New Media & Society*, 13: 114–33.

Meret, S. (2012), 'Denmark', in V. Ramalingam, A. Glennie and S. Feve (eds),
   *Preventing and Countering Far-Right Extremism: European Cooperation. Country
   Reports*, Stockholm: Ministry of Justice, Sweden and Institute of Strategic Dialogue,
   www.strategicdialogue.org/FarRightEM.pdf (accessed 26 June 2013).

Monahan, T. (2010), *Surveillance in the Time of Insecurity*, New Brunswick, NJ: Rutgers
   University Press.

Monahan, T., D. J. Phillips and D. Murakami Wood (2010), 'Editorial: surveillance and
   empowerment', *Surveillance & Society*, 8: 106–12.

Naquin, D. (2007), 'Remarks by Doug Naquin', CIRA Newsletter, 32: 3–9, www.fas.org/
   irp/eprint/naquin.pdf (accessed 23 February 2013).

Nissenbaum, H. (2004), 'Privacy as contextual integrity', *Washington Law Review*, 79:
   119–57.

Obama, B. (2011), *Empowering Local Partners to Prevent Violent Extremism in the
   United States*, The White House, Washington, DC, August, www.whitehouse.gov/
   sites/default/files/empowering_local_partners.pdf (accessed 23 February 2013).

O'Callaghan, D., D. Greene, M. Conway, C. Carthy and P. Cunningham (2012), 'An Analysis of Interactions Within and Between Extreme Right Communities in Social Media', http://doras.dcu.ie/17746/1/XRight_Paper_Long_Version.pdf (accessed 23 February 2013).

Oolo, E. and A. Siibak (2013), 'Performing for One's Imagined Audience: Main Online Privacy Strategies of Estonian Teens', *Cyberpsychology*, 7, www.cyberpsychology.eu/view.php?cisloclanku=2013011501&article=7 (accessed 5 March 2013).

Pino, K. (2007), 'EMT: Rate – Miks Me Seda Ometi Kinni ei Pane?', *Õhtuleht*, 18 May, www.ohtuleht.ee/230332 (accessed 23 February 2013).

Postimees Online (2007), 'Öine Märul: Üks Surnu, 57 Vigastatut, 99 Lõhkumisjuhtu Ja 300 Kinnipeetut', 27 April 2007, http://arter.postimees.ee/270407/esileht/siseuudised/257508_foto.php (accessed 23 February).

Pruul, R. (2007), 'Rahvusäärmuslus Rate.ee Profiilides', Bakalaureusetöö, Tartu Ülikool, ajakirjanduse ja kommunikatsiooni instituut.

Rachels, J. (1975), 'Why privacy is important', *Philosophy & Public Affairs*, 4: 323–33.

Ravik Jupskås, A. (2012), 'Norway', in V. Ramalingam, A. Glennie and S. Feve (eds), *Preventing and Countering Far-Right Extremism: European Cooperation. Country Reports*, Stockholm: Ministry of Justice, Sweden and Institute of Strategic Dialogue, www.strategicdialogue.org/FarRightEM.pdf (accessed 26 June 2013).

Security Police of the Republic of Estonia (2011), 'Annual Review 2011', www.kapo.ee/cms-data/_text/138/124/files/kapo-aastaraamat-2011-eng.pdf (accessed 24 February 2013).

Shachtman, N. (2009), 'Exclusive: US. Spies Buy Stake in Firm that Monitors Blogs, Tweets', *Wired Magazine*, 19 October 2009, www.wired.com/dangerroom/2009/10/exclusive-us-spies-buy-stake-in-twitter-blog-monitoring-firm/ (accessed 23 February 2013).

Siibak, A. (2010), 'Constructing masculinity on a social networking website. The case-study of visual self-presentations of young men on the profile images of SNS *Rate.ee*', *Young*, 18: 403–25.

Simi, P. and R. Futrell (2004),'Free spaces, collective identity, and the persistance of US white power activism', *Social Problems*, 51: 16–42.

—(2009), 'Negotiating white power activist stigma', *Social Problems*, 56: 89–110.

Simi, P., R. Futrell and S. Gottschalk (2006), 'Understanding music in movements: the white power music scene', *The Sociological Quaterly*, 47: 275–304.

Spiegel Online International (2011), 'The Truth About 88: New Book Reveals Secret Meaning of Neo-Nazi Codes', 27 June 2011. www.spiegel.de/international/germany/0,1518,770820,00.html (accessed 23 February 2013).

Taylor, C. (2011), 'Norway Attacks: Suspect's Social Media Trail Examined', Marshable, 22 July 2011, http://mashable.com/2011/07/22/norway-shootings-suspects-social-media-trail-examined/ (accessed 23 February 2013).

Triner, D. (2010), 'Privacy Impact Assessment for the Office of Operations Coordination and Planning: Publicly Available Social Media Monitoring and Situational Awareness Initiative', Department of Homeland Security, www.dhs. gov/xlibrary/asserts/privacy/privacy_pia_ops_publiclyavailablesocialmedia.pdf (accessed 23 February 2013).

Williams, M. (2006), *Virtually Criminal. Crime, Deviation and Regulation Online*, New York: Routledge.

—(2007), 'Policing and cybersociety: the maturation of regulation within an online community, policing and society', *An International Journal of Research and Policy*, 17: 59–82.

Index

2CENTRE 190
10PARIS193 87–8, 97

ACTA (Anti-Counterfeiting Trade
    Agreement) 166
Adobe 33–4
Advanced Persistent Threats (APT) 175
Ahmad, Kenesa 169–70
Al Jazeera 64
Alexander, Keith B. 51
America *see* US
American Civil Liberties Union 94
Andreasson, K. J.: *Cybersecurity: Public
    Sector Threats and Responses* (2011)
    6–7
Andress, J.: *Cyber Warfare* (2011) 8
Annan, Kofi 87
anonymity 61–2, 64
Anti-Counterfeiting Trade Agreement
    (ACTA) 166
Apple iTunes 165
April Unrest 213–14
APT (Advanced Persistent Threats) 175
Arab Spring 213
ARF Work Plan on Cyber Security 55
Assange, Julian 60–3, 65, 70–1, 73–4
AT&T 140, 144
atomic bomb, secrets of the 99–100 *see
    also* nuclear weapons
attacks *see* targets
attribution 49–50, 185
audience, online 216–17

Bank of America 70
barriers 161–2
Bayuk, J. L.: *Cyber Security Policy
    Guidebook* (2012) 6
BGP (border gateway protocol) 28, 30
Binney, William 167
Black Code (2011) (Deibert, Rohozinski
    and Hafner) 8

Blix, Hans 102–3
Bo Xilai 91
border gateway protocol (BGP) 28, 30
Breivik, Anders Behring 222
British Telecom 97
Bronze Night 213–14
budgets 44

Cablegate 59–61, 68, 69, 73–4, 93–4 *see
    also* WikiLeaks
cables 87–8, 97, 194 *see also* Cablegate
capacity-building 51–5
Carr, J. 8
CBMs (confidence-building measures)
    48–51
    bilateral channels 50
CCM (computers cleaned per mille) 195–6
CDSP (Common Security and Defence
    Policy) 43, 46
Centre for Strategic and International
    Studies (CSIS) 50
CenturyLink 143, 144
chain of custody 90–2
'Challenges in Cybersecurity' Conference
    178
Chanel 118–19
child pornography 52, 192–3
China
    confidence-building measures (CBMs)
        and 50–1
    cyber-attacks and 11–12, 115–17
    cyber-espionage and 39, 49–51
    Internet, and the 75, 114–15
    politics and 161
China Institute of Contemporary
    International Relations (CICIR) 50
Choucri, Nazli: *Cyberpolitics in
    International Relations* (2012) 7
CI (critical infrastructures) 113, 184
CICIR (China Institute of Contemporary
    International Relations) 50

CIIs (critical information infrastructures) 1, 24, 184–5
civilization 161–2
Clarke, R. A.: *Cyberwar* (2010) 7–8
classification 65–6, 69, 92, 93–8 *see also* secrecy
CNCI (Comprehensive National Cybersecurity Initiative) 137–8, 187
'Collateral Murder' (2010) 59, 63
Common Security and Defence Policy (CSDP) 43, 46
Comprehensive National Cybersecurity Initiative (CNCI) 137–8, 187
computer networks 2
computers 2
computers cleaned by mille (CCM) 195–6
Conficker 31, 35
confidence-building measures *see* CBMs
Conklin, W. 6
Convention on Cyber-crime 176
copyright infringement 118–19, 164–5
corruption 167
Costigan, S. S.: *Cyberspaces and Global Affairs* (2012) 7
Craft, Perry 6
critical information infrastructures (CIIs) 1, 24, 184–5
'Critical Infrastructure Security and Resilience' (US Policy Directive) 144
critical infrastructures (CI) 113, 184
CSIS (Centre for Strategic and International Studies) 50
'Cyber Atlantic' 53, 55
cyber-attacks 42, 53, 114, 171
   China and 11–12, 115–17
   defences against 174–9
   Iran and 171
   origins of 119–20
   Stuxnet malware and 171–4
cyber capacities 39–40
cyber-crime 3, 48, 52, 55, 117–18
   2CENTRE 190
   Convention on Cyber-crime 176
   IMPACT (International Multilateral Partnership Against Cyber Threats) 191

Octopus 191
cyber-espionage 39
   attribution 49–50
   definition of 194–5
   intentionality 49–50
   US and 39, 41, 49 *see also* WikiLeaks
cyber-exercises 53–5
Cyber Intelligence Sharing and Protection Act 144
cyber-power 170–1
Cyber Security Essentials (2010) (Graham, Olson and Howard) 6
Cyber Security for Educational Leaders (2013) (Phillips and Sianjina) 6
Cyber Security Policy Guidebook (2012) (Bayuk et al.) 6
cyber-war 171
Cyber Warfare (2011) (Andress and Winterfield) 8
cyber-weapons 5
Cyber Working Group 50
cyberconflict 49 *see also* cyber-attacks
Cybercrime Centres of Excellence for Training, Research, and Education 190
Cyberpolitics in International Relations (2012) (Choucri) 7
cybersecurity 1, 3, 23
   challenges 35–6
   definitions of 1, 23, 26–7, 185, 194
   global level 27–31
   individual level 34–5
   measurement of 195–6
   national level 31–2
   organizational level 32–4
   published works on 6–8
   US and 127–9
Cybersecurity Gateway 51–2
Cybersecurity: Public Sector Threats and Responses (2011) (Andreasson) 6–7
cyberspace
   crimes 194
   definitions of 1, 23–5, 27–8
   features of 2
   size of 113
   US and 31
Cyberspace Policy Review 138

Cyberspaces and Global Affairs (2012) (Costigan and Perry) 7
Cyberwar (2010) (Clarke and Knake) 7–8

'Dangers of Surveillance, The' (2013) (Richards) 167–9
darknets 220
data leaks 35
data protection 41–2
Data Protection Directive (DPD) 41–2
deep packet inspection (DPI) technology 128, 132–5, 149
Defense Industrial Base (DIB) 140
Defense Industrial Base (DIB) companies 143–5
Defense Industrial Base Enhanced Cybersecurity Services (DIB/ECS) program 128, 144
Deibert, R.: *Black Code* (2011) 8
Delisle, Jeffrey Paul 93
Denning, Dorothy 7
developing countries 51–2
DHS (US Department of Homeland Security) 6, 128, 135, 142, 149
   'Essential Body of Knowledge' 6
   Joint Cybersecurity Services Pilot (JCSP) and 143–4
   National Cyber Security Division (NCSD) 135
   social media networks (SNS) and 215
Diamond, J.: *Guns, Germs and Steel: The Fates of Human Societies* (1997) 161
DIB (Defense Industrial Base) 140
DIB (Defense Industrial Base) companies 143–5
DIB Cyber Security/Information Assurance (CS/IA) Program 143
DIB/ECS (Defense Industrial Base Enhanced Cybersecurity Services) program 128, 144
DigiNotar 173
Digital Millennium Copyright Act (DMCA) 164
digital rights management systems (DRM) 164
diplomatic cables 87–8, 97 *see also* Cablegate
disarmament researchers 15–16

DMCA (Digital Millennium Copyright Act) 164
DNS (domain name system) 28, 30–1, 118
   sinkholing 143
DNS Changer case 35
DNSSEC (Domain Name System Security Extensions) 118
DoD (US Department of Defense) 128, 144
DoD Defense Industrial Base Opt-in Pilot Exploratory Cybersecurity Initiative 143
domain name system *see* DNS
Domain Name System Security Extensions (DNSSEC) 118
DPD (Date Protection Directive) 41–2
DPI (deep packet inspection) technology 128, 132–5, 149
DRM (digital rights management systems) 164

economics 113, 129, 163–5
ECS (Enhanced Cybersecurity Services) 144–8
education 175–6
Eesti Leegion ('Estonian Legion') 222
Eestlane olen ja eestlaseks jään ('I am an Estonian and will stay an Estonian') 219, 222
Egypt 87–8
Einstein program, the 128, 131–2, 135, 149
   Einstein 1 135–6, 146
   Einstein 2 136–9, 146
   Einstein 3 139–48, 150
   signatures and 134
Ellsberg, Daniel 67
email filtering 143
encryption 90–1
Enduring Security Framework 14
Enhanced Cybersecurity Services (ECS) 144–8
EP3R (European Public-Private Partnership for Resilience) 185, 189–90
'Essential Body of Knowledge' (Department of Homeland Security) 6

Estonia 213–14, 216, 217
   Rate and 213, 218–20, 222–3, 223n. 1
EU (European Union) 41, 43–8, 185
EU-US Working Group on Cybersecurity
   and Cyber Crime 53
European External Action Service 44
European Public-Private Partnership for
   Resilience (EP3R) 185, 189–90
European Union (EU) 41, 43–8, 185
European Union Cyber Strategy 43, 46
Executive Order 8381 65
'Exercise, The' 141–2
external network connections 137–9
extremism 215–23 *see also* Rate

FedCIRC (Federal Computer Incident
   Response Center) 135
Federal Computer Incident Response
   Center (FedCIRC) 135
Federal Information Security
   Management Act (FISMA) 135
FGI (foreign government information)
   98–9
FI-PPP (Future Internet Public Private
   Partnership) 189
FI-WARE 189
firm theory 129–30, 136
FISA (Foreign Intelligence and
   Surveillance Act 1978) 68–9, 135,
   140
FISMA (Federal Information Security
   Management Act) 135
flow record 136
foreign government information (FGI)
   98–9
Foreign Intelligence and Surveillance Act
   1978 (FISA) 68–9, 135, 140
Freedom House 166
'Freedom on the Net' (2012) 166
Future Internet Public Private Partnership
   (FI–PPP) 189

GCA (Global Cybersecurity Agenda) 191
GCHQ (Government Communications
   Headquarters) 68 *see also* Tempora
GGE (UN Group of Government Experts)
   42
Gibson, William 1

Neuromancer (1984) 25
Global Alliance against Child Sexual
   Abuse Online 52, 192
Global Cybersecurity Agenda (GCA) 191
Google 14, 30
governance 40–3, 61, 118
   Internet, and the 40–1, 61, 127–8
   PPPs (public–private partnerships)
   and 184–7
Government Communications
   Headquarters (GCHQ) 68 *see also*
   Tempora
governments 130–1
Graham, J.: *Cyber Security Essentials*
   (2010) 6
Greenwald, Glenn 64
Guardian 59, 63, 68, 72
Gun, Katharine 86
Guns, Germs and Steel: The Fates of
   Human Societies (1997) (Diamond)
   161

hacking 32, 39
Hafner, K.: *Black Code* (2011) 8
hierarchies 130
Hoiame oma kodumaa väärika ja
   puhtana! ('Let's keep our homeland
   dignified and clean') 222
Homeland Security Presidential Directive
   23 'Cyber Security and monitoring'
   (HSPD 23) 137
Howard, R.: *Cyber Security Essentials*
   (2010) 6
HSPD 23 (Homeland Security
   Presidential Directive 23 'Cyber
   Security and monitoring') 137

ICANN (Internet Corporation for
   Assigned Names and Numbers) 28
ICS (industrial control systems) 141, 173
ICTs (information and communication
   technologies) 170
IDS (intrusion detection systems) 132 *see*
   also TIC
IDS/IPS (intrusion detection and
   prevention technology) 128, 131,
   132–3, 142, 148
IGF (Internet Governance Forum) 24, 28

immunity 145
IMPACT (International Multilateral
    Partnership Against Cyber Threats)
    52, 191
'Improving Critical Infrastructure
    Cybersecurity' (US executive
    order) 144–5
in-sourcing 129–30
individuals 5
industrial control systems (ICS) 141, 173
informants 99 *see also* whistleblowing
information and communication
    technologies (ICTs) 170
information security 177
infrastructures 5
    resilience and 30–1
intellectual privacy 167–8
intentionality 49–50
International Code of Conduct for
    Information Security 177
international law 42–4
International Multilateral Partnership
    Against Cyber Threats
    (ITU-IMPACT) 52, 191
international organizations 162
International School on Disarmament and
    Research on Conflict (ISODARCO)
    xvi–xviii, 15–6
'International Strategy for Cyberspace'
    119, 173–4
International Telecommunications
    Regulations 41
International Telecommunications Union
    (ITU) 51
    Global Cybersecurity Agenda (GCA)
    191
international treaties 176, 178
Internet, the 3, 162
    anonymity and 61–2
    economics of 163–5
    extremism and 215–23 *see also* Rate
    governance and 40–1, 61, 127–8
    law enforcement and 165–70
    secret codes and 220–2
    secure access and 145–8 *see also*
        Einstein program, the
    society and 213
    terrorism and 215

Internet Corporation for Assigned Names
    and Numbers (ICANN) 28
Internet Governance Forum (IGF) 24, 28
internet protocol suite 28
internet service providers (ISPs) 137,
    143–4, 149, 162, 194
intrusion 89–90
intrusion detection and prevention
    technology (IDS/IPS) 128, 131,
    132–3, 142, 148
intrusion-detection systems (IDS) 132 *see
    also* TIC
intrusion prevention systems (IPS) 132,
    141–2
IPS (intrusion prevention systems) 132,
    141–2
Iran 171–4
Iraq 85–7
ISODARCO (International School on
    Disarmament and Research on
    Conflict) xvi–xviii, 15–6
ISPs (internet service providers) 137,
    143–4, 149, 162, 194
Israel 172–4
ITU (International Telecommunications
    Union) 51
    Global Cybersecurity Agenda (GCA)
    191
ITU-IMPACT (International Multilateral
    Partnership Against Cyber Threats)
    52, 191

Japan 161
JCSP (Joint Cybersecurity Services Pilot)
    143–4
Joint Cybersecurity Services Pilot (JCSP)
    143–4
journalism 63–5, 66

Kizza, Migga 7
Knake, R. K.: *Cyberwar* (2010) 7–8
Koza, Frank 86
Koza email 86–7

law 42–4
    enforcement 165–70, 185–6
    immunity from the 145
    rule of 121

leaks 89
Leet-speak 221
Leigh, David 68
Lewis, Jeffrey 95
Lieberman, Joseph 70
LinkedIn 33
Lockheed Martin 144
London Action Plan (International
    Cybersecurity Enforcement
    Network) 193, 195
London riots 213

McConnell, Mike 140
Malicious Software Removal Tool 196
malware 32, 35, 171
management costs (MC) 129–30
mandatory reporting 201n8
Manning, Bradley 59, 62, 71–3, 91, 106n6
Marlinspike, Moxie: 'Why "I Have
    Nothing to Hide" Is the Wrong
    Way to Think About Surveillance'
    168
MC (management costs) 129–30
media, the 63, 66 *see also* journalism
media companies 163–4
Migga Kizza, Joseph 7
Moella, R. R. 7
Monde, Le 63

Napster 164
nation-states 4–5
National Cyber Security Division (NCSD)
    135
National Security Agency *see* NSA
National Security Letters 166–7
National Security Presidential Directive
    52 *Cyber Security and Monitoring*
    (NSPD 54) 137
nationalism *see* extremism
NCSD (National Cyber Security Division)
    135
network centres 28
network flow information 135–6
network security 137, 145–8 *see also*
    Einstein program, the
networks 2 *see also* infrastructures
'Networx vendors' 137
Neuromancer (1984) (Gibson, William) 25

New York Times 59, 63, 64, 67, 72
9/11 terrorist attacks 134
NMS-CO (United States National Military
    Strategy for Cyberspace operations)
    119
Northrop Grumman 144
NSA (National Security Agency) *see also*
    PRISM
    data collection programs 60, 75
    deep packet inspection (DPI)
        technology and 134–5
    Koza email and 86–7
    secret surveillance and 151n12, 167
    signatures and 140
    Snowden, Edward and 67, 68–9, 72,
        74–5
NSPD (National Security Presidential
    Directive 52 *Cyber Security and
    Monitoring*) 137
nuclear disarmament 83 *see also* nuclear
    zero
    manufacturing secrets and 99–100
nuclear weapons 83, 85 *see also* nuclear
    zero *and* weapons of mass
    destruction management of 92–3
    secure communications and 96
nuclear zero 11, 93, 96, 100–5 *see also*
    nuclear disarmament

obstacles 161–2
Octopus 191
Olbanian counter-culture 221
Olson, R.: *Cyber Security Essentials* (2010)
    6
one-time pad encryption 91
Operation Atlantic 52
Operation Icarus 52
Organization for Security Co-operation in
    Europe (OSCE) 42
OSCE (Organization for Security
    Co-operation in Europe) 42
out-sourcing 129–30

PAA (Protect America Act) 140
padonki counter-culture 221
País, El 63
pan-EU cybersecurity exercise 190
PAT (principal-agent theory) 4

peace, principle of 120–1
peace researchers 15–16
peer-to-peer protocol 164–5
Pentagon Papers, the 67
Perfect Citizen 141
Perry, J.: *Cyberspaces and Global Affairs* (2012) 7
personally identifiable information (PII) 134
Phillips, R.: *Cyber Security for Educational Leaders* (2013) 6
PII (personally identifiable information) 134
PIPA (Protect IP Act) 166
PKE (public key encryption) 91
PPPs (public–private partnerships) 183–4, 186–9, 194–5
  governance and 184–7
  increased cybersecurity and 195–6
  institutional 191
  international 193–4
  legal frameworks and 196–8, 199
  non-institutional 192–3
  regional 189–90, 198
  societal collateral damage 196–8, 199–200
  taxonomy of 187–9
  transnational 191, 198–9
principal-agent theory (PAT) 4
PRISM 167, 197, 215
privacy 197, 217
  violations 140 *see also* intellectual privacy *and* surveillance
private sector infrastructure 127–8, 139–40, 149 *see also* PPPs
  Einstein program and 140–8
private security 130–1
Protect America Act (PAA) 140
Protect IP Act (PIPA) 166
protocols 28
public key encryption (PKE) 92
public-private partnerships *see* PPPs
public security 130–1
P.W.A. (Preserve White Aryans) 219

Rate 213, 218–20, 222–3, 223n. 1
Raytheon 141, 144
resiliency and redundancy 5

Richards, Neil M.: 'Dangers of Surveillance, The' (2013) 167–9
risk management 32–3
Rock against Communism 219
Rohozinski, R.: *Black Code* (2011) 8
RSA security 173
Russia 176–7, 178

SAIC 144
SCADA (supervisory control and data acquisition) 16n. 4, 141, 173
SCS (sensitive control systems) 141
search engines 118
secrecy 65–72, 97–9 *see also* secure communications
  technology and 75–6, 104
secret codes 220–2
secret surveillance 166–8
secure communications 84–5, 103–4 *see also* classification *and* secrecy
  atomic bomb, and the 99–100
  breakdowns in 85–92, 104
  nuclear weapons and 96, 100–4
sensitive control systems (SCS) 141
Shanghai Cooperation Organization 42
Shoemaker, D. 6
Short, Clare 87
Sianjina, R. R.: *Cyber Security for Educational Leaders* (2013) 6
signatures 132–4, 139–40, 149
SIPRNet 69
Snowden, Edward 60, 64–5, 67–72, 74–5,
  number of files and 104
  PRISM and 167
SNS (social network sites) 118, 177, 213–14
  audiences and 216–17
  extremism and 215–23 *see also* Rate
  music and 219–20, 221, 224n. 3, 224n4
  privacy and 217
  secret codes and 220–2
  surveillance and 214, 215–17
social network sites *see* SNS
social stenography 217–18, 220
software 174–5, 201n. 7
Sony 33
SOPA (Stop Online Piracy Act) 166

sovereignty, principle of 121
Spiegel, Der 59, 63
state cooperation 176, 178
Stop Online Piracy Act (SOPA) 166
Strategy for Partnerships between
    States and Businesses to Counter
    Terrorism 193–4
Stuxnet malware 171–4
submarine cable resilience 30
Suht OI! ('Quite OI!') 219
supervisory control and data acquisition
    (SCADA) 16n. 4, 141, 173
surveillance 166–8
    social network sites (SNS) and 214,
    215–17 *see also* Rate
Swire, Peter 169–70

targets (of cyber-attacks) 4–5, 9–10
TC (transaction costs) 129–30
TCBM (transparency and confidence-
    building measures) 177–8
technology
    organizational relationships and 127–8
    secrecy and 75–6, 104
Telecom Package 200n. 2
Tempora 197
Tengelin Report 2
terrorism 215
thefts 89
threat frame 131
Tianya community, the 116
TIC (Trusted Internet Connections)
    136–9
Track 2 Sino-US Cybersecurity Dialogue
    50–1
transaction costs (TC) 129–30
transparency and confidence-building
    measures (TCBM) 177–8
Trusted Internet Connections (TIC)
    136–9
Twitter 75–6

Udaff 221
UK Home Office 215
UN (United Nations) 42
UN Group of Government Experts (GGE)
    42
unanticipated inference 89

undersea cables *see* cables
United Nations (UN) 42
United Nations Disarmament
    Commission 48
United Nations Office on Drugs and
    Crime (UNODC) 191, 194
United States Computer Emergency
    Readiness Team (US-CERT) 135–6,
    139, 142, 149
United States National Military Strategy
    for Cyberspace operations
    (NMS-CO) 119
UNODC (United Nations Office on Drugs
    and Crime) 191, 194
US 31 *see also* NSA
    classification and 65–6, 69, 93–8
    confidence-building measures (CBMs)
        and 50–1
    cyber-espionage and 39, 41, 49–1, 90
        see also Koza email *and* Cablegate
        and Snowden, Edward *and*
        WikiLeaks
    cybersecurity policy and 127–31,
        134–5, 145–8, 160, 176–7 *see also*
        Einstein program, the
    cyberspace strategy and 119
    Einstein program, and the *see* Einstein
        program, the
    IDS/IPS (intrusion detection and
        prevention technology) and 128,
        131
    nuclear weapons and 92–3
    secret surveillance and 166–7
    state cooperation and 178
    Stuxnet malware and 172–4
US Air Force 92, 95–6
US-ASEAN Cybercrime Capacity–
    Building initiative 55
US-CERT (United States Computer
    Emergency Readiness Team)
    135–6, 139, 142, 149
US-China Strategic and Economic
    Dialogue 50
US Department of Defense (DoD) 128,
    143
US Department of Homeland Security
    (DHS) 6, 128, 135, 142, 149
    'Essential Body of Knowledge' 6

Joint Cybersecurity Services Pilot
(JCSP) and 143–4
National Cyber Security Division
(NCSD) 135
social media networks (SNS) and 215
US National Strategy to Cyberspace 2003
187

VeriSign 173
VGT (Virtual Global Taskforce) 192–3
victims *see* targets
Virtual Global Taskforce (VGT) 192–3
Visible Technologies 215
'Vision Earth Rocked by Isotope Blast'
100

Wall Street Journal 64
Washinton Post 67
weapons of mass destruction 85–7, 98 *see
also* nuclear weapons and nuclear
zero

whistleblowing 66–7, 71–2, 167 *see also*
informants
'Why "I Have Nothing to Hide" Is the
Wrong Way to Think About
Surveillance' (Marlinspike) 168
WikiLeaks 59–5, 68, 69, 70–4, 87–8
Winterfield, S.: *Cyber Warfare* (2011) 8
wiretapping 140
Working Group on Cybersecurity and
Cyber-crime 14, 53, 192
World Conference on International
Telecommunications 41
World Wide Web, the 3, 162

Yahoo 33
YouTube 30

zero-day vulnerabilities 172